PENGUIN  CLASSICS

FOURTEEN BYZANTINE RULERS

ADVISORY EDITOR: BETTY RADICE

MICHAEL PSELLUS (A.D. 1018–96), Byzantine philosopher, historian and man of letters, was born in Constantinople. An infant prodigy, he attracted the notice of important patrons and eventually entered the government service, and, as one short-lived emperor succeeded another, became extremely influential. Falling into disfavour on Constantine IX's death, Psellus for a time became a monk, but finding he had no vocation returned to court to resume a leading role in government, becoming chief minister of the empire under Michael VII Ducas.

Psellus was an intellectual giant, who, more than any other man, laid the groundwork for the 12th-century flowering of art, letters and science. Though there was no branch of knowledge which he did not explore, his main contribution was twofold: a new and deeper understanding of the Platonist, idealist tradition of ancient philosophy and a unique attention to style and elegance of expression. In addition, many of the succeeding generation's most influential figures were his pupils.

His literary output was immense, and not all of it has been identified, let alone published. Psellus's work marks the first break in the old Christian–Aristotelian synthesis which had provided the philosophical and intellectual framework for the Byzantine world since late antiquity; and his creative use of the classical literary heritage paved the way for stylists like Anna Comnena and Nicetas Choniates, as well as for the revived Lucianic satire of the 12th century.

E. R. A. SEWTER was a well-known Byzantine scholar and the editor of *Greece and Rome*. His translation of *The Alexiad of Anna Comnena* is also published in Penguin Classics. E. R. A. Sewter died in 1976.

T0200892

FOURTEEN
BYZANTINE RULERS

The *Chronographia* of
Michael Psellus

*

TRANSLATED,
WITH AN INTRODUCTION, BY
E. R. A. SEWTER

PENGUIN BOOKS

PENGUIN BOOKS

Published by the Penguin Group
Penguin Books Ltd, 80 Strand, London WC2R 0RL, England
Penguin Putnam Inc., 375 Hudson Street, New York, New York 10014, USA
Penguin Books Australia Ltd, 250 Camberwell Road, Camberwell, Victoria 3124, Australia
Penguin Books Canada Ltd, 10 Alcorn Avenue, Toronto, Ontario, Canada M4V 3B2
Penguin Books India (P) Ltd, 11 Community Centre, Panchsheel Park, New Delhi – 110 017, India
Penguin Books (NZ) Ltd, Cnr Rosedale and Airborne Roads, Albany, Auckland, New Zealand
Penguin Books (South Africa) (Pty) Ltd, 24 Sturdee Avenue, Rosebank 2196, South Africa

Penguin Books Ltd, Registered Offices: 80 Strand, London WC2R 0RL, England

www.penguin.com

This translation first published by Routledge & Kegan Paul, UK,
and Yale University Press, USA, 1953
This revised edition published in Penguin Books 1966

036

Copyright © E. R. A. Sewter, 1966
All rights reserved

Printed and bound in Great Britain by Clays Ltd, Elcograf S.p.A.

Set in Monotype Bembo

ISBN-13: 978–0–14–044169–7

www.greenpenguin.co.uk

CONTENTS

THE *CHRONOGRAPHIA*

Contents

BOOK SIX

BOOK SEVEN

PREFACE

THE first edition of this book was published in 1953 by Routledge & Kegan Paul in London, and in the United States by
Yale University Press. It appeared as *The Chronographia of
Michael Psellus* in *Rare Masterpieces of Philosophy and Science*
(edited by Dr W. Stark) – a compliment which would surely
have delighted Psellus himself. I have every reason to be grateful to the London publishers for their courtesy and forbear-
ance; no English translation of the whole work had been
attempted before – in fact, only once had the *Chronographia*
been rendered into any modern language, in Émile Renauld's
Budé version; ten years ago Byzantine studies were still regarded in some quarters with suspicion or even contempt; it
was by no means certain that the book would sell. However,
all went well and for some time now it has been out of print.

This second edition, although the text remains substantially
unaltered, has been thoroughly revised. The notes have been
simplified and where necessary amended. Maps and a brief
glossary have been added. The bibliography has been brought
up to date. In one important respect there has been a change
of a more drastic nature: in Penguin Books it is customary for
authors to write their own Introductions, whereas in the
earlier edition I had not been required to do this, for Professor
Joan Hussey, whose services to *Byzantina* have justly won the
admiration of scholars all over the world, volunteered to carry
out this task herself. Not only did she find time to do this,
despite her many other duties, but she read the text, made
valuable comments, supplied notes for the bibliography, and
interested herself generally in the book's production. To her
I owe a great debt. If this volume contributes anything to our
knowledge of eleventh-century Constantinople, I shall feel

hat some part at least of that obligation has been paid. Others
ave helped me by their encouragement and advice, notably
'. H. Barrow and W. F. Jackson Knight. The former has long
·xercised a beneficial influence on the teaching and study of
he classics; the scholarship of the latter extends far beyond his
avourite Virgil. Neither could have been expected to favour
•ioneer Byzantine research – *tanto magis libentissime gratias
eddo.*

It is proper, too, that tribute should be paid here to M.
' enauld. I have used the Greek text established by him and
here were ample opportunities to observe and respect his
cholarly approach. Nevertheless, our versions do differ con-
iderably. If mine does not meet with everyone's approval I
 all derive some minor comfort from his admission that
'sellus is often utterly obscure: there are '*difficultés insur-
ontables*'.

Newbury, Berkshire
30 September 1964

INTRODUCTION

FIFTY years ago any English schoolboy who professed admiration for things Byzantine would almost certainly have been reprimanded. The Golden Age of Athens, the fifth century before Christ, was the most profitable object of study, and Roman History was respectable enough up to the reign of Hadrian; after that (had not Gibbon said so?) there followed a period of decline and fall. The miserable Byzantines were pale reflections of decadent Greeks: their art was stereotyped, lacking in inspiration, and stiff; their form of government was static and inefficient, their literature debased. *Byzantinus est, non legitur* was the accepted maxim. The boy's mentors probably never bothered to define the term 'Byzantine', which had long been pejorative, but in my schooldays (about that time) we knew vaguely that the ancient city of Byzantium had been founded by a Greek Byzas somewhere about 650 B.C., that it paid tribute to the Delian Confederacy, and that Constantine the Great made it the capital of the Eastern Roman Empire in the year 330 of the Christian Era. We were not encouraged to ask what happened to Rome itself; in fact, looking back on those faraway lessons on Roman History, one wonders if our teachers themselves knew or cared. Once, in an aside, we were told that the first and last rulers of Rome were called by the same name (with a contemptuous reference to 'Augustulus') and further inquiries were dismissed as irrelevant. Obviously something dreadful had occurred in the West two hundred years after Constantine's foundation of his new capital, but many years were to elapse before my contemporaries seriously concerned themselves with the surviving half of the old Roman Empire. It was not even generally agreed whether 'East Romans' or 'Byzantines' was the correct title of its

inhabitants, though most people thought of the Empire as
definitely Byzantine from the time of Justinian to the capture
of Constantinople by the Turks in 1453, a period of some nine
hundred years. However ignorant we may have been, some
of us did ask awkward questions: if they were so inferior, how
did these wretched Byzantines manage to survive so long after
the collapse of the West? and what about Santa Sophia? and
wasn't a millennium rather a long time for a sustained decline?

The attitude to *Byzantina* nowadays has changed radically,
thanks to the fine work of many scholars (Baines, Hussey,
Talbot Rice, Gervase Mathew, Beckwith, Moss, and the historians Vasiliev and Ostrogorsky, to name only a few whose
books have been published in English). The vigour and genius
of Byzantine artists, who were in fact far from stereotyped or
conventional, are now acclaimed. Their craftsmanship is admired, in mosaics and miniatures; in ivories like the famous
Ravenna throne; in silverware like the Kerynia dish; in the
marble sarcophagi to be seen in the Archaeological Museum
at Istanbul; in the silk textiles; in the paintings, superb in conception and design; in the great architectural triumphs which
bear witness to new experiments in light and harmony. Today
it is recognized that the constitution of the Byzantine State
merits detailed study – if for no other reason than that it preserved for so long its outward form more or less unaltered, in
spite of the unremitting hostility of its neighbours. On the
other hand, it has not been so easy to break down prejudice in
the matter of Byzantine literature. One reason for it, no doubt,
is to be found in the English determination at all costs to retain
prose composition in Greek and Latin as an important part of
classical studies. Herodotus and the writers of the New Testa-
ment did not use the pure Attic Greek of Thucydides and
Plato; reading Herodotus and St Matthew in the original
would corrupt our young pupils' style; *ergo* schoolboys are not
urged to read them. Byzantine authors, who were very
numerous and produced volumes on a multitude of subjects,

also used their own brand of Greek and were likewise relegated to the *non legendi*. Now that the whole purpose and content of classical studies are being violently attacked, there may be a change of heart. Indeed, there are signs in some quarters that the object of learning Greek is after all to read Greek authors.

Perhaps the reader will forgive some personal observations at this stage. Like thousands of others who spent six years on active service, I had little time or inclination to read anything beyond newspapers and military manuals. Even the basic elements of Greek and Latin were fast being forgotten. Demobilization was followed by a period of intense and happy study; acquaintance with the old masters was renewed, research in new fields began. Towards the end of 1946 I bought the Budé Psellus, by chance. Of Psellus I knew nothing whatever; even his name was unfamiliar. But I was prepared to read anything in Greek and the Byzantine historians seemed likely to provide something of interest; already Procopius, Agathias, Menander Protector, and Leo Diaconos had proved to be stimulating companions. Psellus surpassed them all, and my pleasure was all the greater because it was unexpected: I felt like stout Cortés on his peak in Darien gazing over unexplored Ocean. We share many emotions with the fifth-century Athenian: a belief in democracy, good sportsmanship, amateur athletics, and so on; but in some ways the Byzantine is nearer to us than Periclean Athens ever could be. To begin with, Psellus was writing when William the Conqueror was making ready his fleet for the invasion of England; Norman churches and cathedrals were soon to be built here, and the Normans had already made themselves known to Byzantine warriors on many battlefields. English and Norman soldiers served in the Varangian Guard at Constantinople. Above all, Psellus was a Christian, writing in a Christian community. It is a refreshing experience to read a Greek author who has so much in common with ourselves and yet is thoroughly conversant with the classical world of ancient Greece (as

Psellus certainly was). However, more of Psellus later. It will be more convenient to say something about the background to his book.

On Christmas Day 1025, Basil II Bulgaroctonos died. For almost fifty years he had been sole emperor. He had won great glory for himself and his people. To men living in Constantinople at that moment it must have seemed that the Byzantine Empire was at the height of its powers. Basil had devoted all his energies to the business of ruling; he had never married, spent most of his time on or near the frontiers, developed a war-machine of terrifying efficiency, coveted autocracy, but despised its outward symbols. He crushed rebellions, subdued the feudal landowners, conquered the enemies of the Empire, notably in the Danubian provinces and the East. Everywhere the might of Roman arms was respected and feared. The treasury was full to overflowing with the accumulated plunder of Basil's campaigns. Even the lamp of learning, despite the emperor's known indifference, was burning still, if somewhat dimly. The lot of ordinary folk in Constantinople must have been pleasant enough. For most of them life was gay and colourful, and if the city's defensive fortifications were at some points in disrepair they had no cause to dread attacks.

Two generations later everything had changed. The rulers who succeeded Basil were either unworthy or largely ineffective. The riches they inherited were squandered on foolish projects, and the standard gold coin, the *nomisma* or *bezant*, had to be devalued; from the 24 carats of Basil's time it was reduced to 18 by Monomachus and to a mere 12 or 13 by Michael VIII. Contemptuous foes violated the borders of the Empire, provinces were abandoned, the armed forces were neglected, and good generals often demoted through jealousy. In the West the Normans threatened; in the North the Uzes, Cumans, and Patzinaks; in the East the Seljuk Turks won a resounding victory at Manzikert and even took prisoner the

Roman emperor. While the armies fell into disorder the civil bureaucrats in the capital itself prospered and gradually their sphere of influence extended. The process of government was being altered in a subtle way. Not many people realized what was happening or knew that the eleventh century was in fact a turning-point in their long history. One man who did partially comprehend the decay in the Empire's fortunes was Constantine Psellus.

He was born of a noble family (there had been consuls and men of patrician rank among his father's ancestors), but in 1018, the year of his birth, his parents were only moderately well-off. We know that he had an elder sister who died young; the providing of her dowry left so little money that his education had to be interrupted and for some time he became a judge's clerk in Anatolia. He owed much to his mother, for she procured for him the best possible tutor. He was taught by John Mauropous, the future Archbishop of Euchaïta. John was a private tutor and obviously a man of culture, devoted to his pupils. If one can deduce anything from their subsequent careers he must have been an inspiring teacher. Three, in particular, distinguished themselves, and all remained life-long friends of Psellus: Constantine Ducas became emperor; Constantine Lichudes was a leading minister, President of the Senate, and finally Ecumenical Patriarch; John Xiphilinus of Trebizond became the first *Nomophylax* of the new University of Constantinople (1045) and later Patriarch. These friends prevailed on Monomachus to endow Chairs of Philosophy and Law. The door was thrown wide open to a renaissance of learning, for education at the University was free and available to all who showed ability. Psellus played a leading part in this. He was chosen Professor of Rhetoric, 'consul of the philosophers'. Promotion had been rapid and he was indebted to Lichudes, who had first introduced him to court in the reign of Michael V, but his own ambition and extraordinary eloquence were responsible for the success he enjoyed thereafter. He soon made himself indispensable at court. Constantine IX admired his eloquence, Michael the Aged 'tasted the honey of his lips', Constantine X regarded his words as 'nectar', Eudocia 'looked upon him as a god'. So he became Secretary of State, Grand Chamberlain, Prime Minister; he led the delegates to offer a crown to Isaac Comnenus – a task which called for diplomacy of a high order; he composed the Accusation against the haughty Cerularius, who as Patriarch had rebuffed a Pope's nuncio and brought about the lasting schism between the Greek Orthodox and Latin Churches; he secured the deposition of Romanus Diogenes and made sure that Michael Parapinaces took his place on the throne. Then, suddenly and inexplicably, he was demoted by the ungrateful Michael. One by one his old friends had died, Lichudes, Ducas, Xiphilinus, Nicetas; he had lost his beloved daughter Styliane; the new emperor, Nicephorus Botaniates, merely ignored him. He died, a lonely and disillusioned old man, in 1078.

Any man who could for so long hold a position of trust under rulers of differing temperaments, but with the absolute authority of Byzantine monarchs, must have been outstanding. In the case of Michael Psellus (Michael was the name he adopted as a monk), the unusual triumphs of a political career are surpassed by his brilliance as a scholar. In the *Chronographia* he tells us of his studies: Homer '*the* poet', of course; Hesiod and the Greek lyric poets; the historians, especially Herodotus and Thucydides; Demosthenes, Lysias, Theophrastus, Plutarch, and the Stoic authors; the Christian apologists, particularly Gregory of Nazianzus; Porphyry, Iamblichus, Proclus; Aristotle, and, above all, his beloved Plato. Nor was this the full extent of his reading: he studied medical treatises (and practised the art); he had a pretty thorough knowledge of military tactics and machines of war, culled from books, but of practical use on at least one occasion; he was acquainted with astrological theories, but gave them no credence; he wrote some poetry, about 500 letters which are still extant, seven *Elogia* (one of which, in honour of his dead mother, Theodote, reveals his love and gratitude to her), many philosophical works and works on theological subjects. Also, much against his will, but to please an old friend (probably Lichudes), he composed the first part of the *Chronographia*, up to the death of Isaac Comnenus. This section of the book was perhaps written about 1063; the rest, which is not impartial and is clearly intended to honour the Ducas, must have been composed in the reign of Michael VII. It was not completed.

It is generally agreed among Byzantine scholars that the *Chronographia* holds a very high place in the catalogue of medieval histories. Apart from its intrinsic value as a memoir of a contemporary witness who is for the most part quite reliable and intelligent, it is undeniably a work of art. Psellus can have few rivals as a vivid narrator of events. His character-studies are masterly, his psychological insight most impressive. As a picture of Byzantine life and particularly of life at the imperial court his work could scarcely be surpassed. On the other hand, there are serious deficiencies (by modern standards) in the *Chronographia*. Far too often Psellus omits to give the names of prominent persons, in a tantalizing and unnecessary way. He is apt to be eclectic, though it is fair to add that nowhere does he profess to tell the *whole* truth. He is not very interested in foreign affairs: the Bulgarian campaigns of Basil II, for example, are barely mentioned. His geography is vague. He fails to record certain plagues, famines, earthquakes, and great fires which other Byzantines consider to have been important and which would have provided much wanted chronological data. His account is too much centred on the Palace.

Psellus himself tells us that the book was intended to be a summary rather than an elaborate treatise.

To meet your wishes [he writes to Lichudes] I have passed over in this work many facts worthy of record. The years have not been numbered by Olympiads, nor divided into seasons (as Thucydides divided his), but I have simply drawn attention to the most important facts and all the things which I have been able to recollect during the writing of it. As I say, I am not making any attempt at the moment to investigate the especial circumstances of each event. My object is rather to pursue a middle course between those who recorded the imperial acts of Ancient Rome, on the one hand, and our modern chroniclers, on the other. I have neither aspired to the diffuseness of the former, nor have I sought to imitate the extreme brevity of the latter.

In comparison with Cedrenus or Scylitzes or Zonaras he may give some impression of vagueness, and there is in the *Chronographia* a somewhat irritating lack of uniformity, but Psellus infuses into his work a colour and variety rarely found in any of his rivals, in language that is racy and sometimes colloquial.

Readers of the work will inevitably be drawn to consider the character of the man himself, for he figures largely in its pages. It would be easy, but unjust, to condemn him for his vanity. In eleventh-century Constantinople it was not thought improper to flaunt one's virtues, and if flattery and high rank did go to his head it is not discernible in his earlier writings. At times he could be humble enough. It is not so easy to defend him against the charges of intrigue and double-dealing. One could, of course, point to the corruption of the age: Psellus could not stand aside, like Lucretius's philosopher, and watch the gathering storm in a mood of calm detachment – he had to protect himself, and in Byzantium the best defence was a violent, but camouflaged, counter-attack. To combat the insidious propaganda of his enemies he was forced to use the subtlety of all unscrupulous politicians, or perish. No doubt he himself would point to his patriotism, his genuine love for the Romans: he was acting in the best interests of his country. So he supported the claims of Isaac Comnenus in 1057, because he knew that Michael Stratioticus was bringing the Empire to the verge of ruin; a few years later the war-like policy of Romanus Diogenes really did appear to him not only unnecessary, but bound to end in disaster; he did sincerely believe that a sound training in rhetoric and logic was the best preparation for the task that confronted the young Michael Parapinaces. Some of his enemies saw that he was mistaken, but he was by then an old man and rather conceited. To him the issue was simple: to govern the Roman Empire was a difficult and complicated matter; nobody had more continuous experience in posts of responsibility than he, none knew better how to advise and influence an emperor, or an empress; for the well-being of the State, therefore, it was essential that he, Psellus, should remain at the helm. It must have been a terrible moment for him when the young emperor, trained so carefully to be a Platonic 'philosopher-king', threw him out and put in his place a literary nobody, one John Italus. Apart from one short interval in the reign of Monomachus, when he retired to the monastery of Narsou, his career had been one of uninterrupted prosperity.

He was a man of warm humanity. The fate of the rebel Vatatzes filled him with compassion; he wept silently as he contemplated the savage fate of the Nobilissimus; the passing of great men is recorded by him with singular tenderness and rarely does he condemn without reservation. Young students, too, had reason to thank him, for he often paid for their tuition out of his own purse, mindful perhaps of his own early struggles. Generosity to the poor and sick was especially commended by him, and in this connexion he expressed unusual admiration for the humility of Michael Paphlagon. He had a doctor's sympathy for all pain and suffering, a trait not always conspicuous in medieval times. He was loyal to his friends, a loving son and father. There was no malevolence in his judgements, though he could be righteously indignant. He had courage and tenacity; maybe the courage had to be screwed up a little, but no one could doubt his determination once the issue was joined: 'I am not the sort of man', he writes, 'who shrinks away when I have started a fight.'

At court the eunuchs were notoriously profligate; bribery, dissimulation, and immorality were rife; manners were corrupt. It would have been surprising if Psellus went altogether unscathed by the evil around him, but on the whole he seems to have been a man of refinement, with high ideals and good intentions. He had inherited from his mother a firm belief in Holy Writ, although he was not afraid to submit Christian doctrine to logical inquiry. In the course of centuries he has not escaped imputations of hypocrisy, but an unbiased reader of the *Chronographia* will probably reject them; his declarations of Christian faith do appear to be heartfelt.

His powers of observation and memory are remarkable. He had the sensitive eye of an artist, whether for the symmetry of some great church, or for the beauty of an Alan princess, or for the glories of nature. Again and again one is delighted by some subtle allusion, some delicate aside, some nice choice of words (in the Greek) which shed a new light on some scene. No Byzantine was a better craftsman of words, though a few wrote better Greek, for it must be admitted that his language, imbued as it is with classical Greek undertones, but overloaded with Byzantine constructions and idioms, often approaches the point of obscurity, and sometimes goes beyond it. He is the most difficult of authors to translate. Yet the dialect is vital and usually unaffected, unlike that of his admirer, the pedantic and consciously artful Princess Anna Comnena. Moreover, Psellus has one saving grace, a charming sense of humour.

His finest achievement was to revive classical learning. He was not unaided in this, for he had earnest collaborators and good friends in Xiphilinus and Lichudes, but it is to Psellus that the main credit must go. His dedication to philosophy was unselfish and life-long. Indirectly the Renaissance owed much to him. He would have wanted no finer epitaph.

A NOTE ON REFERENCES TO
ANCIENT AUTHORITIES

THE quotations from Leo the Deacon, Cedrenus, and Scylitzes in the footnotes are to be found in CSHB (*Corpus Scriptorum Historiae Byzantinae:* Leo Diaconus, Bonn, 1828; Cedrenus and Scylitzes, Bonn, 1839). The works of Cedrenus are published in two volumes, but, as all quotations here are taken from the second, such references as 'Cedrenus, 765B, p. 563' must be understood to give the folio and page reference to that volume. The Bonn Corpus was published with a Latin translation and some notes. These historians may also be found reprinted in J.-P. Migne, *Patrologia Graeca* (with a Latin version).

Adrianopolis
CONSTANTINOPLE
Bosphorus
Rhaedestos
Proconnesus
Chrysopolis
Chalcedon
Nicomedia
Prinkipo
PROPONTIS
Nicaea
Sangares R.
HADES?
Abydos
Didymotichus
Troy
PHRYGIA
0   MILES   100

Adriatic Sea
DALMATIA
SERBIA
Danube R.
BULGARIA
PATZINA
B   L
ITALY
Dyrrachium
(Durazzo)
DO
MACEDONIA
Salonica
THRACE
Adrianopolis   INSET
CONSTANTINOPLE
Propontis
Ostrovo
EPIRUS
MT
ATHOS
MT
OLYMPUS
Troy   MYSIA   PHRYGIA
Dodona
Nicopolis
ACARNANIA
Naupactus
Delphi
Lesbos
Mitylene
Chios
Smyrna
A N
SICILY
(George
Maniaces)
Corinth
Megara
Athens
Samos
Ephesus
Prote Is.
Sparta
Pylos
Halicarnassus
Cos
Rhodes
M
E
D
I
T
E
CRETE
R
R
A
N
E
A

THE
BYZANTINE
EMPIRE
AT THE DEATH
OF
BASIL II
IN 1025

BLACK SEA

UZES or CUMANS

ALANIA

Sinope
Castamon
GUNARIA? ×
PAPHLAGONIA
Amasea
Euchaita
Sangares R.

Trebizond
Colonia

IBERIA

ANI
Araxes R.

ARMENIA

Mantzikert

ATOLIA
CAPPADOCIA

Iconium

Caesarea
TYROPAEUM? ×
Edessa
(George
Maniaces)

PARTHIA

Taurus Mts.
CILICIA
Adana
Tarsus

Antioch
Aleppo

ASSYRIA
or
BABYLONIA

Euphrates R.

Tigris R.

CYPRUS

S
E
A

PHOENICIA
COELE
SYRIA
Damascus

N
S

Halys R.

Miles
0   100   200   300

W.Bromage

21

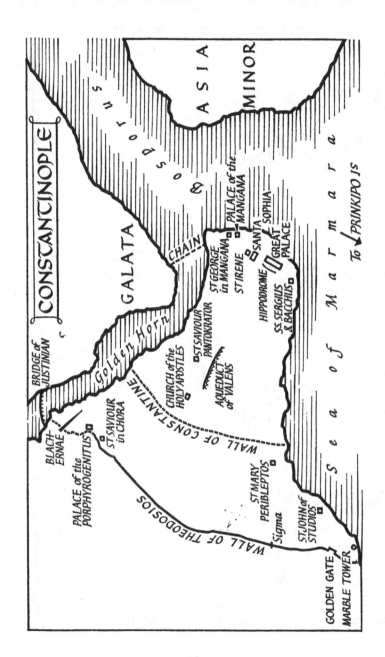

CONSTANTINOPLE

ASIA MINOR

Bosporus

Sea of Marmara

To ↓ PRINKIPO IS

PALACE of the MANGANA

SANTA SOPHIA

GREAT PALACE

ST GEORGE in MANGANA

ST IRENE

HIPPODROME

SS. SERGIUS & BACCHUS

CHAIN

GALATA

Golden Horn

BRIDGE of JUSTINIAN

ST SAVIOUR PANTOKRATOR

CHURCH of the HOLY APOSTLES

AQUEDUCT of VALENS

ST SAVIOUR in CHORA

BLACH-ERNAE

PALACE of the PORPHYROGENITUS

WALL of CONSTANTINE

ST MARY PERIBLEPTOS

WALL of THEODOSIOS

Sigma

ST JOHN of STUDIOS

GOLDEN GATE

MARBLE TOWER

THE *CHRONOGRAPHIA* OF
MICHAEL PSELLUS

THE *Chronographia* composed by the learned and right honour-able monk Michael, in which are recounted the deeds of the following rulers: Basil and Constantine, the Porphyrogeniti; their successor, Romanus Argyropulus; Michael the Paphla-gonian; Michael, nephew of the last-named, who originally had the title of Caesar; the two sisters Zoe and Theodora, also Porphyrogenitae and both princesses; Constantine Mono-machus, who shared the throne with them; the Princess Theodora, one of the aforementioned sisters, who ruled as empress alone; Michael the Aged; Isaac Comnenus.

The History ends with the proclamation of Constantine Ducas.

BOOK ONE

BASIL II

976–1025

THE circumstances in which the Emperor John Tzimisces met his death have already been described [in the history of Leo Diaconus].[1] Basil and Constantine, the sons of Romanus, were now the legitimate heirs to an Empire which through the efforts of their predecessor had won many triumphs and greatly increased its power.[2]

Both princes had seen the last of their boyhood days, but their interests lay far apart. Basil, the elder of the two, always gave an impression of alertness, intelligence, and thoughtfulness; Constantine appeared to be apathetic, lazy, and devoted to a life of luxury. It was natural that they should abandon the idea of joint-rule. By mutual consent all real power was vested in Basil, and Constantine was associated with him as emperor in name only. They planned wisely, for the Empire's well-being depended on the elevation of the older and more experienced brother.

Constantine renounced most of his privileges on this occasion, and perhaps he deserves some commendation here, because legally he was entitled to share his father's inheritance on equal terms – by 'inheritance' I mean the Empire. The sacrifice was all the more remarkable because he was at the time very young, just at the age, in fact, when lust

1. Psellus begins where Leo the Deacon finishes, at the death of John I Tzimisces in 976. Leo (*Hist.* x, 11, p. 177) describes the circumstances of the emperor's death; he may have been poisoned.

2. The young men succeeded on 11 January 976. Basil was eighteen years old, his brother two years younger. They had been crowned during their father's reign and had been under the guardianship of their mother Theophano and John Tzimisces.

for power is most readily kindled. One must remember, too, that Basil was by no means a full-grown man; he was still a mere stripling, 'growing his first beard', as they say. Yet Constantine allowed him to take precedence. It is only right, then, that I should pay this tribute to the younger brother at the outset of this history.

Once invested with supreme power over the Romans, Basil was unwilling to share his designs with anyone else; he refused advice on the conduct of public affairs. On the other hand, having had no previous experience of military matters or of good civil administration, he discovered that to rely on his own unaided judgement was impossible. He was compelled to turn for help to the *parakoimomenus* (Lord Chamberlain).[1] This man, called Basil, happened at that time to be the most remarkable person in the Roman Empire, outstanding in intellect, bodily stature, and regal appearance. Although he was born of the same father as the father of Basil and Constantine, on his mother's side he came of different stock. In early infancy he had suffered castration – a natural precaution against a concubine's offspring, for as a eunuch he could never hope to usurp the throne from a legitimate heir. Actually he was resigned to his fate and was genuinely attached to the imperial house – after all, it was his own family. He was particularly devoted to his nephew Basil, embracing the young man in the most affectionate manner and watching over his progress like some kindly foster-parent. One should not be surprised, then, that Basil placed on this man's shoulders the burden of Empire. The older man's serious nature, too, had its influence on the emperor's character. The *parakoimomenus*, in fact, was like an athlete competing at the games while Basil watched him as a spectator – not a spectator present merely to cheer on the victor, but rather one who trained himself in the running and took part in the contests himself,

1. Son of Romanus I Lecapenus, he was promoted by Nicephorus Phocas.

following in the other's footsteps and imitating his style. Só the *parakoimomenus* had the whole world at his feet. It was to him that the civilian population looked, to him that the army turned, and he was responsible, indeed solely responsible, for the administration of public finance and the direction of government. In this task he was constantly assisted by the emperor, both in word and in deed, for Basil not only backed up his minister's measures, but confirmed them in writing.

To most men of our generation who saw the Emperor Basil he seemed austere and abrupt in manner, an irascible person who did not quickly change his mind, sober in his daily habits and averse to all effeminacy, but if I am to believe the historians of that period who wrote about him, he was not at all like that when his reign began. A change took place in his character after he acceded to the throne, and instead of leading his former dissolute, voluptuous sort of life, he became a man of great energy. The complete metamorphosis was brought about by the pressure of events. His character stiffened, so to speak. Feebleness gave way to strength and the old slackness disappeared before a new fixity of purpose. In his early days he used to feast quite openly and frequently indulged in the pleasures of love; his main concern was with his banqueting and a life spent in the gay, indolent atmosphere of the court. The combination of youth and unlimited power gave him opportunities for self-indulgence, and he enjoyed them to the full. The change in his mode of living dates from the attempted revolutions of the notorious Sclerus [1] and of Phocas. [2] Sclerus twice raised the standard of revolt, and there

1. Bardas Sclerus had been brother-in-law of John Tzimisces, who had married his sister Maria. He had expected to succeed John, for he had been promised the throne by the emperor on his deathbed.

2. The Phocas family came from Cappadocia and for several generations had enjoyed high repute as soldiers. The father of Bardas Phocas was that Leo who won military fame under Romanus II; his uncle was Nicephorus, himself an emperor, and husband of Theophano.

were other aspirants to the throne, with two parties in opposition to the emperor. From that time onward, Basil's carefree existence was forgotten and he wholeheartedly applied himself to serious objects. Once the first blow had been struck against those members of his family who had seized power, he set himself resolutely to compass their utter destruction.[1]

THE REBELLION OF SCLERUS

A policy so drastic, not unnaturally, stirred the nephews of Nicephorus Phocas to bitter revolt. The trouble began with Sclerus, a man who was not only a competent planner, but extremely clever in carrying out his schemes, possessed of vast wealth (no mean asset in one who aimed at a throne), with the prestige of royal blood and of success in great wars, with all the military caste at his side to help on his enterprise. Sclerus's attempted *coup d'état*, in fact, found considerable support. It was the first daring effort to depose Basil and the pretender was very confident of victory. He marched against the emperor in full force, with cavalry and foot-soldiers, thinking he had but to stretch forth his hand to seize the Empire. Actually, the heavy-armed infantry had rallied to Sclerus *en bloc*, and the emperor's advisers, knowing this, at first believed their cause to be hopeless. On second thoughts, however, they changed their minds and the whole affair took on a different aspect. Despair gave way to courage when in a certain Bardas they thought they had found a worthy opponent for the rebel. To them Bardas represented a safe anchorage, a shelter from the storm. He was, indeed, a man of noble birth and great valour, nephew of the Emperor

1. That Basil never carried out his intention of destroying the Phocas family is proved by the fact that as late as 1022 a son of Bardas, another Nicephorus, was in revolt and was actually crowned emperor in Cappadocia. Fortunately for Basil he was assassinated and the rebellion was abortive.

Nicephorus. So they entrusted to this Bardas whatever forces
still remained. He was made commander-in-chief and sent
forth to do battle with the common enemy.

Their immediate difficulties were thus overcome, but their
new general was no less formidable than Sclerus. He was
descended from an emperor. In all probability he would never
be content to occupy a subordinate position, so they stripped
him of his citizen's robes and all insignia of royalty, and forced
him to enter the Church. Then they bound him by the most
fearful oaths never to be guilty of treason, never to transgress
the promises he had made. Having taken these precautions
against any ambitious schemes he might entertain in the future,
they sent him out with the whole of the emperor's forces.

According to the historians, this man Bardas reminded
people of his uncle, the Emperor Nicephorus, for he was
always wrapped in gloom, and watchful, capable of foreseeing
all eventualities, of comprehending everything at a glance.
Far from being ignorant of warlike manoeuvres, he was
thoroughly versed in every type of siege warfare, every trick
of ambush, every tactic of pitched battle. In the matter of
physical prowess, moreover, Bardas was more energetic
and virile than Sclerus. Any man who received a blow from
his hand was dead straightway, and whole armies trembled
even when he shouted from afar. He now divided up his
forces, arranging them in battalions, and more than once –
indeed, on several occasions – put his opponents to flight,
despite their numbers. In truth, Bardas seemed to surpass his
enemies in skill and strategy and vigour, in inverse proportion to his own inferiority in numbers.

Each side was confident in face of its foes, and the two
leaders by common consent decided to engage in single
combat.[1] So, riding out to the space that divided the two lines,
they spied one another and without more ado came to
close quarters. The rebel Sclerus, unable to curb his natural

1. On 24 March 979 at Pancalia.

impetuosity, broke the rules of this kind of fighting, and as he approached Phocas struck him with all his might on the head. The blow gained additional power because it was delivered on the charge. Phocas, dumbfounded at the unexpectedness of this stroke, momentarily lost control of his reins, but collecting his wits again he returned the blow on the same part of his adversary's body. The latter thereupon lost interest in the combat and rode away in flight.

Both patriots and rebels were convinced that here was the decisive point in the war. Certainly no event contributed more to the emperor's victory, for Sclerus was completely embarrassed. He could no longer withstand Phocas in battle and he was too ashamed to beg terms from the emperor. In these circumstances he adopted a policy which was neither very wise nor very safe, transferring his whole army from Roman territories to Assyria. There he made himself known to the King Chosroes and roused *his* suspicions, for Chosroes feared the great numbers of his army and possibly he was nervous, too, in case the Romans planned some sudden attack on himself. The upshot of the matter was that all Sclerus's men were made prisoners and carried off to gaol.

THE REVOLT OF BARDAS PHOCAS

Meanwhile Bardas Phocas returned to the emperor. He was given the privilege of a triumph and took his place among the personal friends of his sovereign. So ended the first revolt. Apparently Basil was now freed from all his troubles, but this seeming collapse of the opposition proved to be only a prelude to the host of evils that were to come. Phocas, after receiving high honours when he first returned to Byzantium, later found himself neglected. His ambitions appeared to be once more slipping from his grasp. This kind of treatment, in his opinion, was undeserved. He had not betrayed the trust reposed in him; he had entered into an agreement, on specific terms, and he had faithfully kept it. So, disgruntled, he broke away in revolt – a revolt more serious and more difficult to counter than the previous attempt of Sclerus – with the greater part of the army ranged beside him against Basil.[1] Having won over the leading and most powerful families, he decided to proclaim himself an open enemy of the régime. An army of Iberians was conscripted; fierce, proud warriors standing up to ten feet in height.[2] It was no longer in imagination, but in very truth, that he put on the imperial robes, with the emperor's crown and the royal insignia of purple.

I will describe what happened next. A foreign war surprised the Babylonian, that same King Chosroes to whom Sclerus and his men had fled and from whom they hoped for assistance. Those hopes, as I have said, had already been dashed. Well, this war proved to be a terrible strain on the king's resources and great numbers of armed men were involved in the struggle. It was impossible for Chosroes to feel any confidence in his own native forces without foreign aid. So he turned for help to the exiled Romans. They were at once released from their bonds, brought out of their prisons, strongly armed and set in battle-array against his enemies. They (Sclerus and his men) being virile and warlike soldiers, acquainted with the disposition of infantry in battle, arranged themselves in two groups, one on either flank. Then, charging on horseback in mass-formation and shouting their war-cry, they killed some of the enemy there on the spot and others they put to flight. The pursuit continued as far as the earthworks and the foe was completely annihilated.[3] On their way

1. This revolt came to a head on 15 August 987 when Bardas Phocas was proclaimed emperor at Chresianus. Sclerus had meanwhile escaped from Baghdad and made terms with him: Phocas was to have the capital and the European provinces, Sclerus Asia Minor. Barely a month later Phocas broke his word and on 14 September Sclerus was imprisoned by him at Tyropaeum and stripped of all insignia.

2. Very tall (a Byzantine saying).

3. This battle apparently took place late in 986.

back the Romans, as if inspired with one common idea, took to flight themselves. The reason for this was that they feared Chosroes. They expected little consideration from him and they believed that he would throw them back into prison. So they made off with all the speed they could muster, and they covered a great distance before the Assyrians noticed they had gone. (These operations took place in Assyria.) Chosroes, whose army had now reassembled, immediately issued an order that all soldiers of the Assyrian army who met these Romans were to join in pursuing them. A large group did indeed fall upon them from the rear, but they soon discovered how inferior they were to the Roman soldier, for the runaways suddenly wheeled about and defeated their pursuers. In fact, the enemy suffered such losses that they retreated fewer in numbers than the Romans, although they had vastly outnumbered them when the engagement started.

Here, Sclerus decided, was the opportunity to revive his struggle for power. The whole Empire, he thought, was ripe for the plucking, for Phocas had already gone away to Anatolia and all the enemy's forces were scattered. Having arrived at the Roman frontier, however, he learnt that Phocas had designs on the throne himself, and since he was in no position to take on both the emperor and his rival, he indulged in a fresh outburst of insolence at the expense of the former, while he presented himself to the latter in the guise of vassal. Phocas's hegemony was recognized and Sclerus agreed to serve under him. Thereupon their forces were divided in two and the rebel army was greatly strengthened. Full of confidence in their soldiers and military dispositions, they came down as far as the Propontis and strongpoints on the seaboard, made their entrenchments secure, and all but tried to leap over the sea itself.

The Emperor Basil was well aware of disloyalty among the Romans, but not long before this a picked band of Scythians

had come to help him from the Taurus.¹ These men, fine
fighters, he had trained in a separate corps, combined with
them another mercenary force, divided by companies, and
sent them out to fight the rebels. They came upon them unexpectedly, when they were off their guard, seated at table
and drinking, and after they had destroyed not a few of them,
scattered the rest in all directions.² The remnants of the
insurgents actually banded together and opposed Phocas
himself, with considerable enthusiasm.

Basil personally took part in these operations with the
Roman army. He had just grown a beard and was learning the
art of war from experience in actual combat. Even his brother
Constantine had a place in the battle-line, armed with breastplate and long spear.

So the two faced one another: on the one side, by the sea,
the emperor's forces; on the higher parts, the rebels, with a
great space between. When Phocas discovered that Basil
and Constantine were in the enemy's ranks, he no longer put
off the battle.³ That day, he determined, was to be the turning-point of the war, the day which was to decide the future
of the Empire. So he committed his cause to fortune. It was
contrary to the advice of the astrologers in his retinue, for
they would have dissuaded him from fighting. Their sacrifices clearly showed the folly of it, but he gave rein to his
horse and obstinately refused to listen. It is said that signs of
ill-omen appeared to him, as well as to the astrologers, for no
sooner had he mounted his horse than the charger slipped
under him, and when he seated himself on a second, that also,
a few paces farther on, suffered the same fate. His skin,

1. This Scythian force of 6,000 arrived at Constantinople in 988.
Vladimir of Russia was persuaded to help: Basil gave him his sister Anna
in marriage and Vladimir was baptized as a Christian. The Scyths (or
Varangians) remained in Greece after Phocas had been defeated.
2. The Battle of Chrysopolis in the summer of 988.
3. The Battle of Abydos, 13 April 989.

moreover, changed colour, his heart was filled with foreboding, and his head was troubled with giddiness. Phocas, however, was not the man to give way once he had set himself to a task, so, riding at the head of his army, and being already somewhat near the emperor's forces, he gathered about him some foot-soldiers. The men I refer to were the finest fighters among the Iberians, all of them young men just growing their first beards, in the flower of their youth, tall men and men of equal height, as though they had been measured off with a ruler, armed on their right with swords, and irresistible when they charged. With these warriors about him, under one standard, Phocas moved forward to the attack in front of his army. Gathering speed he made straight for the emperor with a wild cry, sword uplifted in his right hand, as if he intended to kill Basil there and then.

While Phocas was so boldly charging towards him, Basil rode out in front of his army too. He took his stand there, sword in hand. In his left hand he clasped the image of the Saviour's Mother, thinking this ikon the surest protection again his opponent's terrific onslaught. Phocas swept on like a cloud driven by violent winds, whirling over the plain. Meanwhile those who were stationed on the flanks hurled javelins at him. Among others, slightly in front of the main army, was the Emperor Constantine, brandishing a long spear. After he had galloped forward some distance from his own men, Phocas suddenly slipped from his saddle and was thrown to the ground. At this point the accounts of different authors become contradictory. Some contend that he was hit by the javelin-throwers and fell mortally wounded. Others aver that he was overcome by a sudden faintness, the effect of a stomach disorder, and so fell down from his saddle. Whatever the true explanation may have been, Constantine arrogated to himself the proud distinction of having slain the rebel. The usual story, however, and the one considered to be most probable, is that the whole affair was the result of an intrigue. Poison was mixed, Phocas drank it, and when he moved about the potion became suddenly effective, deprived him of his powers of reason, and caused the giddiness that led to his downfall. The original idea was Basil's, the ministering hand that of Phocas's cupbearer. For my own part, I prefer to express no opinion on the subject and ascribe all the glory to the Mother of the Word.

At all events, he fell, he who until then could neither be wounded nor taken alive, a piteous and mournful sight. As soon as the rival armies saw what had happened, the one was immediately split up and retreated, their close-packed ranks broken, their rout complete. The emperor's forces, on the other hand, after Phocas's collapse, at once leapt upon him, scattered his Iberian bodyguard, and chopped him in pieces with repeated sword-blows. His head was cut off and brought to Basil.[1]

The complete change in the emperor's character dates from that time. While he rejoiced at the death of his enemy, he was no less grieved by the sad condition of his own affairs. He became suspicious of everyone, a haughty and secretive man, ill-tempered, and irate with those who failed to carry out his orders.

THE FALL AND BANISHMENT OF THE
PARAKOIMOMENUS BASIL[2]

Far from allowing the *parakoimomenus* Basil to continue in his general supervision of the government, the emperor from

1. With this defeat opposition to Basil faded away. All the leaders of Phocas's army were put to death except Leo Melissenus, his second-in-command, and Sclerus, who had been set free by Phocas's wife as soon as she heard of her husband's death, was soon reconciled to the emperor.

2. Psellus seems to have misunderstood the chronology of Basil's reign, for the Lord Chamberlain was deposed in 985 and died in exile soon after. Cedrenus (699, p. 443) implies that his downfall coincided with the rise of Romanus, son of Sclerus.

now on decided to supervise everything himself. Further, he proceeded to pursue his minister with a relentless hatred, which he showed in all manner of ways, and refused to see him. Although the *parakoimomenus* was a relative, although the Emperor was greatly indebted to him and the minister had done good service, at no little inconvenience to himself, and despite the very high office that he held, Basil regarded him as an enemy. Nothing on earth would persuade him to change this attitude. The truth is, it offended his pride to think that he, the emperor and a full-grown man, should be given only a share in the government, as if he were an ordinary citizen. One would imagine he had never ascended the throne, but shared authority on equal terms with another man, or held inferior rank in the administration. He gave the subject much thought, and it was only after long vacillation that he finally made up his mind. Once the decision was taken, however, he dismissed the *parakoimomenus* and deposed him at one blow. What made it worse was the fact that this change in the latter's fortunes was not softened by any sign of respect. In fact, the emperor's action was incredibly cruel, for he shipped him off into exile.

Nor did this disgrace prove to be the end of Basil's troubles. Rather was it the prelude to further misfortunes, for the emperor next proceeded to review the events of the reign ever since he acceded to the throne and the *parakoimomenus* began to govern the Empire. He examined the various measures that had been taken during all that period. Whatever happened to contribute to his own (the emperor's) welfare, or to the good of the state, was allowed to remain on the statutes. All those decrees, on the other hand, which referred to the granting of favours or positions of dignity, were now rescinded. The former, the emperor contended, had been approved by himself; of the latter he knew nothing. In everything he strove to bring about the eunuch's downfall and disaster. For example, the *parakoimomenus* had built a

magnificent monastery in honour of Basil the Great, a
monastery that bore his own name too. It had been constructed on a massive scale, at great cost of labour, and it
combined different styles of architecture with beauty. Moreover, the greater part of the material used in its building had
been obtained from generous and voluntary contributions.
The emperor now wished to raze this edifice to the ground.
However, since he was careful to avoid the charge of impiety,
only certain parts of the monastery were removed, and not
all those at once. Other parts he demolished, and the rest
of the building, the movable furniture and the mosaics, he
treated in much the same way. He never rested content until,
to quote his own jesting words, 'he had made of this place of
meditation a place of thought – the thought which those who
dwelt there would now have to take for the bare necessities
of life!'

Naturally, the *parakoimomenus*, tortured like this day after
day, was filled with despair. There was no relief for his suffering, no consolation whatever. Suddenly cast down, in one
brief moment, from his great position of power, this high
and mighty man, whose heart had once been filled with
pride, now became unable to govern his own body. His
limbs were paralysed and he a living corpse. Not long afterwards he died, in very truth a pillar of remembrance, his life
a fine subject for story-tellers, or, shall I say, a proof of the
fickleness of all worldly fortune. Basil the *parakoimomenus*
had fulfilled his destiny.

Let us return to the emperor. Now that he observed the
diverse character of his dominions, and saw that it was no
easy matter to wield such tremendous power, Basil abjured
all self-indulgence. He even went so far as to scorn bodily
ornaments. His neck was unadorned by collars, his head by
diadems. He refused to make himself conspicuous in purple-
coloured cloaks, and he put away superfluous rings, even
clothes of different colours. On the other hand, he took

great pains to ensure that the various departments of the government should be centred on himself, and that they should work without friction. He adopted a supercilious manner, not only in his dealings with other men, but even towards his brother. To Constantine he allotted a mere handful of guards, as though he grudged him protection of a more dignified or imposing nature. Having first straitened himself, so to speak, and having cheerfully stripped off the proud contraptions of monarchy in his own case, he now dealt with his brother and gradually decreased his authority too. He left him to enjoy the beauties of the country, the delights of bathing and hunting, his special hobbies, while he himself went out to the frontiers, where his armies were hard pressed. His ambition, in fact, was to purge the Empire completely of all the barbarians who encircle us and lay siege to our borders, both in the east and in the west.

THE SECOND REVOLT OF SCLERUS AFTER
THE DEATH OF PHOCAS[1]

This project, however, had to be postponed to the future, for Sclerus kept him occupied with a second revolt, and the intended expedition against the barbarians became impossible, at least for the moment. Phocas had died and the men who had been under his command before the alliance with Sclerus, being now foiled of the hopes they had placed in him, dispersed and completely disbanded. Sclerus and his soldiers, who had escaped with him from Assyria, returned home, but voluntarily re-formed their army again. They constituted what might be described as an independent corps, numerically

1. This revolt lasted only a few months; a reconciliation was effected in October 989. It seems likely that Sclerus was supported mainly by the Church and Bardas Phocas by the army. Sclerus died in retirement on 6 March 991, blinded and practically a prisoner of Basil. He had accepted the title of *curopalates*.

the equal of Phocas's army and in the eyes of the emperor
just as menacing.

This man Sclerus, though apparently not to be compared
with Phocas in physical prowess, was a greater exponent of
military strategy and management. It was also said that he
was more resourceful. When his quarrel with the emperor
flared up a second time, he was careful not to come to grips
or risk a battle. His idea was rather to build up his army with
heavy reinforcements and harass the enemy by guerilla
tactics without committing himself to open warfare. No
attempt was made to overwhelm Basil's forces in actual
operations, but his transports were invariably stopped in
convoy, he was cut off from free use of the roads, all mer-
chandise being conveyed to the capital from abroad was im-
pounded – to the great benefit of Sclerus's own army.
Moreover, by maintaining strict vigilance, orders transmitted
through the state couriers were intercepted and never carried
out.

The rebellion began in the summer and dragged on into
the autumn. A whole year passed by and the intrigue was still
not crushed, and, as a matter of fact, this evil troubled the
State for many years to come. Once they had enrolled under
Sclerus, his men were no longer divided in their loyalties;
there were no secret desertions to the emperor. Sclerus inspired them with his own resolute determination and bound
them into one coherent body. By favours he won their
loyalty, by his kindliness he earned their devotion; he reconciled their differences, ate at the same table, drank from the
same cup, called them by name, and by his flattery ensured
their allegiance.

The emperor tried all his wiles and tricks to frustrate him,
but Sclerus easily evaded them. Like a good general, he
answered his opponent's schemes and plans with stratagems of
his own. Seeing that his enemy could never be caught, Basil
sent an embassy to him proposing terms, if Sclerus would

abandon the revolt. Provided he accepted the conditions, he was to occupy rank second only to the emperor himself. At first Sclerus was rather slow to respond. However, he gave the matter deep thought, reviewed the events of the past, examined the present, and guessed what the future might be. He felt the burden of old age and accepted the terms. So he assembled the whole of his army, to support him at the reception of the imperial envoys, and made peace with Basil on the following conditions: he (Sclerus) was to resign his crown and give up wearing the purple, but he was to take precedence immediately after the emperor; the general and others who had revolted with him were to retain their present ranks, and to enjoy as long as they lived whatever privileges he had conferred upon them; they would be deprived neither of property formerly in their possession, nor of any other advantages which had fallen to their lot.

Agreement was reached, and the emperor set out from the capital to one of his most magnificent estates, there to receive the rebel and ratify the treaty.[1] Basil seated himself in the royal tent. Sclerus, some distance away, was introduced by the guards. They led him into the emperor's presence, without preliminaries, not riding on horseback, but escorted on foot. Sclerus was a very tall man, but he was also an aged man, and he came in supported by guards on either side. The emperor, seeing him approaching some way off, turned to the bystanders and made his celebrated remark (everyone knows the story): 'So this is the man I feared! A suppliant dotard, unable to walk by himself!' As for Sclerus, whether because of his eagerness, or because in any case he had forgotten, he had kept on his feet the sandals of purple when he laid aside the other insignia of power, so that it seemed that he was arrogating some share in the royal prerogative. Anyway, he approached the emperor wearing the sandals. Basil saw all this from a distance and shut his eyes in annoyance,

1. At Didymotichus.

refusing to see him at all until he first clothed himself like an ordinary citizen in every detail. There and then Sclerus shook off his purple sandals at the door of the tent and so entered the emperor's presence.

As soon as he saw him enter, Basil rose and they embraced one another. Then they held converse, the one excusing his revolt and explaining the reason why he had plotted and carried it out, the other quietly accepting the apology and attributing to bad luck what had occurred. When they shared a common drinking-bowl, the emperor first put to his own lips the cup offered to Sclerus and took a moderate sip of its contents before handing it back to his guest. Thus he relieved him of any suspicion of poison, and at the same time proved the sanctity of their agreement. After this Basil questioned him, as a man accustomed to command, about his Empire. How could it be preserved free from dissension? Sclerus had an answer to this, although it was not the sort of advice one would expect from a general; in fact, it sounded more like a diabolical plot. 'Cut down the governors who become over-proud,' he said. 'Let no generals on campaign have too many resources. Exhaust them with unjust exactions, to keep them busied with their own affairs. Admit no woman to the imperial councils. Be accessible to no one. Share with few your most intimate plans.'

On this note their conversation came to an end. Sclerus went off to the country estate which had been apportioned him, and soon afterwards he died. We will leave him and return to the emperor. In his dealings with his subjects, Basil behaved with extraordinary circumspection. It is perfectly true that the great reputation he built up as a ruler was founded rather on terror than on loyalty, for as he grew older and became more experienced, he relied less on the judgement of men wiser than himself. He alone introduced new measures, he alone disposed his military forces. As for the civil administration, he governed, not in accordance with the written laws, but following the unwritten dictates of his own intuition, which was most excellently equipped by nature for the purpose. Consequently he paid no attention to men of learning; on the contrary, he affected utter scorn – towards the learned folk, I mean. It seems to me a wonderful thing, therefore, that while the emperor so despised literary culture, no small crop of orators and philosophers sprang up in those times. One solution of the paradox, I fancy, is this: the men of those days did not devote themselves to the study of letters for any ulterior purpose – they cultivated literature for its own sake and as an end in itself, whereas the majority nowadays do not approach the subject of education in this spirit, but consider personal profit to be the first reason for study. Perhaps I should add that though gain is the object of their zeal for literature, if they do not immediately achieve this goal, then they desist from their studies at once. Shame on them!

However, we must return to the emperor. Having purged the Empire of the barbarians, he dealt with his own subjects and completely subjugated them too – I think 'subjugate' is the right word to describe it.[1] He decided to abandon his former policy, and after the great families had been humiliated and put on an equal footing with the rest, Basil found himself playing the game of power-politics with considerable success. He surrounded himself with favourites who were neither remarkable for brilliance of intellect, nor of noble lineage, nor too learned. To them were entrusted the imperial rescripts, and with them he was accustomed to share the

1. Basil was determined to ensure that the great feudal families should never again be able to rebel. By the Novel of January 996, for example, it was enacted that land taken from the people by the rich landowners since the reign of Romanus Lecapenus was to be restored without compensation. The rich were further curbed by the famous *allelengyon*, by which men with money were required to pay taxes for those who were impoverished.

secrets of State. However, since at that time the emperor's
comments on memoranda or requests for favours were never
varied, but only plain, straightforward statements (for Basil,
whether writing or speaking, eschewed all elegance of composition), he used to dictate to his secretaries just as the words
came to his tongue, stringing them all together, one after the
other. There was no subtlety, nothing superfluous in his
speech.

By humbling the pride or jealousy of his people, Basil
made his own road to power an easy one. He was careful,
moreover, to close the exit-doors on the monies contributed
to the treasury. So a huge sum was built up, partly by the
exercise of strict economy, partly by fresh additions from
abroad. Actually the sum accumulated in the imperial
treasury reached the grand total of 200,000 talents. As for the
rest of his gains, it would indeed be hard to find words
adequately to describe them. All the treasures amassed in
Iberia and Arabia, all the riches found among the Celts or
contained in the land of the Scyths – in brief, all the wealth of
the barbarians who surround our borders – all were gathered
together in one place and deposited in the emperor's coffers.
In addition to this, he carried off to his treasure-chambers,
and sequestrated there, all the money of those who rebelled
against him and were afterwards subdued. And since the
vaults of the buildings made for this purpose were not big
enough, he had spiral galleries dug underground, after the
Egyptian style, and there he kept safe a considerable proportion of his treasures. He himself took no pleasure in any of
it; quite the reverse, indeed, for the majority of the precious
stones, both the white ones (which we call pearls) and the
coloured brilliants, far from being inlaid in diadems or
collars, were hidden away in his underground vaults. Meanwhile Basil took part in his processions and gave audience to
his governors clad merely in a robe of purple, not the very
bright purple, but simply purple of a dark hue, with a handful

of gems as a mark of distinction. As he spent the greater part of his reign serving as a soldier on guard at our frontiers and keeping the barbarian marauders at bay, not only did he draw nothing from his reserves of wealth, but even multiplied his riches many times over.

On his expedition against the barbarians, Basil did not follow the customary procedure of other emperors, setting out at the middle of spring and returning home at the end of summer. For him the time to return was when the task in hand was accomplished. He endured the rigours of winter and the heat of summer with equal indifference. He disciplined himself against thirst. In fact, all his natural desires were kept under stern control, and the man was as hard as steel. He had an accurate knowledge of the details of army life, and by that I do not mean the general acquaintance with the composition of his army, the relative functions of individual units in the whole body, or the various groupings and deployments suited to the different formations. His experience of army matters went further than that: the duties of the *protostate*, the duties of the *hemilochites*,[1] the tasks proper to the rank immediately junior to them – all these were no mysteries to Basil, and the knowledge stood him in good stead in his wars. Accordingly, jobs appropriate to these ranks were not devolved on others, and the emperor, being personally conversant with the character and combat duties of each individual, knowing to what each man was fitted either by temperament or by training, used him in this capacity and made him serve there.

Moreover, he knew the various formations suited to his men. Some he had read of in books, others he devised himself during the operations of war, the result of his own intuition. He professed to conduct his wars and draw up the troops in line of battle, himself planning each campaign, but he preferred not to engage in combat personally. A sudden retreat

1. Military ranks, junior officers.

might otherwise prove embarrassing. Consequently, for the most part he kept his troops immobile. He would construct machines of war and skirmish at a distance, while the manoeuvring was left to the light-armed soldiers. Once he had made contact with the enemy, a regular military liaison was established between the different formations of the Roman army. The whole force was drawn up like a solid tower, headquarters being in touch with the cavalry squadrons, who were themselves kept in communication with the light infantry, and these again with the various units of heavy-armed foot. When all was ready, strict orders were given that no soldier should advance in front of the line or break rank under any circumstances. If these orders were disobeyed, and if some of the most valiant or daring soldiers did ride out well in front of the rest, even in cases where they engaged the enemy successfully, they could expect no medals or rewards of valour when they returned. On the contrary, Basil promptly discharged them from the army, and they were punished on the same level as common criminals. The decisive factor in the achievement of victory was, in his opinion, the massing of troops in one coherent body, and for this reason alone he believed the Roman armies to be invincible. The careful inspections he made before battle used to aggravate the soldiers and they abused him openly, but the emperor met their scorn with common sense. He would listen quietly, and then with a gay smile point out that if he neglected these precautions, their battles would go on for ever.

Basil's character was two-fold, for he readily adapted himself no less to the crises of war than to the calm of peace. Really, if the truth be told, he was more of a villain in wartime, more of an emperor in time of peace. Outbursts of wrath he controlled, and like the proverbial 'fire under the ashes' kept anger hidden in his heart, but, if his orders were disobeyed in war, on returning to his palace he would kindle his wrath and reveal it. Terrible then was the vengeance he took on the miscreant. Generally he persisted in his opinions, but there were occasions when he did change his mind. In many cases, too, he traced crimes back to their original causes, and the final links in the chain were exonerated. So most defaulters obtained forgiveness, either through his sympathetic understanding, or because he showed some other interest in their affairs. He was slow to adopt any course of action, but never would he willingly alter the decision once it was taken. Consequently his attitude to friends was unvaried, unless perchance he was compelled by necessity to revise his estimate of them. Similarly, where he had burst out in anger against someone, he did not quickly moderate his indignation. Whatever estimate he formed, indeed, was to him an irrevocable and divinely-inspired judgement.

BASIL'S PERSONAL CHARACTERISTICS

So much for his character. As for his personal appearance, it betrayed the natural nobility of the man, for his eyes were light-blue and fiery, the eyebrows not overhanging nor sullen, nor yet extended in one straight line, like a woman's, but well-arched and indicative of his pride. The eyes were neither deep-set (a sign of knavishness and cunning) nor yet too prominent (a sign of frivolity), but they shone with a brilliance that was manly. His whole face was rounded off, as if from the centre into a perfect circle, and joined to his shoulders by a neck that was firm and not too long. His chest was neither thrust out in front of him, nor hanging on him, so to speak, nor again was it concave and, as it were, cramped; rather was it the mean between two extremes, and the rest of his body was in harmony with it.

As for height, he was of less than normal stature, but it was proportionate to the separate parts of his body, and he held himself upright. If you met him on foot, you would find him much like some other men, but on horseback he afforded a

sight that was altogether incomparable, for in the saddle he
reminded one of the statues which the great sculptors carved,
with their riders adopting a similar pose. When he gave rein
to his horse and rode in the assault, he was erect and firm in
the saddle, riding uphill and downhill alike, and when he
checked his steed, reining it in, he would leap on high as
though he had wings, and he mounted or dismounted alike
with equal grace. In his old age the beard under his chin went
bald, but the hair from his cheeks poured down, the growth
on either side being thick and very profuse, so that wound
round on both sides it was made into a perfect circle and he
appeared to possess a full beard. It was a habit of his to roll it
between his fingers, a gesture to which he was particularly
prone when roused to anger or giving audience, or when he
was engaged in deep thought. That was a frequent habit;
another was to put his fingers on his hips, arms akimbo.
He was not a fluent speaker. The phrases were not rounded off,
nor were they lengthened into periods. In fact, he clipped his
words, with little pauses between them, more like a peasant
than a man of good education. He had a loud laugh, which
convulsed the whole of his body.

The emperor seems to have lived a very long time, more
than all the other sovereigns, for from birth up to his twentieth
year he shared imperial power with his father and Phocas
Nicephorus, and later with John Tzimisces, the latter's successor. During this period he occupied a subordinate position,
but for the next fifty-two years he ruled supreme. He was
therefore in his seventy-second year when he died.[1]

1. Basil died on 15 December 1025. According to Cedrenus he had
reigned as sole monarch for fifty years. He was buried in the monastery
of St John Evangelist in the Hebdomon at Constantinople.

BOOK TWO

CONSTANTINE VIII

1025-8

ON the death of Basil, his brother Constantine became emperor a second time. There was no opposition. As a matter of fact, the dying Basil summoned him to the palace just before the end, and there handed over to him the reins of government. Constantine was at this time in his seventieth year, a person of decidedly effeminate character with but one object in life – to enjoy himself to the full. Since he inherited a treasury crammed with money, he was able to follow his natural inclination, and the new ruler devoted himself to a life of luxury.

According to tradition he was a man of sluggish temperament, with no great ambition for power; he was physically strong, but a craven at heart. Already he was an old man, no longer capable of waging war, and every ill rumour filled him with exasperation. The barbarians encircling our borders had only to stir a finger against us and Constantine would hold them in check – with granting of titles and giving of bribes. If his own subjects rebelled, it was different: they were punished with savage retribution. Suspicion of revolutionary plots, or of party factions, resulted in vengeance, and the suspects were condemned without trial. The Romans became his slaves, not won over by acts of kindness, but subdued by all manner of cruel punishments. No man was ever more quick-tempered. His anger was uncontrolled, and he was ready to listen to any rumour, especially if it concerned those whom he suspected of treachery. On these victims awful tortures were inflicted; it was not a question of temporary restrictions, or of banishment, or of prison; his method was to punish male-factors on the spot, with blinding of the eyes by a red-hot iron. This was the penalty imposed on all and sundry, quite apart from the fact that, in one case, he was dealing with apparently flagrant crime, in another with minor delinquency. No distinction was made between the perpetration of a crime and mere suspicion of wrongdoing. His concern, indeed, was not to award punishment in proportion to the offences, but rather to free himself from his own doubts, and to him it seemed that such torture as blinding was more humane than others. Moreover, it rendered the victims helpless, an excellent reason for its wider use. He maintained this policy irrespective of the high or low rank of his subjects. The evil practice was even extended to include some of the clergy, and the very bishops were not exempt. Once carried away by his anger, the man could only be restored to a reasonable frame of mind with difficulty, and he would turn a deaf ear to all advice. Yet, quick-tempered as he was, Constantine had not been utterly divorced from pity, for at the sight of disaster he would be troubled, and he was often gracious to those who had a woeful story to tell. His anger, too, was not lasting, like that of Basil. He quickly relented and was terribly downcast at what he had done. Better still, if someone could quench the rising fire of his wrath, he would refrain from inflicting chastisement, and even be thankful for some restraining influence. Where there was no resistance, indignation carried him on to any excess. Then, at the first word of apology, he would be grieved, compassionately embrace his victim, let tears fall from his eyes, and beg forgiveness with words full of contrition.

He was generous in his favours, more than all the emperors, but this good quality was not in his case tempered by justice. To members of his court he threw wide open the gates of his favour, heaping gold on them as though it were sand; but to those far removed from the palace this virtue was less displayed. They were his friends most of all whom in their infancy he had castrated and whom afterwards he used as chamberlains and private servants. These men were not of noble birth nor free-born. Actually, they were barbarians and heathens, but they owed their education to the emperor, and because they modelled their own conduct on him, they were accounted worthy of greater respect and honour than others. Their physical degradation was obscured by an adroit and liberal distribution of largess, by their eagerness to confer benefits, by their display of other gentlemanly qualities.

At the time when Basil became emperor, Constantine, while still a young man, had married a lady called Helena. Her father was the renowned Alypius, then a leading man in the city and a member of a noble family held in high repute. This lady, who was not only beautiful but also virtuous, bore him three daughters. The princesses were brought up in the palace and educated in a manner worthy of their exalted rank. The responsibility for their training devolved on Constantine, for although Basil expressed the strongest affection and love for his nieces, he took no further interest in their future. He was too busy guarding the Empire on his brother's behalf.

The eldest of the daughters bore no great resemblance to the rest of her family. She was of a more tranquil disposition, more gentle in spirit, and her beauty was only moderate (in childhood she had been attacked by some infectious illness, and her looks had been marred ever since). The second daughter, whom I myself saw in her extreme old age, was very regal in her ways, a woman of great beauty, most imposing in her manner and commanding respect. About her I will write in more detail at the appropriate point in my history. At the moment I am merely giving a brief outline of their characteristics. The third and last daughter was very tall, curt and glib of tongue, but not so beautiful as her sister. Their uncle, the Emperor Basil, died without making any plans for their subsequent promotion, and as for their father, even he, when he acceded to the throne, failed to reach any wise decision about their future, except in the case of the second sister, the one who was most like an empress. I will tell the story of that decision and of the plan he made on his deathbed, as my narrative proceeds. Actually, this princess and the third sister acquiesced in the ideas of their uncle and father, and made no plans of their own, but the eldest, Eudocia (for that was her name), whether because she had no desire for power, or because she had her affections fixed on higher things, begged her father to dedicate her to the service of God. He readily agreed, and she was presented to the Lord as an offering, the first-fruits so to speak of her parents' marriage. Constantine's intentions for the other two were kept a dark secret. However, I must not speak of that yet.

I would like now to sketch the emperor's character, without bias one way or the other. When the whole government came to depend on himself, he was by no means the man to expend his own energies on cares of State. Putting the wiser of his subjects in charge of affairs, he merely gave audiences to embassies, or administered some other easy matter, seated most royally on his throne. However, when he did have occasion to make a speech, he astonished all hearers by his logical arguments. As a matter of fact, he had not much learning. He had acquired a smattering of culture, just as much as one considers enough for children, but he was endowed with great natural intelligence and more than ordinary grace. He had the added advantage of a tongue both melodious and refined: arguments conceived in his mind were, so to speak, brilliantly delivered by his tongue. He did, indeed, personally dictate some of the imperial rescripts (he made that a point of honour) and the quickest writers could not keep up with him, he spoke so fast, and that despite the fact that he was fortunate in the number and quality of his secretaries, writers so fast that few generations have seen their like. Overwhelmed by the speed of his words, they used to interpret most of his thoughts and expressions by special symbols of their own.

He was a man of enormous size, standing up to nine feet in height. His constitution, moreover, was more than usually robust, and his digestive powers were extraordinary, with a stomach naturally adapted to assimilate all kinds of food with ease. He was especially expert in the art of preparing rich savoury sauces, giving the dishes character by combinations of colour and perfume, and summoning all Nature to his aid – anything to excite the palate. Being dominated by his gluttony and sexual passions, he became afflicted with arthritis, and worse still, his feet gave him such trouble that he was unable to walk. That is why, after his accession, no one saw him attempt to walk with any confidence; he used to ride on horseback, in safety.

For the theatre and horse-racing he had an absolute obsession. To Constantine these things were a matter of real concern, as he changed horses, harnessed fresh mounts, and anxiously kept his eyes on the starting-points in the arena. The *gymnopodia*,[1] long ago neglected, was also revived in his reign. He reintroduced it into the theatre, not content with the emperor's normal role of spectator, but himself appearing as a combatant, with opponents. It was his wish, moreover, that his rivals should not be vanquished simply because he was the emperor, but he liked them to fight back with skill – his own credit for the victory would thus be the greater. He used to chatter away, too, about his contests, and he mixed well with the common people. The theatre also attracted him, and no less the chase. Once engaged in the latter he was impervious to heat, ignored the cold, and never gave way to thirst. Most of all he was skilled in fighting with wild beasts, and it was because of this that he learned to shoot with the bow, hurl the javelin, draw his sword with dexterity, and aim his arrow straight at the mark.

He neglected the affairs of his Empire while he devoted

1. A form of single combat, reminiscent of Roman gladiatorial contests.

himself to his chequers and dice, for so ardent was he in the
pursuit of gaming and so enraptured by it, that even when
ambassadors were waiting to attend on him he would disregard them if he was in the middle of a game. He would
despise matters of the utmost importance, spend whole nights
and days at it, and fast completely, voracious eater though he
was, when he wanted to play at the dice. So, playing away his
Empire, he was surprised by Death, and Old Age reminded
him suddenly of the decay that Nature ordains. When,
therefore, he felt that the end was near, either persuaded by
his counsellors, or through his own recognition of duty, he
began to cast round for an heir to the throne, intending to
betroth the second of his daughters to the man he chose. As,
however, he had never regarded any members of the Senate
with more than a cursory glance before, it was difficult for
him to make a reasonable choice.

One of the persons considered was a man prominent in the
Senate, who had been promoted to the office of Eparch[1] – an
imperial dignity, although it did not carry with it the privilege
of wearing the purple – but since this gentleman had married
while still in his childhood, he hardly seemed a suitable
candidate. In the matter of family and social position, he was
more acceptable than his rivals, but in the eyes of the Church
his previous marriage was an obstacle to further promotion.
It was commonly agreed that he must be passed over. Since
circumstances did not permit of more deliberation, and the
near approach of death prevented the emperor from examining the claims of various men in detail, he condemned every-

1. The Eparch, or City Prefect, ranked eighteenth in the first sixty
great officials. His duties included the maintenance of order in the city,
superintendence of the factions in the Circus, control of the industrial
guilds, and above all the supply of corn. The man here concerned was
probably Constantine Dalassenus (Cedrenus, 722, p. 484) who was
offered the hand of Zoe by the emperor, but Simeon, the *drungarius
vigiliae*, favoured Romanus. There was trouble over the divorce, but the
patriarch soon settled the matter in favour of the new emperor.

one else as unworthy of a royal marriage, and gave his full
support to Romanus. He knew that Romanus's wife opposed
the scheme, so he pretended to be in a most violent, implacable rage with her husband. Messengers were sent,
ostensibly to take awful vengeance on him and to carry
her off to a nunnery. She, not knowing the secret of the plot,
nor seeing that the emperor's anger was only a mask, immediately submitted to her fate. Her hair was cut off, she was
clothed in the nun's robe of black, and admitted into the
nunnery, while her husband was taken up to the palace, to
wed into the imperial family. The most beautiful of Constantine's daughters was no sooner in his sight than she was
made his bride. So her father, having survived just long
enough to see the marriage ceremony performed, passed
away and left the Empire to his kinsman, Romanus.[1]

1. Constantine died on 11 November 1028, aged seventy, after an
illness of only two days.

BOOK THREE

ROMANUS III

1028–34

CONSTANTINE was succeeded as emperor by his son-in-law Romanus, surnamed Argyropulus.[1] The latter was convinced that his reign marked the beginning of a new dynasty. The imperial family descended from Basil the Macedonian[2] had died with his predecessor, and he now looked forward to a new line of monarchs descended from himself. In fact, that line was destined to perish at once, and he, after a short life and that full of suffering, was fated to die suddenly. The story will show all this in more detail as it proceeds. From now on the history will be more accurate than hitherto, for the Emperor Basil died when I was a baby, while Constantine ended his reign just after I had begun my elementary studies. So I was never admitted to their presence, nor did I hear them speak. Whether I even saw them I cannot say, for I was too young to remember at that time. On the other hand, I both saw Romanus and on one occasion actually talked with him. Naturally, therefore, my remarks on the first two emperors are based on information supplied by others, but my account of Romanus is quite independent.

This gentleman, nurtured on Greek literature, also had some acquaintance with the literary works of the Italians. He had a graceful turn of speech and a majestic utterance. A man of heroic stature, he looked every inch a king. His idea of his own range of knowledge was vastly exaggerated, but wishing

1. Romanus's great-grandfather had married a daughter of Romanus Lecapenus. Constantine's grandfather, Constantine VII Porphyrogenitus, had also married a daughter of the same emperor. Thus Zoe and Romanus were distantly related.
2. Basil I, emperor from 867 to 886.

to model his reign on those of the great Antonines of the past, the famous philosopher Marcus and Augustus, he paid attention particularly to two things: the study of letters and the science of war. Of the latter he was completely ignorant, and as for letters, his experience was far from profound: in fact, it was merely superficial. However, his belief in his own knowledge, and this straining beyond his own intellectual limits, led him to commit mistakes on a big scale. Doubtless if there were any sparks of wisdom lying hid beneath the ashes, he added fresh fuel to the fire, and he enrolled a whole new tribe of philosophers and orators and all those who busied themselves in the sciences – or rather, thought they did.

That era produced few men of erudition, and even they stood only at the outer door of the Aristotelian doctrines and merely repeated the Platonic allegories, without any understanding of their hidden meaning or of the philosophers' studies in dialectic or proof by syllogistic deduction. There being no proper criterion, their judgement on these great men was erroneous. However, questions were propounded on religious subjects, questions dealing with the interpretation of Holy Writ. Yet most of the difficult problems were left unsolved. The truth is that they concerned themselves with such mysteries as the Immaculate Conception, the Virgin Birth, and metaphysical problems. The palace indeed clothed itself in the outward form of philosophy for all to see, but it was all a mask and pretence: there was no real test, no real quest for truth.

Abandoning these studies for a while, Romanus returned to strategy, and the conversation now inclined to greaves and breastplates. The plan was to annex the whole barbarian world, east and west alike. Nor was his ambition limited to a subjugation in theory; he wanted to subdue the barbarians by force of arms. Doubtless, had the emperor's two-fold enthusiasm resulted in a genuine understanding of his problems, instead of being mere vanity and make-believe, he would have benefited his empire greatly. As it was, he did nothing more than make projects, or, shall I say, built castles in the air and then, in actual practice, hurled them down again. But there, I am hurrying on because of my exuberance to the end of my story before, so to speak, building up the gateway to his reign. Let us go back, therefore, to the time of his accession.

Having been judged worthy of the crown, in preference to all others, Romanus deceived himself in the belief that he would reign for many years, and leave to succeed him a family destined to inherit the throne for many generations. Apparently it did not occur to him that Constantine's daughter, with whom he lived after his acclamation, was too old to conceive and already barren (she was in her fiftieth year when she married him).[1] Even in the face of natural incapacity, he clung ever more firmly to his ambitions, led on by his own faith in the future. Hence he ignored the physical prerequisite for conception. Nevertheless, he did have recourse to the specialists who deal with sexual disorders and claim the ability to induce or cure sterility. He submitted himself to treatment with ointments and massage, and he enjoined his wife to do likewise. In fact, she went further: she was introduced to most of the magical practices, fastening little pebbles to her body, hanging charms about her, wearing chains, decking herself out with the rest of the nonsense. As their hopes were never realized, the emperor at last gave up in despair and paid less attention to Zoe. In truth, his desires were somewhat dulled and his bodily powers exhausted, for he was more than twenty years older than she was.

He had been most jealous of his reputation in distributing the honours of the Empire, and his generosity in the use of imperial treasures, by way of favours and donations, had won

1. Zoe was forty-eight. She had been born in 980.

him more regard than most sovereigns.[1] Then, suddenly, as if some fresh idea had occurred to him, as if he were another person altogether, this spirit of genial liberality passed; the sudden gust exhausted itself. He lost confidence in his powers and seemed out of place. And when he relaxed there was no moderation about it. From the highest summit he crashed down to the depths, all in one brief moment. As for the empress, two things more than any other vexed her: the fact that Romanus did not love her, and that she herself was unable to squander money. The treasure-chambers were closed to her, sealed by the emperor's orders, and she was compelled to live on a fixed allowance. Not unnaturally, she was furious with him and with the counsellors whose advice he followed in the matter. They, on their part, were aware of her feelings and they took precautions more stringent than ever, especially Pulcheria, the emperor's sister, a woman of great spirit and one who contributed not a little to her brother's success. Romanus, meanwhile, was quite oblivious of this undercurrent of suspicion; apparently he was under the impression that some supernatural power was bound to preserve his throne. His reputation was secure, to be for ever maintained in glory by this power, as if some kind of contract had been made between him and it.

Setting his heart on military glory, he prepared for war against the barbarians, east and west. Victory over the western barbarians, however easy, seemed no great triumph, but an attack on the eastern enemies, he thought, would win him fame. There he could use the resources of his Empire on a colossal scale. For these reasons, although no real pretext for war existed, he made an unprovoked assault on the Saracens, who lived in Coele-Syria and whose capital was Chalep (as

1. Romanus had good reason to reverse his generous policy later on, for apart from Saracen incursions the Empire suffered famine in Asia Minor, plague, loss of crops through the ravages of the locust, and a great earthquake in Constantinople (1031-2).

they pronounce the name of the place in their own language).
The whole Roman army was assembled and organized to
fight these Saracens. The ranks were increased and fresh
formations devised, while the mercenaries were welded into
one force and new troops conscripted. His plan, it appears,
was to overwhelm the enemy at the first attack. He thought
that if he increased the army beyond its normal strength, or
rather, if the legion was made more numerous, when he came
upon the foe with such masses of soldiers, Romans and allies,
no one would be able to resist him. The leading generals tried
to dissuade him from this offensive – they were not a little
fearful of the outcome – but he had the crowns made (at great
expense) with which he was to adorn his head at the proclamation of his triumphs.

So, being satisfied with the preparations, he set out from
Byzantium for Syria. When he occupied Antioch, the entry
into the city was celebrated with much pomp. It was certainly
a royal show, but the equipment was somewhat theatrical,
not worthy of fighting men, nor capable of striking terror into
the hearts of the enemy. On their side, the barbarians took a
more realistic view of the war. First they sent ambassadors
to the emperor. They declared that they had not wanted this
war, nor had they given him any pretext for it. They were
standing by the peace terms already concluded, and they
refused to repudiate the treaty still in force. On the other
hand, seeing that he was now adopting a policy of threats
and since he persisted in parading his strength, they themselves, if he proved obdurate, would from now on make their
own preparations for conflict: they committed themselves
to the fortunes of war. Such was the purport of this embassy.
Despite the warning, the emperor to all appearances had one
object only – to draw up his line of battle, to set his men in
array against the enemy, to lay ambushes, to go out foraging,
to dig trenches, to drain off rivers, to take fortresses. In fact,
he wanted to imitate the traditional deeds of the famous

Trajans and Hadrians, or (still farther back in history) of the
Augusti and Caesars, or of *their* predecessor, Alexander the
son of Philip. The ambassadors were therefore dismissed with
a conciliatory message while still more strenuous preparations
were made for war. To attain his object, however, he did
not choose the best men. He thought war was decided by
the big battalions, and it was on the big battalions that he
relied.

When he left Antioch and went on farther, a detachment of
barbarian soldiers, all equipped in their own fashion, daring
bareback riders, lay in ambush on either side of the army's
route. Suddenly they appeared on high ground. Yelling their
war-cry and filling their opponents with consternation at this
unexpected sight, they made a tremendous din as their horses
charged to the attack. By not keeping in close order, they
created the illusion of great numbers, running about in
scattered groups and with no regular formations. This so
terrorized the Roman soldiery and spread such panic in this
mighty and famous army, and so shattered their morale,
that they all ran away, dressed just as they were, and not a
thought did they give to anything but flight. Those who
happened to be on horseback wheeled about and made off as
fast as they could, while the rest did not even wait to mount
their horses, but left them to the first master who claimed
them, and every man, running off or wandering away,
sought his own safety to the best of his ability. It was an
extraordinary sight. Here were those same men, who had
brought a continent to terms, who in their preparations for
war and in their military dispositions had made themselves
invincible before the whole might of Barbary, now daring
not even to look their enemies in the eye. As if the thunder of
barbarian cries had deafened their ears and smitten their
hearts with fear, they turned and ran off like men in utter
defeat. First to feel the effects of the hubbub were the Imperial
Guards. Without so much as a backward glance they deserted

their emperor and fled.[1] Indeed, if someone had not helped
him on to his horse, given him the reins, and counselled him
to escape, he would have been almost captured himself and
made prisoner by the enemy – he who had hoped to shake a
whole continent! The truth is, if God had not at that moment
restrained the barbarian onrush, and had He not inspired
them to moderation in the hour of victory, nothing could
have saved the Roman army from complete annihilation, and
the emperor would have fallen first of all.

So the Romans ran off in disorder. Meanwhile the enemy, as
if amazed at the sight of Romans routed and fleeing for no
reason, merely stood and watched this astounding triumph.
Later on, after taking a handful of prisoners on the field, and
those men whom they knew to be of some importance, they
told the rest to go free, and turned to the loot. First they seized
the imperial tent, which was nearly as valuable as the palace of
today, for it was filled with necklaces and bracelets and
diadems, pearls and precious stones even more costly, all
kinds of glorious booty. To count the multitude of these
treasures would have been no easy task, nor to admire enough
their beauty and magnificence, so great and luxurious was the
profusion of wealth in the emperor's tent. Next they proceeded to collect the rest of the spoil, and loading themselves
with it they rejoined their compatriots. The emperor was
meanwhile riding on ahead of the Saracens, wandering on
wherever the whim of his charger bore him. He came by a
certain ridge and here he was seen by some men who were
running past and recognized who he was by the colour of his
sandals. Many of these fugitives he stopped there, and stood
surrounded by them. Thereupon the rumour spread far and
wide that Romanus still lived, and others joined him. More
important than that, somebody came up with the ikon of the

1. This reverse took place in 1030, near Chalep (Aleppo). It was partially avenged in the next year by the capture of Edessa by George
Maniaces, who first became prominent in these campaigns.

Theometor,[1] the image which Roman emperors habitually carry with them on campaign as a guide and guardian of all the army. This alone had not been taken by the enemy.

When the emperor saw this beautiful sight (he was particularly reverent in his veneration for this ikon) he immediately took heart, and holding it in his hands – but no words can describe how he embraced it, how he bedewed it with his tears, how heartfelt were the terms in which he addressed it, how he recalled Our Lady's kindnesses in the past and those many times when she, his ally, had rescued and saved the Roman power in moments of crisis. From now on he was full of courage. He who had but lately been a fugitive himself now rebuked others who were running away. With loud cries and the vigour of a man years younger than himself he stopped their aimless wandering, made himself known to them by his voice and appearance, and quickly gathered together a considerable force. Then, going on foot with them, he retired to a tent hastily erected to shelter him, and there he bivouacked. After a brief rest, at dawn he called for his generals and suggested that they should decide what to do. Without exception they advised him to return to Byzantium. In the capital a thorough inquiry into the whole affair should be held. Romanus agreed with them – it was a course of action likely to benefit himself – and hurried back to Constantinople.

There followed bitter repentance for what he had done, and self-pity for the sufferings he had endured. Then, all at once, his mood changed. His career now entered on a new and, for him, somewhat unusual phase. He hoped that by careful management of public funds he would completely recover his losses. So he became more tax-gatherer than emperor. Reviving, as the proverb has it, 'pre-Euclidean history', and subjecting it to careful scrutiny, he proceeded to pry into the accounts of sons, long after their fathers were dead and gone –

1. The Mother of God.

a cruel thing to do. Verdicts in law-suits were not given according to the evidence submitted by the contesting parties, but he would personally take the part of one or the other. Sentence of the court, therefore, was not so much in favour of plaintiff or defendant as of himself. In his view the whole populace was divided into two classes. On the one hand there were the reasonable folk who preferred to live a simple, honest life and took no part in public affairs; for them the emperor cared not a straw. On the other there were the dare-devils who enriched themselves at the expense of the rest. These latter added their own quota of evil as fuel to the general conflagration fired by their ruler, and the result was nothing but confusion and trouble. What made it more terrible was the fact that while the great majority were being plundered and stripped, the imperial treasury enjoyed not a penny of the profits built up from these embezzlements, for the rivers of money were being diverted elsewhere. The truth of this will be shown more clearly as the story progresses.

This particular emperor aspired to a reputation for piety. It is quite true that he was interested in religious matters, but there was more pretence about it than real piety. Anyway, he appeared to be a pious man. In the first place, this led to extravagance in discussions about problems of divinity. He would examine causes and arguments which could not be explained by mere knowledge; only if one had recourse to Mind, without any interpreting medium, could the mysteries be made intelligible. In natural philosophy, however, he showed little interest, nor did he discuss such matters with the professors, except with those who claimed (unjustly) that they were disciples of Aristotle. Romanus's studies, as one of our wise men said, were more profound, and dealt with objects comprehensible by Mind alone.

That was the first way he devised of showing his piety. Later on, being jealous of the great Solomon, for his building of the much-vaunted Temple, and envious of the Emperor

Justinian, because of the mighty church that was named after the Holy and Ineffable Wisdom, he determined to build and found, by way of recompense so to speak, another in honour of the Mother of God.[1] It was a great mistake, for what was intended to be an act of piety, turned out to be the cause of evil and the occasion for many injustices. The expenditure incurred over this church was constantly increased. Every day he collected more contributions than the work necessitated, and woe betide the man who tried to limit the building. On the other hand, anyone who invented fresh extravagances and new variations of style was sure of winning the emperor's friendship at once. Every mountain was bored for material, and the miner's art esteemed higher than philosophy itself. Of the stones thus obtained, some were split, others polished, others turned for the sculptures, and the workers on these stones were reckoned with the like of Pheidias and Polygnotus and Zeuxis.[2] Nothing in the whole world was thought good enough for this church. All the royal treasure was made available, every golden stream poured into it. The monies were exhausted, and yet the construction went on, for one on top of another new parts were added, and at the same time some other part would be pulled down. Often, too, the work would cease and then suddenly rise up afresh, slightly bigger or with some more elaborate variety. When rivers flow into the sea, most of their water is drained away before ever it reaches the mouth, and so it was with this money, for most of what had been collected for this church was appropriated in advance and wasted on other things.

While Romanus manifested his piety in these activities, he

1. He also began rebuilding the Church of the Holy Sepulchre at Jerusalem and spent much money on gold and silver decorations for St Sophia. The foundation stone of the latter was laid in 532, and again in 537 after the destruction of the cathedral by fire.

2. Famous Greek artists of the fifth century B.C. Pheidias was a sculptor; Polygnotus and Zeuxis were painters.

showed himself a rogue from the very start, because he used money which had been contributed for quite different purposes than the building of this church. Doubtless it is a beautiful thing to love the House of the Lord, and make it magnificent, as the psalmist tells us, and it is a fine thing to love the Tabernacle of His Glory. It is better to suffer disgrace many times in the eyes of men by serving God thus than to gain worldly riches. Such devotion is indeed noble, and who, of those that are zealous in His service and filled with the Spirit of the Lord, would bring themselves to despise it? But, surely, there should be nothing to mar this devotion. It cannot be right, in order to show one's piety, to commit great injustices, to put the whole state in confusion, to break down the whole body politic. He who rejects the harlot's offering, who utterly despises the sacrifice of the ungodly, as though the wicked were no better than a dog – how could he in any way draw near a building, however rich and glorious, when that building is the cause of many evils? The symmetry of walls, the encircling columns, the hanging tapestries, the magnificent offerings, and the other things of like splendour – what can they contribute to the sacred object of piety? Surely it is enough that a man's soul be clothed in godliness, that his heart be dyed in the spiritual purple, that his deeds be righteous, his thoughts full of grace. In a word, it is sufficient if a man be without guile, and because of this simple faith there is builded up within us a temple of another sort, a temple acceptable to the Lord and beloved by Him. The philosophy Romanus knew was concerned with the scholar's inquiries, the syllogisms '*sorites*' and '*outis*',[1] but in his works he had no idea at all how to show forth that philosophic spirit. Even if the emperor felt compelled to build on a more imposing scale than anyone else, it was still his duty to care for his palace, to glorify the acropolis, to repair what had fallen

1. Arguments of the Megarian School, called *Eristikoi* because of their fondness for dialectic.

in ruins, to replenish the imperial treasury, and to dedicate
the money to the upkeep of his armies. Yet he neglected all
this, and in order that his church might surpass all others in
beauty, he reduced everything else to ruin. To tell the truth,
he was mad on the work and could scarcely tear himself away
from it. So he surrounded the place with all the paraphernalia
of a court, set up thrones there, adorned it with sceptres, hung
up purple cloth, and spent the greater part of the year in this
church, glorying in the beauty of it and beaming with
pleasure. It was his wish to honour the Theometor with
some name of more than ordinary beauty. Unfortunately
he failed to notice that the epithet he gave her was in fact
more suited to a woman than a saint, if the name '*Peribleptos*'
does indeed mean 'Celebrated'.

To these buildings a further addition was made and the
church became a hospice for monks, so once more there
began fresh wrongdoings and greater excesses than before.
He was not sufficiently trained in arithmetic or geometry to
diminish the size or the number of his buildings, in the same
way that geometricians simplify a complex pattern. So, wishing to have buildings of enormous size, he must needs have
greater numbers of monks. The rest was proportionate: as
there were multitudes of monks, so there were contributions
in multitudes. Another world was ransacked, and the sea
beyond the Pillars of Hercules[1] was explored; the former was
to provide seasonable sweetmeats, the latter fish of enormous
size, even whales. Since it seemed to him, moreover, that
Anaxagoras[2] had lied when he said that the worlds were
infinite, he dedicated the greater part of this finite world of
ours to the glorification of his church. Piling grandeur on
grandeur, multitude on multitude, surpassing the first super-

1. The Straits of Gibraltar.
2. Anaxagoras of Clazomenae, Ionian philosopher of the fifth century B.C., thought that other *kosmoi* (universes) contemporaneous with
our own might and did exist *ad infinitum*.

lative with a second, and setting no bound nor limit to these things, he would never have stopped adding to them in his boundless ambition, had not the measure of his own life been shortened.

There is a tradition, in fact, that his life was cut short by a certain event. I wish to speak of it, but only by way of preface at this moment. In some matters the emperor showed little respect for the accepted standards of morality. For one thing, he lived with a mistress. Perhaps, at the beginning of his reign, he wished to live chastely. Maybe – and most folk contend that this was the truth – he turned to fresh amours. Whatever the cause of his behaviour, he came to despise the Empress Zoe. Not only did he abstain from sexual intercourse with her, but he was loath to consort with her in any way at all. She, on her side, was stirred to hate him, not only because the blood royal, meaning herself, was treated with such little respect, but, above all considerations, by her own longing for intercourse, and that was due not to her age, but to the soft and sensual manner of her life at the palace.

THE INTRODUCTION OF MICHAEL TO THE
EMPEROR BY HIS BROTHER

There, then, is the preface to the story; the sequel came about as follows. Among other persons who served this emperor, before his accession to the throne, was a certain eunuch,[1] a man of mean and contemptible fortune, but endowed with an extremely active and ingenious mind. In his time the Emperor Basil had treated this man with great familiarity

1. John the Orphanotrophus had been protonotary under Basil II. He had four brothers: Michael, Nicetas, Constantine, and George, the last two also being eunuchs. The family came from Paphlagonia and appears to have been engaged in some disreputable business, Cedrenus (733, p. 504) hints that it was forgery. Through John's influence Michael was promoted Archon of the Pantheon.

and had shared secrets with him. Without promoting him to
any exalted positions of responsibility, he still used him with
genuine respect. This eunuch had a brother, a mere youth
before Romanus became emperor, but now in his early manhood. He was a finely-proportioned young man, with the
fair bloom of youth in his face, as fresh as a flower, clear-eyed,
and in very truth 'red-cheeked'. This youth was led by his
brother into the emperor's presence when he was seated with
Zoe that they might see him, at the express command of
Romanus. When the two men came in, the emperor, casting
him one glance and asking a few questions, brief enough,
bade him retire but stay on in the court. The effect of the
interview on Zoe was quite different. Her eyes burned with a
fire as dazzling as the young man's beauty and she at once fell
victim to his charm. From some mystic union between them
she conceived a love for him. But most people knew nothing
of that at the time.

Zoe could neither regard the young man with philosophic
detachment, nor control her desires. Consequently, though in
the past she had more than once shown her dislike for the
eunuch, she now approached him frequently. Her conversations would begin with reference to some extraneous matter,
and then, as if by way of digression, she would end with some
remark about his brother. Let him be bold, she said, and visit
her whenever he wished. The young man, so far knowing
nothing of the empress's secret, supposed the invitation was
due to her kindness of heart, and he accepted it, although in a
modest and timorous fashion. This bashful reserve, however,
only made him the more dazzling. His face, suffused with
blushes, shone with a glorious colour. She eased his fear,
smiling on him gently and forgetting her usual grim arrogance. She hinted at love, tried to encourage him, and when
she proceeded to give her beloved manifest opportunities to
make love on his part, he set himself to answer her desire, not
with any real confidence at first, but later his advances became

more brazen and he acted as lovers will. Suddenly he threw his arms about her, kissing her and touching her hand and neck, as his brother had taught him he should do. She clung to him all the closer. Her kisses became more passionate, she truly loving him, he in no way desiring her (for she was past the age of love), but thinking in his heart of the glory that power would bring him. For this he was prepared to dare anything, and bear it with patience. As for those who lived in the palace, they at first only suspected or conjectured what was going on, but afterwards, when the affair broke all bounds of modesty, everyone knew of it. There was nobody who did not perceive how it was going, for their embraces had already ended in carnal union, and they were discovered by several people sleeping together on the same couch. He blushed with shame and was filled with apprehension for the outcome of this, but she did not conceal it. In the eyes of all she clung to him and offered her kisses, boasting that she had more than once had her joy of him.

That she should adorn him, as if he were some statue, cover him with gold, make him resplendent with rings and garments of woven gold cloth, I do not regard as anything remarkable, for what would an empress not provide for her beloved? But she, unknown to the world, sometimes went so far as to seat him, turn by turn with herself, on the imperial throne, to put in his hand a sceptre; and on one occasion even deemed him worthy of a crown. Thereupon she would throw her arms about him all over again, calling him her 'idol', 'the delight of her eyes', 'the flower of beauty', 'the comfort of her soul'. As she repeated this again and again, she was observed by one of those who have eyes for everything. This fellow was a eunuch who had been put in charge of the imperial court, a man respected for his dignified bearing, as well as for his exalted position, and a family retainer of the empress. When he saw this extraordinary sight, he was so amazed that he almost expired; Zoe, however, called him to

her side and reassured him (by that time he was utterly confounded and at his last gasp). She told him to attach himself
to Michael, for he was in fact emperor already and soon
everyone would acknowledge his promotion.

Although nobody else had failed to notice this, it did not
come to the knowledge of the emperor. Romanus was so
completely blind. However, when the flash of the lightning
and the roar of the thunder did eventually play round his
eyes and deafen his ears, when he himself saw some things
going on and heard of others, even then, as if he preferred to
be blind and deaf, he closed his eyes again and refused to
listen. Worse than that, many a time when he was sleeping
with the empress and she, clothed in some garment of purple,
was waiting for him to lie down on their couch, he would
call for Michael, bidding him come alone, and order him to
touch and massage his feet. In fact, he made him servant of the
bed-chamber, and, in order that the young man might do
this office, deliberately abandoned his wife to him. When
his sister Pulcheria and some of the chamberlains discovered a
plot against his life and told him of it and warned him to be
on his guard, still he did not destroy the secret adulterer and
cut short the whole drama, as he could have done. He could
have suggested any reason but the real one and still have had
his way, but he refused. He made no effort to combat the
intrigue. Once he did send for the lover – or the beloved –
and questioned him about the affair; however, as Michael
pretended to know nothing about it, Romanus made him give
his word of honour and swear by the Holy Relics, and after
the other had completely perjured himself, the emperor
looked upon the stories of the rest as mere calumny, listening
only to Michael and calling him 'his most faithful servant'.

Another factor helped to confirm the emperor in his attitude, so that Michael's guilt seemed even more unlikely.
Ever since his childhood the young man had been afflicted by
a terrible illness. This malady took the form of a periodic

derangement of the brain. Without any previous symptoms he would be suddenly confused, roll his eyes, throw himself down on the ground, bang his head, and suffer prolonged and convulsive fits. Then he would become himself again and gradually return to his normal appearance. The emperor had seen him afflicted by this illness and was sorry for him. He thought the young man unfortunate. His madness, therefore, he did recognize, but he failed to recognize his indulgence in the pleasures of love. To most folk it seemed that this malady was a pretext and veil for Michael's scheming, and the suspicion would have been justified were it not for the fact that when he became emperor he still continued to suffer from this derangement. However, discussion of that problem must be postponed to the part of my history concerned with Michael's reign. We can say that the trouble was not self-induced. Equally we can say that the malady, which had no pretence about it, served as a veil to hide his designs.

To convince the emperor, therefore, that those who loved one another were not really in love, was no great task, for he was very easily convinced. I had a conversation with one of the gentlemen who regularly attended the imperial court at that time, a man well acquainted with the whole question of Zoe's love-affairs, and one who supplied me with material for this history, and he told me that Romanus did wish, in a way, to be convinced that she was not Michael's paramour. On the other hand, he knew that she was greatly attracted to the opposite sex, on fire with passion, so to speak. So, to prevent her sharing her favours among many, he was not particularly disgusted at her association with one. Although he pretended not to see it, he allowed the empress to satisfy her desires to the full. I have been told another version of the story. The emperor, according to my other informant, was indulgent towards his wife's amorous intentions or their consummation, but his sister Pulcheria was enraged, and so were all those whom she treated as her confidants. So she and they waged war with Michael and the empress. The arrangements for the struggle did not pass unnoticed, but their anticipated triumphs never came to pass, for the sister died not long after, while, of her friends, one also died suddenly and another left the palace at the express desire of the emperor. As to the rest, some approved of the business, others held their tongues. Zoe and Michael, therefore, far from consummating their love in an underhand way, did so with an almost legal sanction.

THE EMPEROR'S ILLNESS

What happened next? I will tell you. An illness of an unusual and painful character befell Romanus. Actually, the whole of his body became festering and corrupted inside. At any rate, from then onwards he lost most of his appetite, and sleep, poised on his eye-lids, quickly flitted away. All the ill-humours fell upon him together – harshness of character, peevishness of spirit, anger and wrath and shouting, things unknown in him hitherto. All his life, from his earliest years, he had been a friendly sort of man; now it became not only hard to be admitted into his presence, but hard to get a civil reply to one's questions. Laughter deserted him, along with his former graciousness and pleasant nature. He trusted nobody at all, nor did he seem to others trustworthy himself. Each party suspected and was suspected by the other. His lack of generosity now became more pronounced. The distributions of money that he made were niggardly in any case, and he was savagely angry at every request for it. Every tale of pity only succeeded in irritating him. Yet, despite the dreadful condition of his health, he neither neglected the usual court ceremonial nor did he overlook the importance of the imperial processions. He even clothed himself in magnificent robes shot with gold and put on the rest of the paraphernalia proper to those occasions. It was like a heavy load to him, in his weakened state, and after returning to the palace with difficulty he was more ill than ever.

I have often seen him myself when he was distressed during these processions (at the time I was just under sixteen years of age) and he differed little from a man who was dead. His whole face was swollen and the colour of it was no more pleasant to look upon than that of men three days dead in the tombs. His breathing was fast, and after moving a few paces he had to rest. Most of the hairs on his head had fallen out, as though he were a corpse, but a few strands, scattered here and there, were tousled round his forehead, moved, I suppose, by his breathing. The others despaired of his life, but he himself was by no means without hope. He had put himself in the hands of the doctors and he expected to be restored to health by their skill.

THE EMPEROR'S DEATH

Whether the loving couple themselves, and their accomplices, committed a very horrible crime against him, I would not say with any certainty, because it is no easy thing for me to bring accusations in matters that I still do not thoroughly understand.[1] However, it was universally accepted among the rest that they first bewitched him with drugs, and later had recourse to a mixture of hellebore as well. I am not disputing that for the moment – it may or may not be true – but I do maintain that Zoe and Michael were the cause of his death. His state of health being what it was, the emperor made his preparations for the Resurrection that awaits all of us alike. At the same time, he was making himself ready for the public services on the morrow (Good Friday). Before dawn he set out to bathe in one of the baths situated near the imperial quarters. There was no one to assist him, and he was certainly

1. Cedrenus (733, p. 505) definitely says that Zoe was slowly poisoning him.

not at death's door then. He got up in a perfectly normal way
to anoint and bathe himself and take his aperitives. So he
entered the bath. First he washed his head, then drenched his
body as well, and as he was breathing strongly, he proceeded
to the swimming pool, which had been deepened in the
middle. To begin with, he enjoyed himself swimming on the
surface and floating lightly, blowing out and refreshing himself with the greatest of pleasure. Later on some of his retinue
came in to support him and give him a rest, according to his
own orders. Whether they made an attempt on the emperor's
life after they entered the bath I cannot say with any conviction. At any rate, those who see some connexion between
these events and the rest of their version say that when
Romanus plunged his head under the water – his usual
custom – they all pressed his neck and held him down for
some considerable time, after which they let him go and went
away.[1] The air inside him, however, caused his body to rise
and it brought him to the surface, almost breathless. There he
floated about in a haphazard way, like a cork. When he had
recovered a little and saw in what an evil plight he was, he
stretched out his hand and begged someone to take hold of
it and help him to his feet. In pity for him, and because of his
sad condition, one man did indeed go to his aid. Putting his
arms round him, he drew him out of the water and carried
him to a couch, where he laid him, just as he was, in a pitiable
state. At this an uproar ensued. Several persons came into the
room, among them the empress herself, without any bodyguard and apparently stricken with grief. After one look at
him, however, she went off, having satisfied herself with her
own eyes that he was a dying man. Romanus gave one strong
deep moan, and then kept looking round, this way and that,
without being able to speak, but showing by signs and nods

1. Cedrenus (ibid.) says he was drowned deliberately by Michael's
friends. The date was 12 April 1034 (Good Friday). The emperor was
over seventy years of age.

what he wanted. Then, as still nobody could understand him, he shut his eyes and began to breathe more fast again. Suddenly his mouth gaped open and there flowed gently from it some dark-coloured, coagulated matter, and, with two or three gasps, he died.

BOOK FOUR

MICHAEL IV

SUCH was the manner of Romanus's death, after a reign of five and a half years. The Empress Zoe, learning of his death – she had not herself been present while he was dying – immediately took control of affairs, apparently under the impression that she was the rightful heir to the throne by divine permission. In point of fact, she was not so much concerned to seize power on her own behalf; all her efforts were directed to securing the crown for Michael, the person I have already described. There was opposition,[1] for those courtiers who had been allotted positions of dignity – most of them were old family retainers – joined with her husband's friends and his retainers, who had served his family ever since his father's time, in trying to prevent her from any precipitate or drastic action. They advised her to consider the noblest course for herself before making any decisions. One of the people, they said, should be promoted to the crown, some man pre-eminent among themselves and a man willing to treat her, not as his consort, but as empress in her own right.

All kinds of argument were produced to persuade her. They believed their influence would quickly prevail and she would come over to their point of view. To their surprise, she persisted in her support of Michael, with unwavering loyalty; there was no question of reason in the matter, for her judgement of the man was inspired by sentiment. It remained to set a time for the ceremony of coronation and for the assumption

1. The only man to oppose the accession of Michael was the patrician Constantine Dalassenus, at least according to Cedrenus (734D, p. 506). The Patriarch Alexius was induced to agree to the marriage by substantial bribes.

of the other insignia of power. Michael's elder brother approached her on the subject privately (he was the eunuch John, a man of outstanding intellect, as well as a man of action). 'We shall die,' he argued, 'if there is any further delay in promoting Michael.' Zoe, now completely won over, at once sent for the young man, clothed him in a robe interwoven with gold, placed on his head the imperial crown, and set him down on a magnificent throne, with herself near him in similar dress. She then issued an order that all those who were living in the palace were to prostrate themselves before both of them and hail them both as sovereigns in common. Of course, the order was obeyed, but when news of it reached those outside the palace also, all the city wanted to share in the rejoicings at her command. To flatter their new monarch, the majority feigned approval of the proceedings. As for the old emperor, they cast him off as though he were some heavy burden. So, light-hearted and blithe, with pleasure and satisfaction, they acclaimed Michael as emperor.

This proclamation was arranged in the evening by the new emperor's personal friends. Immediately afterwards a twofold order was sent to the City Eparchus. He, with all the Senate, was to come to the palace at dawn, and with them he was to prostrate himself before Michael; next, he was to carry out, also with their cooperation, the customary obsequies for the dead Romanus.[1] Accordingly they presented themselves for these duties. Entering one by one, they bowed their heads to the ground before the royal pair, who were seated on thrones. To the empress, only this homage was rendered; in the emperor's case the ceremony of kissing the right hand was performed as well. Thereupon Michael was proclaimed emperor and sovereign, and without more ado he set himself to consider the best interests of his Empire. The funeral ceremony for the defunct Romanus, who had been laid out on a

1. Romanus was buried on Good Friday in the church of St Mary Peribleptos.

superb bier, was already prepared, and the whole assembly went out to pay their respects to their late emperor in the usual fashion. One of those who preceded this bier was John the eunuch, whom I will discuss at the appropriate point in my history.

I saw this funeral procession myself. I had not yet grown a beard and only recently had I applied myself to the study of the poets. Examining the dead man, I did not really recognize him, either from his colour or outward appearance. It was only because of the insignia that I guessed the corpse had once been emperor. His face was completely altered, not wasted away, but swollen, and its colour was altogether changed. It was not that of a corpse, but rather reminiscent of men bloated and pale from drinking of poison, so that they appeared absolutely bloodless beneath the cheeks. The hair on his head and the hair of his beard were so thinned out that his corrupted frame was like a cornfield ravaged by fire, where the baldness of it can be seen from afar. If anyone wept for him, it was for that reason alone that their tears fell, for the whole populace, some because of the many evils they had received at his hands, others because they had enjoyed no favour, watched him go by, or escorted the procession with their eyes fixed upon him, without one single word of respect.

So lived Romanus and such was the funeral with which he was honoured. Despite the work and expense involved in the building of his monastery, he himself had joy of only one tiny part of the church – the spot where his body was laid.

Till now, Michael had played a part: his attitude and the look in his eyes showed love for the empress. It was not long, however, before all this was changed, and her love, as well as her favours to him, were repaid with base ingratitude. I can neither praise nor blame him for it; though I can scarcely commend this hatred for his benefactress or his behaviour towards her, yet I cannot fail to applaud his fear of the lady, fear lest he too should be involved in catastrophe, like Romanus.

The chief objection to any forthright condemnation of the man lies in his own character, for if you acquit him of this one crime committed against Romanus, and acquit him also of the charge of adultery and of accusations that he exiled persons on mere suspicion, this man will take his place in the forefront of Roman emperors. He was, it is true, entirely devoid of Hellenic culture; on the other hand, he was more harmonious in his nature than the philosophers who professed that culture. Even in the fullness of manhood and the flower of youth he mastered his body. Far from the physical passions beating down his reason, it was reason that exercised severe control over the desires. Nor was it merely his eye that was grim – his soul was too. He was ready, moreover, with the witty retort, and his tongue was well equipped to this end, for it lacked monotony, and he spoke fluently, with a voice both fine and resonant.

So far as reference to laws or canons was concerned, whether he had to pass judgement or prove a case, he was in difficulties, and glibness of tongue did not avail him very much. But if the point in question had to be settled by reasoning, he would immediately take it up, with a host of suggestions and intricate arguments. The practised expert was overwhelmed by the man's extraordinary natural ability. Of course he had no time for that yet, and I must go back to the start of his reign. My object is to show how carefully, from the very day of his enthronement, he watched over the administration of public affairs.

Clearly it was not a noble beginning for a man promoted to supreme power, as I have shown. Nevertheless, for a short period after he became master of the Empire, he treated the governing of it as a kind of joke. He would put off decisions until some crisis arose or some unexpected turn of events, while he passed the time in amusing his wife and in organizing pleasures and pastimes for her. Once he saw the magnitude of the Empire, however, and recognized the diverse quality of

forethought required for its managing and the multitudinous
difficulties involved in the cares of state – difficulties with
which a man who is truly an emperor must be faced – then
his character was suddenly and radically changed. It was as
if he had grown to manhood, no longer a boy, and from that
moment he governed his Empire in a fashion at once more
manly and more noble.

There is one more trait in the emperor which I cannot
refrain from admiring. It is this: although his origin was
humble, in the hour of his great good fortune he did not lose
his sense of balance, nor was he overwhelmed by his power.
None of his usual habits was changed. You would think he
had been carefully trained for the task long before, and he
seemed to approach it naturally. On the day of his accession
he behaved like a man who had been acclaimed emperor
years before, and men regarded him as such. He made no
innovations in established customs, rescinded no laws, introduced none that was contrary to the spirit of his predecessor,
removed no member of the Senate – changes which normally
occur when a new reign commences. As to those who had
befriended him before his promotion, or men to whom he
was under obligation, when he became emperor he did not
cheat them of their hopes, except inasmuch as their promotion
to the highest offices was not immediate. He employed them
first, by way of trial so to speak, in the lesser and humbler
duties, and so gradually prepared them for positions of greater
importance. I must admit that if his brothers had not been
born under some evil star – and it was for this reason that he
could neither wipe out the family root and branch, nor make
honest men of them, because of their wicked nature – had it
not been for this, not one of the famous monarchs would have
been his equal.

Not one of the emperors in my time – and I say this with
experience of many in my life, for most of them only lasted a
year – not one of them, to my knowledge, bore the burden of

Empire entirely free from blame *to the end*. Some were
naturally evil, others were evil through their friendship for
certain individuals, and others again for some other of the
common reasons. So it was with this man; in himself he was
good, but in the way he treated his brothers he was hard to
excess. Apparently Nature, when she brought them to birth,
accorded the nobler qualities to Michael, but in the others she
produced characteristics exactly the opposite. Each of them
wanted to usurp the place of his brothers, and, allowing none
of them to live either on sea or even on land, to dwell alone
in the whole wide world, as if by some dispensation of God
both sea and land were his own inheritance. Often Michael
tried to restrain them, not by warnings, but with harsh invective, angry reprimands, and the use of violent and frightful
threats. All to no purpose, for the eldest brother, John,
administered their affairs with great dexterity. It was he who
assuaged the emperor's wrath and he who won for his brothers
permission to do what they liked. And he did this, not because
he exactly approved of their attitude, but because, despite it,
he cared for his family.

It is my desire in this history to give a somewhat fuller
description of John, without recourse to empty or lying statements. You see, when I was starting to grow a beard, I saw
the man himself and I heard him speak and witnessed his
actions. I marked his disposition closely, and I am aware that
although some of his deeds are praiseworthy, there are other
things in his life which cannot meet with general approval.
At that time there were many sides to his character. He had a
ready wit, and if ever a man was shrewd he was; the piercing
glance of his eyes betrayed those qualities. He paid meticulous
care to his duties; in fact, he went to extremes of industry in
their performance. His experience in all branches of government was great, but it was in the administration of public
finance that his wisdom and shrewdness were especially evident. He bore no one ill-will; yet, at the same time, he was

irritated if anyone underestimated his (John's) importance. If he did no harm to a soul, yet in his dealings with the people he assumed a fierce expression which terrified one and all. As far as looks were concerned, he really hurt them. Most of them shuddered at the sight of him – and refrained from their evil practices. Thus John was a veritable bulwark to the emperor and a real brother, for he never relaxed in his vigilance, either by day or by night. He never forgot his zeal for duty, even at the times which he devoted to pleasure or on those occasions when he took part in banquets and public ceremonies and festivals. Nothing ever escaped his notice and nobody even so much as tried to elude him, because everyone feared him and trembled at his superintendence, for at untimely hours in the night he would suddenly ride off on his horse and scour every nook and cranny of the metropolis, traversing all the inhabited districts at once, like a flash of lightning. No one would ever know when he would carry out these inspections and so they all became nervous and subdued and cautious. It being impossible to meet in public, men remained in their homes, living their own lives in private.

Such were the qualities in the man that one can admire, but there were others of the contrary sort. His moods were changeable. He accommodated himself to every shade of opinion in those who conversed with him, presenting many facets at each interview. When men approached him, he criticized them while they were still far away, but as they drew near addressed them in an affable manner, as if it were then that he saw them for the first time. Again, if anyone brought news likely to be of great service to the State, in order to avoid obligation to his informant he used to pretend that he had known it a long time ago, and then upbraid the man for his slowness. The latter would go away covered with confusion, while John took the necessary action and by suppressing the trouble, perhaps in its initial stages, was able to root it out altogether. A desire on his part to achieve greater magnificence, and to manage the affairs of the Empire in a manner more befitting an emperor, was thwarted by his own natural habits, for, to tell the truth, he never succeeded in ridding himself of his inveterate greed. Thus, once embarked on drink – a besetting sin in his case – he would plunge head-long into all kinds of indecency. Even then, though, he did not forget the cares of Empire, nor relax that fierce-beast look on his face or the sternness of his expression.

It has often been a cause of surprise to me, when I have sat with him at banquets, to observe how a man, a slave to drink and given to ribaldry, as he was, could bear the burden of power. In his cups he would carefully watch how each of his fellows behaved. Afterwards, as if he had caught them red-handed, he would submit them to questioning and examine what they had said and done in their drunken moments. They came to fear him more, therefore, when he was tipsy than when he was sober. Indeed, the fellow was an extra-ordinary mixture. For a long time he had garbed himself in a monkish habit, but not even in his dreams did he care one jot for the decent behaviour that befits such a dress. Yet he acted the part, if long-established custom demanded a certain ritual. As for those libertines who indulged unrestrainedly in sensual pleasures, John had nothing but scorn for them. On the other hand, if a man chose to live in a decent way, or pass his time in the free exercise of virtue, or profit his mind with scientific studies, he would find in John an implacable foe. The eunuch would wilfully misrepresent the other's worthy ambitions in some way or other. This paradoxical conduct in his dealings with other men was not repeated when he had to do with the emperor, his brother, for with Michael he pre-served one and the same attitude, never varying, never changing. In his presence there was no dissimulation at any time.

There were five brothers in all. As far as character was concerned, the Emperor Michael was the antithesis of the others, but John the Eunuch, whom I have just described, was inferior in virtue only to him. To compare him with the others would be impossible, for the man was *sui generis*. To put it more clearly, I would say that his attitude towards the three others was exactly opposed to that of the emperor. In comparison with him, John was vastly inferior, but there were certain resemblances: he too was displeased with the brothers' incorrigible outlook. On the other hand, he felt the deepest affection for them: no man ever showed more brotherly love. He was reluctant, therefore, to call them to account for their misdeeds. He was inclined rather to conceal their wrongdoings and claim for them still greater liberty, in the belief that Michael would never notice what was happening.

So much then for the brothers. Let us return to the emperor. For some time he treated Zoe with marked consideration, but that phase soon passed. He suspected her motives – there were reasons for suspicion in that house – and he proceeded to deny her any liberty whatever. Permission to leave the palace in her usual way was refused, and she was shut up in the women's quarters. No one was allowed to approach her, unless the captain of the guard had first given authority after careful scrutiny of the visitor's identity, origin, and purpose – so close was the watch kept over her. She was, quite naturally, embittered by this sort of treatment. Surely it was hardly to be wondered at, when the benefits she had conferred upon the emperor were being repaid with such hatred. Nevertheless, she retrained herself, reflecting that to rebel against Michael's decisions would be improper, and in any case she had no opportunity, even if she wished, to take any action or oppose his will, for she was deprived of all protection from the Imperial Guard and bereft of all power. Anyway, she avoided the despicable feminine trait of talkativeness and there were no emotional outbursts. She neither reminded the emperor of the love and belief in her that he had shown in the past, nor did she evince anger against his brothers when they attacked her with their threats and abuse. Not once did she look with bitterness on the captain of the guard or dismiss him from her presence. On the contrary she was gentle to all and, like the cleverest orators, adjusted herself to different persons and different conditions.

The others, however, by no means modified their own attitude to please Zoe. In fact, they were exceedingly afraid of her, as if she were some lioness which for a while had laid aside her ferocity. It was inevitable that they should consult their own safety, and every kind of barrier, every kind of rampart, was erected to protect them from her attacks. They kept unceasing vigil, while the emperor, for his part, gradually stopped seeing her at all. There were, I know, many reasons for this. Marital relations with her had become impossible, now that the malady which threatened him had already made its appearance. His health was undermined and his bodily condition poor. Then, again, he was covered with shame whenever he looked at Zoe, and it was beyond his power to meet her gaze, knowing how he had betrayed his love, forsworn his promises, and broken his word. In the third place, having conversed with certain saintly persons about the deeds he had committed in order to gain the throne, and having received some wholesome advice from these gentlemen, he now eschewed all kinds of excess and refrained even from legitimate intercourse.[1] There was something else that he feared, too – something that further prevented him from visiting Zoe. The brainstorms no longer attacked him, as before, at lengthy intervals, but they occurred more frequently, whether through some outside influence which altered the nature of the illness, or because of some internal

1. Michael spent much of his time in Salonica at the tomb of St Demetrius. No doubt the 'saintly persons' conversed with him there, and among them was the monk Cosmas Tzintzuluces through whose influence he was induced on his deathbed to accept the tonsure.

affection which brought on the fits. In front of others he was not so embarrassed when these came on, but before her he blushed deeply, and, since the malady afflicted him in circumstances that were unpredictable, he kept out of her sight. If she had seen him like that, he would have felt disgraced.

For these reasons he rarely appeared in public and he lacked self-confidence in the society of others. Whenever he wished to give audience or to carry out any other of the usual ceremonies, certain persons were entrusted with the duty of observing and keeping watch over him. These officials hung red curtains on either side of him, and as soon as they saw him turn his head ever so slightly, or nod, or use whatever other signs they knew to herald the onset of his trouble, they immediately asked those who came into his presence to retire, drew together the curtains, and so attended him behind them, in private. The attacks came on quickly, but he recovered even more quickly, and afterwards there was no trace of illness in his conduct. He would swiftly become master of himself and reason clearly. If ever he went out on foot or on horseback, a circle of guards used to escort him, and when he felt ill they would gather round him on all sides and so look after him, without fear of strangers seeing his distress. There were many occasions, however, when he was seen being thrown from his horse. Once, while he was crossing a stream of water on horseback, an attack came on; the guards, anticipating no trouble, were some distance away at the time, when suddenly he rolled off his saddle and was seen by the mob, lying on the ground there in one of his spasms. Nobody attempted to lift him up, but they were full of pity for his misfortune.

The sequel to these events will be related at the proper place in this history. We have seen the emperor in sickness; now let us see what kind of man he was in good health. In the intervals between his fits, when his reason was sound, he devoted himself entirely to thought for his Empire. Not only did he ensure the good government of cities within our boundaries, but he stopped the nations beyond our borders from invading Roman territory. This he did, partly by the dispatch of envoys, partly by bribery, partly by annual displays of military strength. Thanks to these precautions, neither the ruler of Egypt nor of Persia, nor even of Babylonia, broke the terms of treaties they had made with us. Nor did any of the more distant peoples openly show their hostility. Some were actually reconciled altogether, while others, apprehensive of the emperor's watchful care and fearful of his vengeance, followed a policy of strict neutrality. The organization and control of public finance had been deputed to his brother John. To John also was left the greater part of civil administration, but the remaining affairs of state Michael managed himself. Now some subject of civil government would claim his attention; at other times he would be organizing the 'sinews' of the Roman Empire, that is, the Army, and building up its strength; but all the time that the disease which had begun to affect him was growing to its climax and reaching its zenith, he still supervised the whole administration of the Empire, just as if no illness were weighing upon him at all.

When his brother John saw his gradual decline, he was fearful for himself and all his family. After the sovereign's death, in the general disorder, the Empire might forget him; he might be compelled to face all kinds of trouble. Therefore he adopted a policy that was, to all appearances, most prudent, but in fact most perilous, as the outcome of the affair was to prove. Indeed, it was the immediate cause of their shipwreck, with the loss of all hands, in what can only be described as complete and utter ruin. However, that story must come later. Well then, John, having abandoned all hope of the emperor's recovery, had an interview with him unknown to his brothers. The suggestions made by him at that meeting were more specious than honest. It came about

like this. One day he found Michael alone, and cloaking his
thought in periphrasis, began to address him in the following
manner, obviously with the idea of compelling him to ask
questions. 'That I have continued to serve you,' he said, 'not
simply as a brother, but as Master and Emperor, Heaven
knows, and all the world knows it too; you yourself could
scarcely deny it. That, however, I also pay some small attention, to put it mildly, to the desires of the rest of the family,
to their opinions of the common good and to their interests,
you, more than anyone else, also know. So I am not worried
about your present tenure of the throne. What I want to
guarantee is the future as well, and I wish to ensure that the
crown can continue free from attacks. If I have been unable
to restrain the tongues of the people, at least my policy has
consistently directed everyone's attention to you, and to you
alone. If then you have received sure proof of my loyalty, if
you know that I have faithfully done my duty, do not, I beg
of you, thrust aside this idea of mine. If you do – well, I will
hold my tongue. Where our fortunes will end I will not say
now, lest I leave you offended. . . .'

At these words the emperor was thoroughly disturbed.
He asked what in the world all this meant, what could be the
object of such a speech. 'Your loyalty to me is admitted;
forget that for a moment.' The other, seizing on this admission, went on, 'Do not imagine, Sir, that the people have
failed to hear, or see with their own eyes, that you are
afflicted with a disease which is obvious, and yet kept secret.
I know quite well, of course, that you will suffer no dreadful
effects from it, but men's tongues constantly spread rumours
that you have died. My anxiety, then, is this: through their
belief in your imminent death, there may be a revolt against
you. Men may set up as their champion one of the people and
elevate him to your throne. For my own affairs, and for the
affairs of the family in general, I am less concerned, but I do
fear for you. It would be dreadful if so good and so just an

emperor should be accused of thoughtlessness. Of course, he would escape the danger himself, but he will not evade the charge of failing to provide for the future.' Michael had a ready reply to this. 'And what, may I ask,' he said, 'what is this prevision? And how are we to check the people's gossip? Tell me more about these desires for revolution.'

THE EMPRESS'S ADOPTION OF MICHAEL[1]
AND HIS PROMOTION TO CAESAR

'A very easy measure,' answered John, 'and all ready. If our brother[2] were not dead, you would have granted him the second highest dignity in the state – the office of Caesar. Since death has taken him from us, there is our sister's son, Michael, who as you know has been entrusted with the command of your bodyguard. Why not make him Caesar? He will be of more service to you than before, and as for the position, he will regard that as merely nominal. Apart from holding the title, he will be no more than a slave to you, occupying the lowest rank.' With these persuasive arguments he won over the emperor, and, once agreed on the new policy, they debated the manner of carrying it out. John again was ready with advice. 'You know, Sir, that the Empire belongs by inheritance to Zoe, and the whole nation owes greater allegiance to her, because she is a woman and heir to the throne. Moreover, being so generous in her distribution of money, she has won the hearts of the people completely. I suggest, therefore, that we should make her

1. Michael Calaphates, the future Michael V, was adopted by Zoe in 1040.

2. Stephen, husband of John's sister Maria, was father of the young Caesar. He had been admiral in Sicilian waters in 1035 and heavily defeated. George Maniaces was rightly indignant at his inefficiency and Maniaces was recalled through Stephen's intrigues (cf. Constantine IX, Chapter 76). He soon nullified Maniaces' good work.

mother to our nephew – if she adopts him it will be more
propitious – and at the same time persuade her to promote him
to the dignity and title of Caesar. She will not refuse. Zoe is
accommodating enough, and in any case she cannot oppose us
in any way.'

The emperor agreed that the plan was a good one, and,
when they informed Zoe of the scheme, they found it a very
simple matter to win her over. So at once they proceeded to
put it into practice. An announcement was made about the
public ceremony, and all the dignitaries were gathered in the
church at Blachernae. When the sacred building was full, the
Empress-Mother, accompanied by her adopted son, was
brought from the palace. The emperor congratulated him on
his new relationship to the empress and formally promoted
him to the dignity of Caesar. The assembly thereupon
acclaimed him, and the usual rites and ceremonies proper to
such an occasion were performed in his honour. After this
the meeting was dismissed. As for John, believing that all his
troubles were now at an end and that the family fortunes
were now secured, he hardly knew how to contain himself for
the greatness of his joy.

What had taken place was, in reality, the beginning of
mighty disasters in the future, and what was, to all appearances, the foundation stone of the family's glory proved really
to be its utter destruction. I will demonstrate the truth of that
later in the history. Let it suffice now that the emperor's
friends settled the matter in the way I have described and put
this young Caesar, the heir-presumptive, in a position where
he would accede to the throne, as soon as the emperor suc-
cumbed to his illness. Having done so, they ceased to concern themselves with the permanence of their own position,
convinced that their interests were now thoroughly assured.
I do not know whether the emperor immediately repented
of his action, but he did not treat him as Caesar, and far from
respecting his lofty rank, he failed to accord him even the

recognized honours, and took care that he should enjoy only the outward symbols of power.

I myself have seen the Caesar stand aside among the palace dignitaries, so that someone might pass on some good story at his expense to the emperor. Nor did he share the emperor's table, except when he occupied the Caesar's place at official banquets. If ever a tent was pitched for him, with guards at the entrance and with some semblance of a Caesar's headquarters, it would lie in some inconspicuous spot and looked much like the tent occupied by the emperor's brothers. The similarity was not accidental, for they, fearing now for their brother's life and pinning their hopes on the nephew, treated the latter with extraordinary deference. They insinuated themselves into his good graces and lavished on him honour befitting an emperor. In other ways, too, their actions were designed to secure for themselves a pre-eminent place in the future government, and to prepare the way for it. So it came about that they assigned him a residence, not in Constantinople, but in some part of the suburbs. Apparently they designed this as some signal honour, but really it was a kind of disguised exile, for he came and went, not when he himself wished, but when they ordered him. Not even in his wildest dreams did he reap the slightest benefit from his uncle's patronage.

Let me now give some account of the man. His family, on his father's side, was altogether insignificant and completely obscure. His father came from some absolutely deserted country place or from some other odd corner of the world. His activities included neither the sowing of crops nor the planting of vineyards – in truth, he could not call a single acre of land his own. There was no herd of cattle to drive, no flock of sheep to tend. He was not a farm-bailiff. He had no other livelihood there, or even a sign of one. No, the fellow turned his attention to the sea. He had no mind to engage in commerce, or to act as navigator on a ship, or to pilot vessels at a fee when they put into harbour or sailed out to sea. How-

ever, as he had turned his back on the land and now looked to
the sea for his living, he became something big in the ship-
building line. Please do not imagine that he cut timber or
planed off the wood they use in the ships, nor did he fit and
fasten together the planks. Not a bit of it. What he did was
this: when others had done the assembling, he very skilfully
smeared the assembled parts with pitch. There was not a
boat, freshly-built, which could ever be launched on the deep,
unless this fellow, with his cunning skill, had first given it the
finishing touch.

Later on he became the plaything of Fortune and his whole
manner of life was changed. I saw him after the metamorphosis, and there was nothing whatever about him in
harmony or congruous with the part he was playing; his
horse, his clothes, everything else that alters a man's appearance – all were out of place. It was as if a pygmy wanted to
play Hercules and was trying to make himself look like the
demi-god. The more such a person tries, the more his appearance belies him – clothed in the lion's skin, but weighed down
by the club! So it was with this man: nothing about him was
right.

Well, that was Michael's family on his father's side. If
anyone cared to trace his descent on the maternal side, he
would find, with the exception of his uncle, no essential
difference from the ancestors of his father. That was the sort
of folk from whom he was sprung. As for the man himself, in
all matters that contribute to one's self-respect – superior
standing and rank in society, or at least its outward form – he
bore little resemblance to his parents. He had an extraordinary
flair for concealing 'the fire beneath the ashes', that is to say,
he hid an evil disposition under a kindly exterior. He was
expert in the conception and planning of unlikely designs.
He showed no consideration for benefactors, no gratitude to
anyone for friendship or solicitude or devotion on his behalf.
But his powers of dissimulation were such that he could hide

all that. After his promotion to Caesar, there was a fairly long interval before he became emperor, and he began to imagine in his own mind, secretly of course, what it would be like to rule. He began to plot the things he would do, picturing the scene to himself. Every member of the family was considered in turn. All those who had shown him favour and helped to promote him he planned to destroy. With the empress he would be bitterly angry, some of his uncles he would kill, others he would drive into exile. And all the time he was imagining these things he was even more careful than usual to appear friendly towards them. The eunuch John was the principal object of his treacherous designs, but there was no hint of them in Michael's behaviour. Indeed, the dissimulation in this case was even more adroit, for the nephew persisted in acting like an inferior and called John 'Sir'. His hopes of life and safety, he said, rested in John's hands.

The others were unaware of the Caesar's artifice and they knew nothing of the hidden depths of his soul, but John's perception was more acute than Michael's play-acting. To John the whole business was suspicious. Despite this, he thought no immediate change of policy was called for; he would act when a favourable opportunity presented itself. The Caesar, on the other hand, was not deluded by *his* manoeuvres. So both lay in wait for each other, each secretly plotting, but simulating benevolence. Each thought he was deceiving his rival, yet neither was ignorant of the other's designs. It was John, however, who was caught, because he failed to make full use of his cunning. By putting off the chance to depose and overthrow the Caesar, he brought down on his own head the sum-total of the family misfortunes. I will tell that tale later.

It is my custom to attribute to Divine Providence the governance of great events, or rather I consider that all occurrences derive from Providence, if only our human nature is not corrupted. This event also, in my opinion,

derived from a more than human prescience and direction –
the fact, I mean, that the succession to the throne fell to the
Caesar, and not to any other member of the family, because
God knew it was through the Caesar that the whole family
would be annihilated. However, that is a subject with which I
will deal later.

It was now evident that the whole of the emperor's body
was swollen, and nobody could fail to notice the hydropsy
from which he was suffering. He tried various methods, such
as prayers and purifications, in the hope of being cured, but
he was confident of recovery for one reason in particular –
the building of a church in honour of the Anargyroi,[1] in a
suburb of the city on the east side. It was a glorious monu-
ment. Actually, not all the foundations were laid by Michael,
but he threw them over a wider area. There had been a sacred
building on the spot before, although it was not noted for
any magnificence, nor was it remarkable for its architectural
style. This erection he now beautified, built additions on to it,
and surrounded it with walls. The new chapels enhanced its
glory. When all the work was done, he dedicated this church
as a monastery. So far as the building of sacred churches was
concerned, Michael surpassed all his predecessors, both in
workmanship and in splendour. The depths and heights of
this edifice were given a new symmetry, and his chapels
harmonized with the church to bestow on it an infinite
beauty; the most wonderful stones were used in the floors and
walls, and the whole church became radiant with gold mosaic
and the painter's art. Images that seemed almost to live, set
in every possible part, filled the sacred building with glory.
Besides all this, there were near this church, and practically
incorporated into its precincts, lovely baths, numerous

1. St Cosmas and his brother St Damian were put to death in the
Diocletian persecution in the fourth century. They had been physicians
and made no charge for their medical services (hence their name *Anargyroi*). Justinian built the church in their honour.

fountains, beautiful lawns, and whatever else can delight or attract the eye.

The object of all this was, in some measure, to honour the Deity, but the emperor also hoped to propitiate the 'Servants of God'; perchance they might heal his affliction. It was all in vain though, for the measure of his life was fulfilled, and his health still continued to break up. At last, therefore, he abandoned all hope of recovery. It was the Judgement to come that now engrossed all his attention; he must free himself, once and for all, from the sins that were besetting his soul.

There are some people, not exactly well disposed to the family, but prejudiced in their opinions, who say that, before Michael came to power, certain mysterious rites influenced him to seek the Principate. Ghostly apparitions, seen only by himself (so they say), prophesied his future exaltation, and, in return for these services, they demanded that he should deny his faith in God. According to their story, it was this transaction that now distressed him, giving him no respite and driving him on to make his peace with the Almighty. Those who took part in these ceremonies with him and faked the apparitions will know whether the story is true or false. If it is a mere fabrication, then my opinion on the subject cannot be disregarded. Obviously, where history is concerned, men are prone to invention and for that very reason slanders current among ordinary folk do not readily convince me. Before I trust what I hear, I always put such stories to the test.

I do know that the man was a pattern of piety after his accession. Not only did he regularly attend Holy Church, but he paid particular heed to the philosophers. By the word 'philosophers' here I do not mean those who have tried to discover the principles of the universe – and neglected the principles of their own salvation – nor those who have examined the essence of nature. I mean those who have

scorned the world and who live with the beings above this
world. Who, then, that have lived such a life, escaped the
emperor's notice? What land and sea did he not thoroughly
search, what clefts in the rocks, what secret holes in the earth,
that he might bring to the light of day one who was hidden
there? Once he had found them, he would carry them off
to his palace. And then, what honour did he not pay them,
washing their dust-covered feet, even putting his arms about
them and gladly embracing their bodies, secretly clothing
himself in their rags and making them lie down on his
imperial bed, while he cast himself down on some humble
couch, with a hard stone for a pillow? That by no means
exhausts the catalogue of good deeds, but my purpose here
is not to compose a eulogy: I am narrating simple events.

The truth is that while most men usually avoid the society
of persons suffering from disease, this man did an extraordinary thing, for he frequented their company, put his face
to the festering sores on their bodies, then – even more
amazing – embraced them, folded them in his arms, tended
them, bathed and waited on them, as though he were a slave
and they his masters. What right, then, have the wicked to
slander him? Why should an emperor be exposed to their
calumnies? But I am deviating somewhat from the main
course of my narrative.

The emperor desired forgiveness of his sins. He set himself,
therefore, to do all such things as would please God, and he
encouraged the clergy to help him in this object. In fact, a
considerable part of the imperial treasure was set aside for the
foundation of monasteries and nunneries throughout the
continent. A new hospice was built too, called by him *The
Ptochotropheium*,[1] and in this way a mighty stream of gold
was poured out for the benefit of those who preferred a life
of meditation. One idea followed another, and among other
schemes he devised a plan for the salvation of lost souls.

1. 'Hospice for Beggars.'

Scattered all over the city was a vast multitude of harlots, and without attempting to turn them away from their trade by argument – that class of woman is deaf anyway to all advice that would save them – without even trying to curb their activities by force, lest he earn the reputation of violence, he built in the Queen of Cities a place of refuge to house them, an edifice of enormous size and very great beauty. Then, in the stentorian notes of the public herald, he issued a proclamation: all women who trafficked in their beauty, provided they were willing to renounce their trade and live in luxury, were to find sanctuary in this building: they were to change their own clothes for the habit of nuns, and all fear of poverty would be banished from their lives for ever, 'for all things, unsown, without labour of hands, would spring forth for their use'.[1] Thereupon a great swarm of prostitutes descended upon this refuge, relying on the emperor's edict, and changed both their garments and their manner of life, a youthful band enrolled in the service of God, as soldiers of virtue.

The emperor's efforts to work out his own salvation did not end even there. He put himself in the hands of those who were dedicated to the worship of God, men who had grown old in the ascetic life. He believed that they were in immediate contact with the Almighty and endowed with all power. To some of these he looked for spiritual guidance, or conversion, while from others he exacted promises that they would pray to the Deity on his behalf and for the remission of his sins. This led to further trouble, for evil-minded folk indulged in malicious gossip, especially when some of the monks were hesitant on this point – not all of them complied with Michael's demands. As a matter of fact, the majority gave up the task because they were afraid that the emperor, having committed some dreadful crime and being ashamed to confess it, might force them to transgress Holy Writ.

1. Homer, *Odyssey*, ix, 108–9.

However, that was merely conjecture, and to all appearances he was eager and anxious to obtain forgiveness of his sins from God.

I am aware that many chroniclers of his life will, in all probability, give an account different from mine, for in his time false opinions prevailed. But I took part in these events myself and, besides that, I have acquired information of a more confidential nature from men who were his intimate friends. My conclusions, therefore, are fair – unless someone is tempted to quarrel with my interpretation of things that I have seen myself and heard with my own ears. Maybe the greater part of my account will present the evil ones with an opportunity to indulge in their idle chatter, but I do not believe that anyone will dispute the truth of what I am going to say now. It would take a long time to describe in full his various activities and measures in times of civil discord or foreign wars, but I will select one deed alone. I am referring to the struggle he waged against the barbarians. I will run over it in a brief summary.

The people of Bulgaria, after many vicissitudes of fortune and after frequent wars in the past, had become subjects of the Roman Empire. That prince of emperors, the famous Basil, had deliberately attacked their country and destroyed their power. For some time the Bulgarians, being completely exhausted after pitting their strength against the might of the Romans, resigned themselves to defeat, but later they reverted to the old arrogance. There were no immediate signs of open revolt, however, until the appearance among them of a political agitator; thereupon their policy at once became hostile to the Empire.[1]

1. The Bulgarian Revolt broke out in 1040. The Slav leader was Peter Delyan, who claimed to be a grandson of Samuel. He had been a slave at Byzantium, but escaped. The rebellion prospered at first and the emperor was nearly killed at Salonica. The Bulgars were enraged because of John's exactions.

The man who moved them to this folly was, in their eyes, a marvel. He was of their own race, member of a family unworthy of mention, but cunning, and capable of practising any deceit on his compatriots, a fellow called Dolianus.[1] I do not know whether he inherited such a name from his father, or if he gave himself the name for an omen. He knew that the whole nation was set on rebellion against the Romans; the revolt had hitherto been merely a project only because no leader had risen up among them able to carry out their plans. In the first place, therefore, he made himself conspicuous, proved his ability in council, demonstrated his skill in the conduct of war. Then, having won their approval by these qualities, it only remained for him to prove his own noble descent in order to become the acknowledged leader of the Bulgarians. It was their custom to recognize as leaders of the nation only men of royal blood, so, knowing this to be the national custom, he proceeded to trace his descent from the famous Samuel and his brother Aaron, who had ruled the whole people as kings a short time before. He did not claim to be the legitimate heir of these kings, but he either invented or proved that he was a collateral relation. He readily convinced the people with his story, and they raised him on the shield. He was proclaimed king. From that moment Bulgarian designs became manifest, for they seceded openly. The yoke of Roman domination was hurled from their necks and they made a declaration of independence, emphasizing the fact that they took this course of their own free will. Whereupon they engaged in attacks and plundering expeditions on Roman territory.

Had the barbarians dared to do a thing so foolish immediately after Michael's accession, they would very soon have learnt what kind of a sovereign they had assailed. In those days he was strong in body and virile in face of danger. It was nothing at all for him to take up arms in a minute, and

1. His name would remind a Greek of δόλος, 'treachery'.

with the *élite* of his generals to invade their land; it would have been a simple matter to teach them not to revolt against Rome with temerity. However that may be, when this particular rebellion came to birth, he was already failing and his bodily condition was desperate. It came at a time when even the slightest movement caused him pain, and when he found it hard even to put on his clothes. That was the moment when the Bulgarians, for a brief interval, decided to play at ruling themselves, like actors on a stage, and to enjoy themselves with a bit of make-believe. And so they did – until a burning ambition for glory suddenly gave the emperor strength, and in a burst of exultation carried him against his foes.

As soon as the news became known to him, and actually before the full account was received, he determined to carry the war to the Bulgars. He would march against them himself, at the head of his army. It was impossible, of course, to do this because of the state of his health, and in any case the Senate altogether opposed the project. Michael's family, too, begged him not to leave the city – much to his disgust, for he had set his heart on the war. It was extremely disappointing – he emphasized this point – if his reign was not only destined to witness no aggrandizement of the Roman Empire, but actually some loss of territory. He suspected that he was personally responsible before God and man, if, after what had occurred, he should through any carelessness on his part allow the Bulgars to secede with impunity.

THE EMPEROR'S BULGARIAN EXPEDITION

This thought afflicted the emperor much more than physical suffering, and the harm it produced in him was quite different, for whereas the disease caused his body to swell, the mental agony he endured over this revolt had the opposite effect and wasted him. So he was torn between two evils which

tortured him in exactly opposite ways. His first battle, however
– a battle in which he was victorious – was against his own
intimate friends before he ever came to grips with the
barbarians, and the first trophy of the war was set up to commemorate his triumph over his own kinsmen and his associates – and himself. Bodily weakness, in his case, was more
than compensated by strength of purpose, and in this strength
he committed his cause to God. So preparations for the war
began. The first move was to take counsel, determine his
objectives, and direct all his efforts to the attainment of them.
The enterprise was certainly not taken in hand rashly, or
without due precautions. I need not go into details, but the
military rehearsals were adequate. Not all the army was
mobilized and mere numbers were discounted; the best
soldiers were selected and generals with most experience in
the field. With them he set out to meet the Scyths,[1] advancing
in due order, his army disposed with proper regard for the
rules of strategy.

Camp was pitched in a suitable spot when the expedition
arrived at the enemy borders. A council of war was held, and
after it the emperor decided to engage the Bulgars – an
extraordinary plan, about which even his commanders
there present had contrary opinions. Nor is this surprising,
for during the night he was under medical treatment and
nearly died. Yet at daybreak he at once got up, some power
apparently giving him the strength, mounted his horse, sat
firm in the saddle, and managed the animal with clever use
of his bridle. Then, an object of wonder to all who saw him,
he rode to the rear and formed up the various divisions of his
army into one coherent force.

1. Psellus uses the name 'Scyths' indiscriminately for all Slavs.

THE ESCAPE OF ALOUSIANUS TO BULGARIA[1]

The war had not yet broken out when a most astonishing thing happened – something nearly as remarkable as the emperor's own actions. The more agreeable of Aaron's sons (Aaron had been king of the Bulgars), one Alousianus by name, a man of gentle character, with a fine intellect and a position of great dignity, proved chiefly responsible for Michael's victory. This was not because of any desire on his part to help the emperor; in fact, he was far from well-disposed. The truth is, God moved him to do what he did, and thus brought about the emperor's triumph, in despite of his enemies.

Now this Alousianus was by no means in favour at court, and was neither consulted on matters of policy nor honoured in any way with the others. Indeed, an order was issued that he must remain in his own home and he was forbidden to enter Byzantium except by direct command of the emperor. Naturally the restriction depressed and irritated the man, but for the moment he was powerless. However, the events in Bulgaria were reported to him, and he knew that the people there had supported the claims of an illegitimate pretender to their throne for one reason only – because no one else in the country was of royal blood. Under these circumstances he ventured on rather a childish expedition. Ignoring the claims of his own offspring and forgetting his love for his wife – none of them was allowed to know anything of his plans – he boldly marched from the extreme east to the west with a handful of servants, men whom he knew to be reckless dare-devils, ready for all hazards. To avoid recognition in the city, he adopted a thorough disguise. It was not a matter of discarding some of his clothes and retaining others, but he dressed

1. September 1041. Alousianus was the second son of Aaron. John had fined him without trial on some unknown charge and had imprisoned his wife.

himself as a common mercenary soldier, and so escaped detection altogether.

On two or three occasions he visited my informant in the Great City. The latter gentleman told me about it afterwards. 'The fellow was quite well known to me,' he said, 'and he greeted me in a friendly way, but even so I failed to recognize him, and so did all the others whom he visited.' Thus he evaded the vigilant John (the Orphanotrophus, the Many-Eyed) – no mean feat. Yet his sudden disappearance had roused suspicion, and the authorities were on the watch to find and arrest him, if they could. However, to cut a long story short, he deceived them all and reached Bulgaria in safety. Now he did not make himself known to his people at once, but first approached certain individuals, on different occasions. He referred to his father in an impersonal way, as though he himself was a member of another family. He then spoke with pride of his father's ancestry, and made some tentative inquiries: if any of his sons turned up in the country, would the rebels choose the legitimate heir as their king, or the pretender? Or, now that the latter had already assumed the leadership, was the rightful heir completely forgotten?

When it was obvious that the acknowledged son was universally preferred to the doubtful one, he ventured, in a somewhat mysterious way, to reveal his true identity to one of the persons he had consulted, a man of whose warm loyalty to his family he felt reasonably sure. This man, fixing his eyes steadily on Alousianus (he had known him quite well in the past) and recognizing him, fell on his knees and kissed his feet. Then, to avert any possible doubt, he asked him to show a certain secret mark. This was a dark patch on the right elbow, with a thick tuft of rough hair grown over it. When he saw that, he fell on Alousianus's neck even more vehemently and covered his breast with kisses. The two men then set about their design cleverly. They approached others one by one, and little by little the story was spread abroad.

The majority of the Bulgars transferred their allegiance to him, the real heir, and the monarchy became a 'polyarchy' as some preferred this and others that son, but both parties were anxious to maintain peace and they reconciled the two protagonists. Thereafter they lived on equal terms, with frequent meetings but mutual suspicion.

Nevertheless, it was Alousianus who got in the first blow and frustrated the plans of his rival, for quite unexpectedly he arrested Dolianus, cut off his nose and blinded his eyes, using a cook's knife for both operations. Thus the Scythians once again became subject to one master. This event was not followed immediately by negotiations with the emperor. In fact, Alousianus mobilized his forces and marched against the Romans, but the attack proved unsuccessful and he had to seek refuge. It was clear that further opposition to Michael, in open warfare, would involve great difficulties. There was also the question of his beloved wife and children. So, having summed up the whole business, he conveyed secret information to the emperor. If Alousianus won his favour and if he received other honours that were his due, he was willing to commit himself and his belongings to the Roman. This proposition being acceptable to the emperor, further communications passed between them, in great secrecy, as Alousianus had desired. In accordance with the terms of agreement, the latter advanced, apparently with the intention of joining battle for a second time, but suddenly abandoning his army he surrendered. Michael treated him with signal honour, and he was sent back to Byzantium. As for his people, now torn asunder with war on all sides and still without a leader, after inflicting a crushing defeat, Michael again made them subject to the Empire from which they had revolted. Then he returned to his palace in glory with a host of captives, among whom were the most notable men of the Bulgars and the pretender himself, their leader, minus his nose and deprived of his eyes.

The entry into the city was a brilliant affair. The whole populace thronged out to meet him. I myself saw him on this occasion, looking as if he were attending a funeral and swaying on his horse. The fingers that gripped his bridle were like those of a giant, for each of them was as thick and large as a man's arm – the result of his internal trouble. His face, too, preserved not a trace of its former likeness. Riding thus, he led a wonderful triumphal procession to the palace. The prisoners were compelled to march through the centre of the Theatre – a reminder to the Romans that ardour breathes new life into the dead, and that desire for glory is stronger than physical weakness.

Nevertheless, the power of nature could not be mastered indefinitely, nor could the emperor vanquish and overwhelm this disease for ever. Secretly and step by step it advanced to the final dissolution. For a while his friends attempted to hide his condition and they took counsel for the State, to forestall any revolutionary movement, but when the whole city was talking about his illness and the report of it spread everywhere, they altered their former plans. Their new policy was rather directed to the consolidation of their own control of the Empire. Let us leave them for the moment in that occupation.

THE EMPEROR'S TONSURE[1]

The emperor, before the decease of his body, sought another, more spiritual, change. He disdained the imperial rank which he was in so short a time to relinquish, mastered all his natural impulses, and turned to God. In order that he might not be interrupted while thus changing his life and making his confession to the Deity, he set out from his palace and retired to the monastery he had built, or rather he was conveyed thither by his bearers. Inside this place of meditation, kneeling

1. 10 December 1041, at the monastery of the Holy Anargyroi.

on the floor of the church, he prayed to God that he might appear a well-pleasing sacrifice and be received pure after his consecration. Thus he conciliated the Almighty and won His favour. Then he put himself in the hands of his priests, asking them to sacrifice a willing victim – auspicious omen – and they, grouped round him on either side, chanted the opening prayers of the Sacrifice to the Lord. They took off him the imperial robe and the purple, and they garbed him in the Holy Mantle of Christ. Then they took from his head the diadem and put on the Helmet of Salvation,[1] armed his chest and back with the Cross, and, bravely girding him against the spirits of evil, let him go. So much for his zeal and determination.

In the thought that he was now changed to a higher life, he rejoiced and was exceedingly glad. He had become swift-footed, as it were, and nimble for the spiritual journey. His own household, on the other hand, and especially the elder brother, were covered in a cloud of despair, so much so that they were unable to restrain their sympathetic laments. Not even the empress controlled her emotion. When she heard from someone about his tonsure, she dared to leave the women's quarters, overcoming every natural disinclination, and went on foot to see him. But Michael, whether through shame at the evils he had brought upon her, or because in his attention to God he had forgotten her, refused her permission to enter his presence.

She returned to the palace, and he, when the hour of prayer summoned and it was time for him to attend for the usual hymns, quietly rose from his couch. When he was about to put on his shoes and found that the footwear he had formerly worn was still unchanged (because the customary leathern sandals of the monks had not been prepared for him), he was angry at this lack of prevision and went barefoot to church, supported on either side. His respiration was laboured

1. Epistle to the Ephesians, vi.

already and he was beginning to breathe his last, so he again went to his couch and lay down. For a little while he was silent, for he had lost the power of speech and his breathing was difficult. Then he gave up his soul to God. In the course of his reign, Michael had done and planned many things; in few had he met with failure. For my own part, when I examine his deeds and compare successes with failures, I find that the former were the more numerous, and it does not appear to me that this man failed to attain the higher life. In fact, I am sure that he did obtain a better lot.

So he died, in the moment of great victory, after a reign of seven years,[1] and on the very day when he received the tonsure. Yet there was no magnificent funeral or burial-place for him when his life on earth was done, for he was buried in the church itself, on the left side as you enter, beside the holy altar.

1. Michael had reigned seven years and eight months.

BOOK FIVE

MICHAEL V

1041-2

THEODORA

1042

His nephew, whom I have mentioned several times in the last book, succeeded him as emperor. In fact, when John and his brothers perceived that Michael was at death's door, and when they really understood that he was past all hopes of recovery, they issued an order, professedly from the emperor, authorizing their nephew to enter the palace. They did this because they were afraid they might lose their own hold on the government and lest the Empire should pass into the hands of some other family. They even anticipated the old emperor's death, and as one sovereign went out of the palace to die (as I have described) another came in to take his place.

The late emperor had three brothers. Of these the Orphanotrophus John was at that time solely responsible for the administration. He had more affection for his brother than the rest, and, when Michael died, he did not leave him at once, but stayed by the corpse for three days, as though he were still alive. The other two surviving brothers meanwhile escorted the Caesar, their nephew, to the palace. The object of this was partly to defend and take care of him, partly to win greater commendation for themselves. John's intellectual capacity was wider and deeper than their own, and without his help it was beyond their powers to formulate any policy on the grand scale, either with regard to the succession or to affairs of State. Their activities were therefore limited to a display of fellowship and kindred feeling. As for John, having had his fill of lamentation, or rather when he grew alarmed at the prospect of any further delay in declaring Michael emperor, which might well wreck all their hopes completely, he returned to the palace.

I myself witnessed his return, and having seen with my own eyes what really happened, I am now committing the story to writing. I will describe the scene exactly. When the brothers heard that John had crossed the threshold of the outer palace entrance, they approached him as if they were about to meet God Himself. The ceremonial was prepared beforehand: they gathered about him and smothered him with kisses, all kissing different parts of his body at once. Even his nephew stretched out his right hand for him to lean on, as if there were some virtue to be gained from his very touch. The demands of flattery having been satisfied, John without more ado took the first step in his master plan. He urged them to do nothing without the empress, to build on her the foundations of their own greatness and of their future, to do all things that they saw were likely to win her over.

So with one accord they straightway banded together for the contest. With the artillery of their logic they laid siege to her soul – an easy capture. They reminded her of Michael's adoption, put the young man under the protection of his mother and mistress, and threw him at her feet. Heaping upon her all the flattering names suitable to such a moment, they assured her that their nephew would be emperor only in name, while she, apart from the title, would have, besides, the power that she inherited by right of descent. If she so desired, she would administer the State in person; if not, she would give her orders to him and use him as a slave-emperor to do her bidding. They took solemn oaths and pledged their loyalty by the Holy Relics, and so made her their prisoner at the first shot. What else, indeed, could she do, bereft as she was of outside assistance and spellbound by their sorcery, or shall I say rather, led astray by their trickery, beguiled by their ruses, and converted to their desires?

THE PROCLAMATION OF MICHAEL AS
EMPEROR

Well, she entrusted them with the government and she
quieted the city, which was meanwhile in suspense awaiting
her decision, by an exhortation to keep the peace. Then the
ceremony of the Caesar's enthronement was completed. The
procession followed, then the entry into the church; the
Patriarch gave his blessing, the coronation and all the other
customary rites were duly performed. For the first day, at any
rate, the emperor was not forgetful of his proper station,
either in word or in deed. Constantly on his lips were the expressions 'the empress', 'my mistress', 'I am her servant', and
'whatever decision she makes'.

With similar cajolery he set out to charm John too, no less
than the empress. 'My master', he would say, and gave him a
throne to sit on near to himself. If ever he wished to speak, he
first sought some sign of approval from John, saying that he
himself was like a tool in the craftsman's hands, and that the
melody was not of the lyre but of him who played it in harmony. All, therefore, were amazed at the wisdom of the man
and marvelled at the success of John's scheming. Now the
man's deceitfulness was unperceived by the others, but his
uncle knew well that his smoothness went no deeper than
words: the hardness of his heart was hidden deep inside and
covered over. The more he acquiesced in John's plans, the
more John suspected his motives. He plumbed the hollow
depths of the young emperor's mind, but he still did not know
what to do, nor how he might most easily deprive him of
power, once having been foiled of this hope when opportunity had assured him of certain success. However, he held his
peace for a while, not by any means because he had abandoned his scheme, but intending to try it out if the other took
the initiative and wronged him first. In fact, Michael did begin
to change, little by little, from the excessive modesty he used

to evince in John's presence at the beginning of his reign. Sometimes he did not wait for John's opinion on his actions as emperor; sometimes he deliberately opposed him and spoke with persons whom he knew John did not tolerate.

He had an ally to encourage this enmity towards his uncle: Constantine, the latter's brother, who for a long time had been jealous of John. The reason for this was that John, alone among the brothers, held an active post in the government: he was like their master, not their kinsman. At that time Constantine was unable to show hatred for him openly, because the late emperor had great affection for the man, not only as the eldest of the family, but also as the most intelligent, and as a man thoroughly proved in the conscientious performance of his official duties. On the other hand, he abominated and loathed the rest of the family, because they neither loved moderation nor made any useful contribution to the government of the Empire. Consequently, when the emperor had been angry with the brothers, it used to be John who interceded on their behalf, John who coaxed him to look on them again with benevolence. Naturally then, despite the brothers' jealousy at John's reputation, and although Constantine in particular felt chagrin, yet it was impossible for them to dare or do anything to oppose him.

But after their brother Michael died and succession to the throne fell to the nephew, Constantine had a very convenient starting-point for his attack on the Orphanotrophus, for he carefully cultivated the new emperor while he was still only the Caesar and allowed him to draw on his own personal treasures to his heart's content. Constantine's money was there to be used, and the young man looked upon his wealth as a kind of storehouse instituted for his own convenience. Certainly this was the way Constantine bought his favour, and, while fortune obviously smiled on his efforts, he continued to court his friendship with an eye to the future. They shared their secrets. They stood side by side in their campaign against

John, knowing that he, on his part, was scheming against them. If he had his way, then their plans would be frustrated and some other members of the family would sit on the throne. Under those circumstances it was to be expected that the Caesar would promote Constantine to the dignity of Nobilissimus, as soon as he himself had been crowned emperor. Constantine became his boon companion, amply rewarded for the loyalty he had displayed before Michael's accession.

At this stage I will interrupt the narrative for a few moments while I make some preliminary comments on the emperor's mental and spiritual outlook. My readers may possibly be saved from a feeling of perplexity when I describe his actions later; they will not be surprised when they see in them a lack of premeditation and a certain irrelevance, qualities which had their origin in the complex fortunes of his life. The outstanding characteristic of the man, indeed, was his interest in a great variety of subjects and an extraordinary facility in moving from one subject to another. A second peculiarity was the contradiction in the man between heart and tongue – he would think one thing and say something quite different. Men would often stir him to anger and yet meet with a reception of more than usual friendliness when they came to him, while he assured them most solemnly that he had their interests close at heart and regarded them with feelings of sincere attachment. There were several examples of men, who, at dawn the next morning, were destined by him to undergo the most horrible tortures, being made to share his table at dinner the evening before, and to drink from the same cup as himself. As for the names denoting family-relationship – I would go further than that and say even the relationship itself – to him they were so much nonsense. He would not have cared one jot if a single wave had overwhelmed and engulfed the lot of them, all his kith and kin at once. He was not only jealous of them in the matter of government – that was natural enough – but he grudged them the elementary necessities of life and any little luck that came their way. If power was to be shared, it would be with someone quite insignificant, or with nobody at all. In fact, more than that, he seems to me to have felt envy even for the supernatural, so great was his dislike and suspicion of all men in all circumstances. When fortune was adverse, no man was ever more cringing, in deed and in word, no man more base in spirit. Yet fortune had but to change a little for the better and at once he threw off the mask of servility. The counterfeit appearance was put aside and immediately he was full of courage. Terrible deeds were done, others were saved up for the future. The man was a slave to his anger, changeable, stirred to hatred and wrath by any chance happening. So there burned secretly in his heart a loathing for all his family, but to get rid of them was a different matter. For the moment he made no attempt to do so, because he still feared his uncle; he knew that John was still in the position of a father to the whole family.

After this interruption in my opening remarks on this reign, I now return to the simple narrative. Well, when Constantine became Nobilissimus, he shook off the awe which he felt for his brother. His former attitude of reverence was forgotten, his conversation became bolder, and he attacked John's policy with more recklessness. On several occasions he reproached the emperor for his deference to John's will and threw the young man into much confusion. There were other reasons why Michael's composure was rudely shattered, there were other influences which urged him to rebel, but Constantine's intervention added fresh fuel to the fire, and the emperor began to treat John with contempt in nearly everything. The prospect of losing his place and the supremacy he wielded over the family was particularly distasteful to the Orphanotrophus, but as it was no easy matter to depose one who had already acceded to the throne, he adopted a new policy to get his way. I myself witnessed what was going on then and I guessed that he had changed his ideas, but most people knew nothing about it. In my opinion, his ambition was to transfer the government to one of his nephews, a man called Constantine, who held the rank of Magister. His plan was not to attack the emperor himself, but to give this Constantine the chance of plotting against him instead. Later, fearing lest the nephew should be caught and have to stand trial on charges of sedition, and being afraid that he himself might not escape destruction, or fail to bring down destruction on the rest of the family at the same time, he decided to preclude any such possibility in the future; the important thing was that the present should go according to plan. He proceeded to effect a reconciliation between the emperor and his kinsmen. He persuaded him to grant certain privileges to them, with the promise of others later on. He was especially insistent that they should be provided for in the event of those troubles which men commonly meet with in life. So far the emperor granted his requests and his promises were confirmed in writing, in order that John might have an assured guarantee for the future. However, no sooner were these promises put into writing than John added a secret clause of his own, to the effect that if any of his nephews should be convicted of plotting against the emperor, he should be neither punished nor condemned, but that the special privilege of exemption from trial was to be granted by his uncle.

Having added this clause, he waited for a favourable opportunity, and when he saw Michael not particularly interested in certain papers, he handed him this manuscript for signature. The emperor read it through in a cursory way and confirmed it in his own handwriting. Naturally John was filled with exultation. It was a great triumph, and the realization of his secret ambitions was brought appreciably nearer. And no doubt he was ready to put his plans to the test. In reality, though, this was the start of his tribulations, as a detailed

examination of these events will show, for before the
Orphanotrophus could take the initiative, the emperor suspected what was afoot, partly because of his own forebodings,
partly from the remarks of his courtiers, who told him what
they thought about the proceeding. They made it clear that
his continued subjection to John was intolerable. There were
now two alternatives and they would move heaven and earth
to bring about one or the other: either they must preserve the
emperor's authority intact or they would perish with the
State.

   This ultimatum had an immediate effect. Michael not only
ceased to pay John the honour that was due to him, but he
even differed with him on questions of policy. They rarely
met in conference, at long intervals, and when they did meet
it was clearly against their will. Once, when they were dining
together, Constantine directed the conversation to a certain
affair, and having heard both men express an opinion on the
subject, he praised the emperor's estimate of the matter,
acclaiming it as 'an excellent judgement, one really worthy of
an emperor', but rejected his brother's opinion as a 'crafty
bit of intrigue'. He gradually developed this theme and
presently launched a big-scale attack. He recalled John's
arrogance in the past, exposed his ill-will and deceit in the
present. The Orphanotrophus, quite incapable of listening to
such an onslaught with patience, got up at once and went
away. He took himself off, not to his usual place of residence,
but to some spot far away from the city. This change of abode,
he imagined, would compel the emperor to pray and beseech
him to return; he would very soon bring him back to the
palace. When he went off, his own private bodyguard
followed him, and a considerable body of senators went
away with him too, not through any feelings of friendship for
John, but in most cases because they believed that he would
be back again in his old haunts almost immediately, and they
were trying to make sure of his favour in advance. Their

departure from the capital would be an excellent method of reminding him of their services.

John's defection was, no doubt, extremely gratifying to Michael, but it could not compensate the painful suspicions roused in him when the greater part of the city populace was flocking out to join the Orphanotrophus in his retreat. He feared a possible revolution, so, with extreme craftiness and no little malevolence, he wrote him a letter. In it he upbraided the other for his excessive pride and recalled him, presumably in order to discuss certain secret matters connected with the government. John at once returned. He had assumed from the tone of the letter that the emperor would come out to meet him. He expected to be addressed in terms befitting his high office and treated with the respect to which he had been accustomed. What actually happened was quite different. A performance was going on in the Theatre and the emperor, without waiting to see his uncle, left for the entertainment earlier than usual. What is more, he left no message for John. When the latter perceived what had occurred, he considered himself even more insulted than before: the emperor had cast him off. So, in high dudgeon, he returned to the place from which he had come, without delay. There was no doubt now as to the emperor's intentions. From his actions it was clear to John that he had to deal with an enemy. The bond of friendship was now absolutely broken and each plotted the other's downfall. John, especially, was engaged in con-spiracy – naturally, for he was at a disadvantage as an ordinary citizen – and schemed ways and means of attacking the emperor, without the knowledge of others and without ex-posing himself to arrest. Michael, on the other hand, being the supreme ruler of the Empire, was in a superior position and made good use of it. There was no secret about his hatred for John, for the days of pretence were over. He simply ordered his foe to embark on a ship and appear in his own defence. He would have to explain why he treated

the emperor with gross contempt and why he refused to obey
his orders.

Accordingly John set sail. The emperor, meanwhile,
watched the sea from a high vantage-point in the palace, and
when the ship carrying his uncle was about to anchor in the
Great Harbour, he gave a signal from above to the sailors, as
they were putting in, to turn about. Actually, this signal had
been arranged beforehand. A second trireme, ready to put to
sea and in the wake of the first, then hailed John's ship, took
him on board, and carried him off to a distant place of exile.[1]
It was through this man's efforts that Michael had become
first Caesar and subsequently emperor, yet the reverence he
formerly felt for John now meant so little to him that he
inflicted punishment on his uncle without so much as a blush
of shame. In fact, he banished him to a place reserved ex-
clusively for convicted pirates. It is only fair to add that afterwards, when his anger had died somewhat, he did consider it
proper to allow him certain small favours. So John went
away, not merely to satisfy the emperor's vengeance, but
destined to see misfortunes one after the other, for the fate
which by the decree of Providence fell to his lot – I will
speak in moderate terms – never gave him a single respite;
evil followed evil, till finally fate laid on his eyes[2] the hand of
the executioner and brought him, with terrible swiftness, to a
most violent death.[3]

The rascally Michael now took upon his own shoulders
the sole control of the Empire. His intentions were anything
but moderate, for his first efforts were directed to a complete

1. The Guardian of the Orphans was banished to the monastery of
Monobatae. Cedrenus (749D, p. 535) has a different account. According
to him John was exiled by Zoe before Michael was crowned.

2. John was blinded in prison on the orders of the Patriarch Cerularius (1043).

3. Constantine IX Monomachus put him to death, after banishing
him to Mitylene.

reversal of policy: everything had to conform to his wishes.
Government officials were treated with no sign of friendliness
whatever. The emperor's hostility to them was evident both
in his look and in his general attitude. In fact, his arrogant
speech and manners terrified them. His ambition centred on
one object: to make his realm in very truth 'subject' to himself; most of the officials were to be stripped of their customary
privileges and the people were to have their freedom restored;
he would then have the support of the people, who were
many, rather than of the nobility, who were few.[1] As for his
personal bodyguard, he filled the corps with new soldiers,
Scythian youths whom he had bought some time previously.
Every one of them was a eunuch. They understood what he
required of them and they were well fitted to serve his
desires. Indeed, he never questioned their allegiance, because
it was to himself that they owed their promotion to the
highest ranks. Some he employed in actual guard-duties,
while others were engaged in various tasks that he wished to
be done.

In this way his plans were brought to fruition. There remained, however, the problem of the rest – the pick of the
city populace and all those who belonged to the merchant
class or were manual workers. Their adherence, too, was
assured and the hearts of the people won over by his favours.
It was a necessary expense, for one day, if need arose, he might
want their backing for his projects. The people, on their side,
were genuinely attached to him and their sentiments found
expression in certain obvious marks of goodwill. For instance,
they would not let him walk on the bare ground; it would
be a dreadful thing, they thought, if he did not tread on

1. Despite this criticism, Michael did restore George Maniaces and
Constantine Dalassenus, both men of great ability. The future Patriarch
Lichudes also first won promotion in this reign. The historian Michael
Attaliates altogether differs from Psellus in his estimate of Michael V
(cf. Schlumberger, *L'Épopée byzantine*, iii, p. 383).

carpets. His horse, too, must needs revel in covers of silk. These compliments, not unnaturally, gave him pleasure, and in his elation he began to reveal what his secret designs were. The truth is, the empress was the object of his wrath, the woman who had become his mother by adoption, contrary to all propriety and reason. This feeling of his, moreover, was no new one, for it dated back to the time when through her efforts he had been made emperor. He had once called her his 'mistress' and the very thought of it made him feel like biting off his own tongue and spitting it away in disgust.

THE EMPEROR'S HATRED FOR THE AUGUSTA AND HIS ENVY OF HER

In the public proclamations he heard her name mentioned before his own, and after that indignity he could no longer hide his chagrin. It led him, in the first place, to adopt an attitude of defiance. When she approached him, he turned a deaf ear; the council-chamber was closed to her, and, worse still, she was denied all access to the imperial treasury. In fact, the empress was held in contempt everywhere. Indeed, I would go further than that – he made her an object of ridicule, for he treated her like a prisoner of war. She was kept under surveillance, in the most ignominious manner, her ladies-in-waiting controlled by the emperor and no corner of her private apartments free from inspection. Not one of the agreements made with her was respected by Michael, and when even these restrictions failed to satisfy him, he brought upon her the final disgrace – nothing less than expulsion from the palace. Such was his plan. There was no honest excuse for such action, but the beast had a foul lying story all ready, so determined was he to have the whole palace to himself. Of course, once this idea was conceived, all other duties of State were neglected: all his energy, all his ingenuity was devoted to the accomplishment of his daring project.

To begin with, therefore, he disclosed his plans to the more enterprising of his accomplices. Later on, as his scheme gradually advanced, he sounded other persons as well. In every case they were known to himself personally as men of keen judgement and endowed with other intellectual qualities. Some of them secretly encouraged him. Their advice was to follow his own inclination. Others counselled him to give up the whole idea, while a third party suggested that the proposed course of action should be studied first in greater detail. Another group thought that the astrologers ought to be consulted: it would be wise for Michael first to assure himself that the time was propitious for the attempt; some aspect of the heavens might be unfavourable. Seated in front of them, he listened gravely to all these monitors, prepared to take up anything whatever which could help him to realize his ambitions. Nothing was allowed to stand in the way of success. In the end, however, he rejected the arguments of all other counsellors and turned to the astrologers. Through them he would learn what the future held for him.

At that time there was a group of distinguished men engaged in the study of that science, men with whom I myself had dealings. These gentlemen were not specially concerned with the position or movement of stars in the celestial sphere (actually they had no training in the proof of such things by the laws of geometry, and certainly this power of demonstration was not acquired by them before they studied astrology); they confined themselves rather to the setting up of astro-logical centres, the examination of the rise and fall of the zodiacal signs above or below the horizon. Other phenomena connected with these movements also became the objects of their study – the ruling planets, the relative positions and limits of the planets, together with those aspects considered favourable and those which were not propitious. Certain predictions were then offered to persons who asked for advice and their questions were answered. In some cases, too, they did indeed hit on the correct answer. I say this, because I myself have some knowledge of the science, a knowledge acquired after long and diligent research, and I have been of some assistance to many of these men and helped them to understand the planetary aspects. Despite this, I am no believer in the theory that our human affairs are influenced by the movement of the stars. That, however, is a problem that must form the subject of inquiry in another work – it gives rise to too many controversies on either side.

Let us return to the reigning emperor. Without disclosing the nature of the deed he had in mind, he submitted a vague question to the astrologers. The only information he asked for was whether the heavenly aspects were inauspicious to a man who took a great risk. Observations were taken and the general position of the stars was carefully examined at the proper moment, and when the astrologers saw that everything portended blood and sorrow, they warned him to abandon the enterprise. The more circumspect among them advised him to put off the deed until some later occasion. At this the emperor burst into a loud laugh. He mocked their science, calling it a fraud. 'To blazes with you!' he said. 'And as for your wonderful knowledge, my daring venture will make child's-play of it!'

So at once he got to work and went over to the attack without delay. Certain charges[1] were fabricated against his adopted mother, who was innocent of any plot aimed at himself, and the wretched boy condemned her as a poisoner. She, still knowing nothing of his machinations, was driven

1. The text of the proclamation of 19 April 1042, made in the Forum of Constantine the Great by the City Prefect Anastasius, is preserved in Cedrenus (750D, p. 537). In it Zoe was accused of treachery and of collaborating with Alexius the Patriarch. Cedrenus's account of the whole episode is different. According to him Michael was persuaded by the Nobilissimus and the Orphanotrophus not to trust Zoe, because she was preparing to poison him. She was sent to Prinkipo on 18 April as an exile.

from her bedchamber – she who had been born there, driven out by a *parvenu*! She, the daughter of a most noble family, was dispossessed by a man sprung from the gutter. Witnesses were suborned to give false evidence and he proceeded to question her on matters of which she knew nothing. She was compelled to account for her actions and was then convicted of the most abominable crimes. At once she was put on board ship, together with certain persons who were given full liberty to insult her. Exiled from the palace, she was landed on one of the islands lying off Byzantium, called Prinkipo.

Afterwards I talked with some of those who took her away there and they told me that when the ship had put out to sea for the voyage, Zoe looked back at her royal home and apostrophized the palace in a kind of dirge. She spoke of her father and her ancestors (her family had occupied the throne for four generations before she inherited the Empire) and when she recalled her uncle – I am speaking now of the famous Basil, that treasure and glory of the Roman Empire who outshone all other sovereigns who ruled over it – then her eyes suddenly filled with tears and she exclaimed: 'It was you, my uncle and emperor, you who wrapped me in my swaddling clothes as soon as I was born, you who loved me, and honoured me too, more than my sisters, because, as I have often heard them say who saw you, I was like yourself. It was you who said, as you kissed me and held me in your arms, "Good luck, my darling, and may you live many years, to be the glory of our family and the most marvellous gift to our Empire!" It was you, also, who so carefully brought me up and trained me, you who saw in my hands a great future for this same Empire. But your hopes have been brought to nothing, for I have been dishonoured. I have disgraced all my family, condemned on most horrible charges and expelled from the palace, driven away to I know not what place of exile, convicted of crime. For all I know, they may throw me a prey to wild beasts, or drown me in the sea. I beg you,

watch over me from Heaven and with all your strength
protect your niece.' After reaching the island that was to be
her place of exile, however, she recovered somewhat from
her mood of despair. She thanked God that she was still alive,
and at once offered up prayers and sacrifices to Him who had
saved her.

She had no intention of meddling in State affairs. Indeed,
how could she, spending her life in exile, with one lady-in-
waiting? Yet that rascal cherished even more terrible designs
against her and trouble was heaped on trouble. In the end, a
party was dispatched to cut off her hair – perhaps it would be
more correct to say that they were sent to kill her. She was
to be offered up, so to speak, as a whole burnt-offering, not to
please the Lord maybe, but certainly to appease the wrath of
the emperor who gave this order. However, once the design
was satisfactorily carried out, he left her alone. So far as he
was concerned, the empress was already dead, but he gave a
dramatic account of the whole affair to the Senate. It was like
a scene from a play. Her so-called plots against himself were
revealed, while he told them how for a long time past he had
suspected her; worse than that, he had more than once
caught her red-handed, but had concealed her misdoings out
of respect for the Senators. After inventing such lies – sheer
nonsense it was – and after winning their approval (they
passed remarks suited to the occasion), he considered his
defence before them was adequate, and next put his case to the
people. Some of the latter were already quite prepared to
dance to his tune, and to them he told his story. They gave
him their verdict. There was obviously support for his
policy in that quarter as well, so this second meeting was dismissed, and he, like a man who has accomplished some mighty
exploit, took a rest from his great labours and gave himself up
to childish delight, all but dancing and leaping from the
ground in his pleasure. Yet retribution was near; the usurper's
pride was to meet its downfall in the not distant future.

As for the events that followed, words are inadequate to describe them. The human mind cannot comprehend the working of Providence. When I say this, I am judging other people's reactions by my own. Certain it is that no poet, with his soul animated by the divine afflatus and his tongue inspired by God; no orator who had attained the height of spiritual and rhetorical perfection, and had moreover adorned with the skill of artifice his own natural abilities; no philosopher, even, who had thorough knowledge of the ways of Providence and of their revelation, or who had learnt by the power of his wisdom any other thing that surpasses our human understanding; none of these would be capable of describing the events that took place at this crisis, at least in a manner that would do them justice. Such a task would be impossible, even if the poet dramatized the story with subtle touches of character; even if the orator made a glorious speech, with his periods harmonized and altogether fitted to the vastness of his theme; even if the philosopher, denying the spontaneous origin of these events, explained them by reason and produced causes from which that great and far spread mystery – for one cannot describe it as anything else – was derived. Naturally, therefore, it was not for me to mention that extraordinary social upheaval. Nor would I have done so, unless I had realized that by holding my peace the supreme crisis of my history would be neglected. So, in my tiny skiff, I have ventured to cross a mighty ocean. At all events, to the best of my ability, I will tell my story – an account of all those strange happenings that followed the empress's exile, events that Divine Justice brought to pass at this moment in history.

Up to this time the emperor had lived in the height of luxury and he was extremely proud of his achievements. Throughout the city, however – and I am speaking here of persons of every kind and fortune and age – a feeling of dissatisfaction and confusion gradually became more apparent. It was as if the natural harmony of the city had been interrupted. There was at first an undercurrent of anxiety which slowly made itself felt everywhere. Everyone was concerned over the empress's conviction. Deep in their hearts men had grim forebodings and they began to speak freely about them. As the story of her new position in the State became generally known, the whole city quite obviously went into mourning. Just as in the great upheavals of nature all men are sad at heart and know not how to recover their spirits – for some terrible evils they have already endured and others they still await – so then a certain awful dejection seized on every soul and a sense of misfortune that was beyond comfort. On the second day no one any longer held his tongue. The ruling classes, the clergy, even the emperor's family and household staff, were talking about it. Those engaged in business, too, prepared themselves for deeds of daring, and not even the foreigners and allies whom the emperors are wont to maintain by their side – I am referring to the Scyths from the Taurus – were able to restrain their anger. The indignation, in fact, was universal and all were ready to lay down their lives for Zoe.

As for the common mob, it was already on the move, greatly stirred at the prospect of exercising tyranny over him who had himself played the tyrant. And the women – but how can I explain this to people who do not know them? I myself saw some of them, whom nobody till then had seen outside the women's quarters, appearing in public and shouting and beating their breasts and lamenting terribly at the empress's misfortune, but the rest were borne along like Maenads,[1] and they formed no small band to oppose the offender. 'Where can she be,' they cried, 'she who alone is noble of heart and alone is beautiful? Where can she be, she who alone of all women is free, the mistress of all the imperial family, the rightful heir to the Empire, whose father was

1. Women inspired to ecstatic frenzy by Dionysus (Bacchus).

emperor, whose grandfather was monarch before him – yes, and great-grandfather too? How was it this low-born fellow dared to raise a hand against a woman of such lineage? How could he conceive so vile a thought against her? No other soul on earth would dream of it.' Thus they spoke and hurried together as though they intended to fire the palace. As there was no longer anything to stop them, for all men had already rebelled against the tyrant, they took up their positions for battle, at first in small groups, as if they were divided by companies. Later, with all the citizen army, they marched in one body to the attack.

Every man was armed; one clasped in his hands an axe, another brandished a heavy iron broadsword, another handled a bow, and another a spear, but the bulk of the mob, with some of the biggest stones in the folds of their clothing and holding others ready in their hands, ran in general disorder. I myself was standing at the time in front of the palace entrance. For a long time I had been acting as secretary to the emperor and had recently been initiated into the ceremonies of Entry to the Imperial Presence. I was in the outer porch dictating some of the more confidential dispatches, when suddenly there assailed our ears a hubbub like the sound of horses' hooves and the hearts of most of us trembled at the sound. Then there came a messenger with the news that all the people were roused against the emperor; they were gathered in one body; they must be marching under one common standard, with one single purpose. To most of the others it seemed a senseless revolt, but I, knowing from what I had seen before, and from what I had heard, that the spark had flared up into a fire, and that it needed many rivers and a fast-flowing current to put it out, straightway mounted my horse and going through the midst of the city saw with my own eyes the sight which now I can hardly believe.

It was as if the whole multitude were sharing in some superhuman inspiration. They seemed changed persons. There was more madness in their running, more strength in their hands, the flash in their eyes was fiery and impassioned, the muscles of their bodies more powerful. As for prevailing on them to behave in a more dignified manner or dissuading them from their intentions, nobody whatever was willing to try such a thing. Anyone who gave advice of that sort was impotent.

It was decided first to attack the emperor's family and tear down their proud and luxurious mansions. With this object they advanced to the general assault, and all was razed to the ground. Of the buildings some were covered over, others were left open to the sky; roofs falling to the ground were covered with débris, foundations thrust up in ruins from the earth were stripped, as if the soil were throwing off its burden and hurling away the floors. It was not the hands of strong men in the prime of youth that pulled down the most of it, but young girls and children of either sex lent aid in the work of destruction. Every building fell straightway at the first onslaught and the destroyers carried away what had been smashed or pulled down, with utter indifference. The objects were put up for sale, without a thought for the mansions from which they had come.

Such then was the state of affairs in the city and so quickly had its usual appearance been altered. As for the emperor, he sat in the palace, at first by no means alarmed at the course of events. His idea was to end civil war without the shedding of blood, but when the revolution was afoot beyond all doubt and the people adopted military formations, with quite a respectable battle-array, then he was fearfully troubled. Hemmed in on all sides, he was at a loss what to do. He was afraid to sally forth and he was no less suspicious of remaining where he was to sustain a siege; he had no ally in the palace nor could he send out for help, and even the mercenaries maintained by him were, some of them, of doubtful allegiance and not invariably obedient, while others were openly hostile, and, when their discipline broke, they broke out with the mob.

In his utter perplexity an ally did come to his aid – the Nobilissimus. At that moment he happened to be away from the palace, but when he learnt of the danger, being filled with alarm, he at first stayed in his home. He was terribly afraid of the crowd standing at his gates and would not venture outside, for he believed he would die on the spot if he did. Later on, however, he armed the whole of his household staff, without putting on defensive armour himself, and with their help he gave the door a sudden shove, got outside without attracting any attention, and went through the city like lightning. His retinue were armed with daggers, so that if anyone met them, they could slay him at once. Charging thus through the city they dashed to the gates of the palace and entered it. The emperor, whom they had come to help in his hour of danger, received them with joy, and almost embraced his uncle for choosing to die with him. They determined then to recall the empress from exile at once – it was through her that the mob had broken out in revolt and the war was being fought on her behalf. With regard to themselves, they came to the conclusion that they should use the multitude then in the palace, the javelin-men and stone-throwers, against anybody who had the effrontery to attack them. Urgent necessity dictated it. So these men hurled down their missiles and shot their arrows from concealed positions in the high parts of the palace, and they slew a considerable number of the enemy. Their close formation was indeed broken up, but seeing what the idea of the emperor's men was, they rallied again and formed up more tightly than before.

In the meantime the empress was carried into the palace, full of joy at the thought that God was working for her. But there was a shadow – she feared punishment still more awful at the hands of the wicked Michael. It was for that reason she neither seized the chance of revenge nor blamed the tyrant for her misfortunes nor changed her demeanour. She even gave him her sympathy and shed tears at his distress. But instead of taking from her the nun's habit and clothing her in a robe of purple, as he should have done, he compelled her to promise that once the storm had died down she would live as she was then, with the same nun's habit; she would moreover acquiesce in the decisions he had already made about her future. Every proposal he offered she agreed with, and they made a covenant to face the danger together. On these conditions they carried her up to a balcony on the Great Theatre and there they showed her to the rebel people; they thought it would quench the fire of the rebels' anger if they saw their mistress had been recalled from exile, but the people were in no hurry to recognize the lady. Those who did know her were all the more incensed at the tyrant's stratagem; they thought it monstrous that even in the midst of danger he still could not forget his natural ferocity and wickedness.

The war, therefore, flared up against him all the more bitterly. But the rebels were afraid lest the combined efforts of Michael and Zoe might yet prove their undoing, and most of their supporters might be persuaded by her and give up the struggle. So a new plan was adopted, a plan which was a sufficient and complete answer to Michael's scheming.

At this stage I would like to go back a little, so that the story can be told in a methodical way. I shall have to refer to events previous to this outbreak and link them with it. As I have said before, Constantine (VIII) had not one daughter, but three. The eldest of these ladies was dead. The youngest for a short time continued to live with her sister after she became empress and, to a certain extent, shared the throne with her. The privilege of acclamation was not extended to her, but she did enjoy exceptional honours and she had her share of splendour in the palace, although her position was inferior to that of her sister. Their close relationship, however, and the fact that they were born of the same mother, were not sufficient to avert jealousy, and even her lower rank excited the empress to envy Theodora (that was the younger sister's name). At the same time certain persons maliciously spread rumours about her and prevailed on Zoe to remove her from the palace, cut off her hair, and give her one of the more stately imperial houses to live in.[1] The place would be a kind of prison, but it would be veiled under a fine name. This advice was followed at once. Jealousy divided the two sisters and kept one in a position of greater importance, the other in an inferior condition, but Theodora at least retained the semblance of majesty.

Yet she (Theodora) resigned herself to her lot. Neither the donning of a nun's robe nor separation from her sister provoked her to anger, and as for the emperor, he still treated her with some of his former courtesy. He even granted her certain imperial favours. But when he died and Michael (Paphlagon) ascended the throne, the latter, as I have already shown, soon forgot Zoe and completely despised Theodora. In his turn he too fulfilled the allotted span of life and departed, to be succeeded by his nephew, Michael Calaphates. This emperor did not know who Theodora was, or if she was born of royal stock, but, as far as he was concerned, she might never have been born, might never have passed this way at all. Although she was in this plight – perhaps I should say, despite the attitude of the emperors towards her – she never opposed their wishes. This was no enforced obedience; she submitted of her own free will. I had to explain all this before I could return to my narrative.

THE MOB IS LED AWAY TO THE AUGUSTA THEODORA

As I have said, the people revolted against the tyrant, but they were afraid their efforts might be wasted. His force might get the better of them and the affair might develop into nothing

1. Theodora had been exiled to the convent of Petrion during the reign of Romanus III Argyrus.

more than an uproar. Since, therefore, they could not lay hands on the senior empress – the tyrant had anticipated that move and he was watching her with all the vigilance of a tax-gatherer waiting to collect dues from a ship in harbour – they turned their attention to her sister. She was, after all, the second child of an emperor. There was no confusion, no disorderly tumult. On the contrary, they appointed one of her father's retainers[1] to act as general at the head of their column, a man who was not a Greek by birth, but a person of the noblest character and a man of heroic stature, whose high-born ancestry inspired respect. With this brave leader they departed in full force to find Theodora.

Astounded by the unexpectedness of this sight, she refused at first to give way to their pleading and shut herself up in the church, deaf to every entreaty. The citizen army, however, giving up all hope of persuasion, used force, and some of their number, drawing their daggers, rushed in as if to kill her. Boldly they dragged her from the sanctuary, brought her out into the open, and clothed her in a magnificent robe. Then they made her sit on a horse, and forming a circle all about her, they led her to the great church of St Sophia. Homage was paid to her, not now by a mere fraction of the people, but by all the *élite* as well. Everyone, with utter disregard for the tyrant and loud applause for her, proclaimed Theodora empress.

THE FLIGHT OF THE EMPEROR AND HIS UNCLE, AND THE BLINDING OF THEIR EYES

When news of this reached Michael, fearing that the rebels would suddenly come upon him and lay violent hands on him there in the palace, he embarked on one of the imperial ships and landed with his uncle at the holy Studite monastery. There he laid aside his emperor's garments and put on the

1. Constantine Cabasilas.

clothes of a suppliant and refugee. As soon as their flight
became known in the city, the hearts of all men, hitherto
filled with fear and grim forebodings, were now relieved of
anxiety. Some made thank-offerings to God for their deliverance, others acclaimed the new empress, while the common
folk and the loungers in the market joined in dancing. The
revolution[1] was dramatized and they composed choral songs
inspired by the events that had taken place before their eyes.
More numerous still was the crowd that rushed in one wild
swoop upon the tyrant himself, intent on cutting him down,
on slitting his throat.

So much for them. Theodora's companions meanwhile
sent a guard for him. The guard commander[2] was one of the
nobles and I myself accompanied him (I was a personal friend
of the man). Actually, he had invited me to advise him and
help in the carrying out of his orders. On our arrival at the
doors of the church, we saw another guard, composed of
volunteers, a company of citizens who had completely surrounded the sacred building. They were ready to do everything but tear it down. So it was not without difficulty that
we made our way into the church. Along with us a great
multitude of folk poured in, roaring abuse at the accursed
fellow. All manner of indecent epithets were hurled at him.

Up till then I too had gone along with the mob, having no
particularly moderate feelings about him. I was not indifferent
to his treatment of the empress, and a certain mild resentment
against the man stirred me on my own account. But when I
reached the sacred altar where he was, and saw both the
refugees, one, who had been emperor, clinging to the Holy

1. Heavy casualties were suffered on both sides in the battle of 19–20
April. As many as 3,000 men were killed.

2. The newly-appointed City Prefect, Campanares. Zoe (Cedrenus,
752C, p. 540) was inclined not to punish Michael; Theodora, on the
other hand, was bitterly opposed to him. The Patriarch Alexius seems
to have played a leading part in the revolt.

Table of the Word, the other, the Nobilissimus, standing on the right of the altar, both with their clothes changed, their spirit gone and utterly put to shame, then there was no trace whatever of anger left in my heart. I stood there dumbfounded, mute with astonishment, as if I had been struck by a hurricane. I was transformed at the strangeness of the thing. Then, recovering my spirits, I began to curse this life of ours, in which these strange and terrible things so often come to pass, and as if some spring had welled up within me, a flood of tears beyond control poured from my eyes. This outburst finally gave way to groans.

Now the mob that had entered the church gathered in a circle round the two men, like wild beasts longing to devour them, while I was standing by the latticed gate on the right of the altar, lamenting. Both of them saw that I was greatly distressed and not entirely hostile to themselves. They detected in me some signs of moderation. Both therefore converged on me. Changing my manner somewhat, I began with gentle censure of the Nobilissimus. Among other faults I charged him with voluntarily supporting the emperor in his persecution of Zoe. Then I turned to him who had formerly been all-powerful, asking him what possible hurt he could have suffered at the hands of his adopted mother and mistress, that he should add such wrongs to her tragic story. Both answered me. The Nobilissimus denied that he was privy to his nephew's plot against Zoe. He had encouraged him in no other designs. 'If I had wished to restrain him,' he said, 'my reward would have been some calamity. The fellow was so headstrong' – and here he turned to the emperor – 'so headstrong in all his desires and ambitions. Had I been able to check his enthusiasms, the whole of my family would not have been mutilated, a prey to fire and sword.'

I would like to interrupt the history for a moment and explain what he meant by this 'mutilated'. When the emperor exiled the Orphanotrophus, thereby bringing down, as he

thought, the pillar of the family, he hastened to the destruction of the rest. All his relatives, most of whom had already
reached their full stature and were bearded men, who had
become fathers and been entrusted with offices of great
dignity in the State, he compelled to undergo castration,
making of their life a semi-death. The truth is, he was ashamed
to kill them openly: he preferred to compass their destruction
by mutilation, a punishment apparently less severe.

Such was the reply of the uncle. The tyrant, however,
slowly shaking his head and forcing a tear from his eyes (not
without some difficulty) said, 'Truly, God is not unjust' –
those were his very words – 'and I am rightly paying the
penalty for what I have done.' With these words he again laid
hold of the Holy Table. Then he prayed that his change of
garment might receive legal sanction, and the ceremony of
reception into the Church was performed in respect of them
both. Nevertheless, they were utterly dejected, filled with
apprehension and dread lest the mob should attack them. For
my own part, I thought their turbulence would go no further.
I was still fascinated by the drama of the thing. The unravel-
ling of the plot bewildered me, but this proved to be indeed
only a short prelude to the worse tragedies which followed.
However, I will describe what happened in detail.

Day was already drawing to a close when suddenly there
arrived one of the newly-appointed officials, saying that he
had received an order from Theodora to remove the refugees
to some other place. He was accompanied by a crowd of
citizens and soldiers. Approaching the altar at which they had
sought sanctuary, he invited them, in a somewhat peremptory
manner, to leave the church. Despite this, when they saw the
mob talking of public execution and when with their own
eyes they perceived the mob leader signalling that the moment was at hand, and when they observed the change in the
man – he was more insolent than usual – they refused to
come forth and clung even more resolutely to the pillars that

support the altar. The other thereupon laid aside his arrogance and addressed them with greater respect. He swore by the Holy Relics and used all manner of persuasion, saying that they would neither suffer any evil nor would he, the empress's envoy, treat them with any more severity than the occasion demanded. Even so, they remained deaf to his arguments, filled with terror and expecting all kinds of disaster to follow their present distress. It was better, they thought, to be slain in the sanctuary than meet with any and every outrage in the open.

So the official abandoned all hope of reasoned persuasion and resorted to violence. At his command the mob laid hands on them and without more ado proceeded to break the law, hounding them out of the church like wild beasts. The victims emitted cries of anguish unrestrained. They lifted their eyes to the Holy Lamb, praying fervently that they might not be disappointed of their hopes, that they might not be cruelly driven away after seeking refuge in the house of God. And most of those who were there with us were indeed put to shame by their sufferings. They did not dare to resist outright – affairs were now hurrying on to the climax – but they did make a bargain with the mob and relied on the sworn word of their leader. So they handed them over to him, with the air of men who have concluded a treaty, and then continued to escort them, presumably in order to give assistance once they were driven from the church. In reality, nothing could help them; circumstances were far too unfavourable and the people's hatred too general.

Theodora's adherents were aware of Zoe's jealousy. They knew that she would be quite willing to see a stable-lad on the imperial throne rather than let her sister share power with herself. They drew the natural conclusion that she would in all probability scorn Theodora completely and promote Michael to the throne a second time, by underhand means. Their unanimous decision, therefore, was to do away with the fugitive emperor. The moderate element, however, was not disposed to favour sentence of death; the ambitions of Michael and his uncle would have to be extinguished by some other device, and, after careful consideration, they determined their course of action. Bold, resolute men were dispatched with all speed. Their instructions were to burn out the fugitives' eyes, as soon as they saw them outside the sacred building.

Actually they had already left the church, and a shameful reception awaited them outside, where the rabble made fun of them, naturally enough under the circumstances. Sometimes the insults were tempered with laughter, but malice inspired others. Anyhow, they brought them out, intending to drive them through the centre of the city, but they had not gone far on the journey when they were encountered by the man who had been commanded to blind the two criminals. His party showed their instructions to the mob and they began preparing for the execution; the iron was sharpened for the branding. Meanwhile the victims heard what wretched fate was in store for them. There was no longer any hope of escape, for while some applauded the sentence, the others did nothing to oppose it, and the two were instantly struck dumb with fright. In fact, they would have nearly died, had not one of the senators stood by them to help. He offered consolation in their misery and little by little restored some courage in their hearts.

In spite of this encouragement the emperor, overwhelmed by the situation and his dreadful misfortunes, showed the same weakness of character throughout the whole time of his tribulation. He moaned and wailed aloud, and whenever anyone approached him, he begged for help. He humbly called on God, raised hands in supplication to Heaven, to the Church, to anything he could think of. His uncle, on the other hand, although at first he followed his companion's example, once he was convinced that safety really was out of the question, braced himself for the trial and, having armed himself, as it were, against the shock of catastrophe, faced suffering bravely. The fact is, he was a man of more dignified and steadfast character than his nephew, a man who would not willingly surrender to adversity. Seeing the executioners all ready for their work, he at once offered himself as the first victim and calmly approached them. They waited with hands athirst for his blood. As there was no clear space between himself and the mob – for everyone there present wished to be the first witness of their punishment – the Nobilissimus quietly looked round for the man to whom the miserable job had been entrusted. 'You there,' he said, 'please make the people stand back. Then you will see how bravely I bear my calamity!'

When the executioner tried to tie him down, to prevent movement at the time of blinding, he said, 'Look here. If you see me budge, *nail* me down!' With these words he lay flat on his back on the ground. There was no change of colour in his face, no crying out, no groaning. It was hard to believe that the man was still alive. His eyes were then gouged, one after the other. Meanwhile the emperor, seeing in the other's torment the fate that was about to overtake him, too, lived through Constantine's anguish in himself, beating his hands together, smiting his face, and bellowing in agony.

The Nobilissimus, his eyes gouged out, stood up from the ground and leaned for support on one of his most intimate friends. He addressed those who came up to him with great courage – a man who rose superior to the trials that beset him, to whom death was as nothing. With Michael it was different, for when the executioner saw him flinch away and lower himself to base entreaty, he bound him securely. He held him down with considerable force, to stop the violent twitching when he was undergoing his punishment. After his eyes, too, had been blinded, the insolence of the mob, so marked before, died away, and with it their fury against these men.

They left them to rest there, while they themselves hurried back to Theodora.[1] One of the two empresses was in fact in the palace, the other in the great cathedral of St Sophia.

The Senate was unable to decide between them. Zoe, who was in the palace, they respected because she was the elder; Theodora, who was in the church, because it was through her that the revolt had been brought to an end and to her they owed their preservation. Each, therefore, had a claim on the Empire. However, the problem was settled for them by Zoe. For the first time, she greeted her sister and embraced her with affection. What is more, she shared with her the Empire they both inherited. The question of the government was thus resolved by agreement between them. Next, Zoe brought her to live with herself, escorted by a procession of great magnificence, and made her joint-ruler of the Empire. As for Theodora, she lost none of her respect for her sister, nor did she encroach on her prerogatives. On the contrary, she allowed Zoe to take precedence and, although both were empresses, Theodora held rank inferior to the older woman.

1. The execution took place at the Sigma on 21 April 1042. Afterwards Michael was banished to the monastery of Elcimon. Where Constantine went, we do not know.

BOOK SIX

ZOE AND THEODORA

1042

CONSTANTINE IX

1042-55

So the Empire passed into the hands of the two sisters, and for the first time in our lives we saw the transformation of a *gynaeconitis*[1] into an emperor's council chamber. What is more, both the civilian population and the military caste were working in harmony under empresses, and more obedient to them than to any proud overlord issuing arrogant commands. In fact, I doubt if any other family was ever so favoured by God as theirs was – a surprising thing, when one reflects on the unlawful manner in which the family fortune was, so to speak, rooted and planted in the ground with murder and bloodshed. Yet the plant blossomed out and sent forth such mighty shoots, each with its royal fruit, that no others could be compared with it, either in beauty or grandeur. But this is a mere digression from my main story.

For a while the sisters preferred to govern alone. The Empire was administered without the appointment of new officials, and no immediate reforms were brought in to affect the constitution already established.[2] After dismissing only the members of the rebel family, Zoe and Theodora maintained in their position of authority the other ministers of state, who were men of proved loyalty and known for their

1. 'Women's quarters.'
2. The custom of buying high offices was now forbidden and letters to this effect were sent to the provinces (Cedrenus, 753, p. 541).

traditional allegiance to themselves.[1] These men, because they were afraid lest at some future time they should be accused of introducing new ideas into the constitution, or of making foolish decisions, or of acting illegally, were meticulously careful in their conduct of state affairs, both military and civil, and as far as possible they treated the empresses with all due honour.

Court procedure, in the case of the sisters, was made to conform exactly to the usual observance of the sovereigns who had ruled before them. Both of them sat in front of the royal tribunal, so aligned that Theodora was slightly behind her sister. Near them were the Rods and Sword-bearers and the officials armed with the *rhomphaia*.[2] Inside this circle were the special favourites and court officials, while round them, on the outside of the circle, was the second rank of the personal bodyguard, all with eyes fixed on the ground in an attitude of respect. Behind them came the Senate and the privileged class, then persons of the second class and the tribes, all in ranks and drawn up at proper intervals. When all was ready, the other business was carried on. There were lawsuits to be settled, questions of public interest, or contributions of money, audiences with foreign ambassadors, controversies or agreements, and all the other duties that go to fill up an emperor's time. Most of the talking was done by the officials concerned, but sometimes, when it was necessary, the empresses also gave their instructions, in a calm voice, or made their replies, sometimes being prompted and taking their cue from the experts, sometimes using their own discretion.

For those who did not know them it may be instructive if I give here some description of the two sisters. The elder, Zoe, was the quicker to understand ideas, but slower to give them

1. Nicolaus was appointed to high office in the east and Constantine Cabasilas in the west. George Maniaces became *magister* and was sent back to Italy as supreme commander (Cedrenus, ibid.).

2. See Glossary.

utterance. With Theodora it was just the reverse in both respects, for she did not readily show her inmost thoughts, but once she had embarked on a conversation, she would chatter away with an expert and lively tongue. Zoe was a woman of passionate interests, prepared with equal enthusiasm for both alternatives – death or life, I mean. In that she reminded me of sea-waves, now lifting a ship on high and then again plunging it down to the depths. Such characteristics were certainly not found in Theodora; in fact, she had a placid disposition, and in one way, if I may put it so, a dull one. Zoe was open-handed, the sort of woman who could exhaust a sea teeming with gold-dust in one day; the other counted her *staters* when she gave away money, partly no doubt because her limited resources forbade any reckless spending, and partly because inherently she was more self-controlled in this matter.

To put it quite candidly (for my present purpose is not to compose a eulogy, but to write an accurate history) neither of them was fitted by temperament to govern. They neither knew how to administer nor were they capable of serious argument on the subject of politics. For the most part they confused the trifles of the harem with important matters of state. Even the very trait in the elder sister which is commended among many folk today, namely, her ungrudging liberality, dispensed very widely over a long period of time, even this trait, although it was no doubt satisfactory to those who enjoyed it because of the benefits they received from her, was after all the sole cause, in the first place, of the universal corruption and of the reduction of Roman fortunes to their lowest ebb. The virtue of well-doing is most characteristic of those who govern, and where discrimination is made, where the particular circumstances and the fortune of the recipients and their differing personal qualities are taken into account, there the distribution of largess is to be commended. On the contrary, where no real discernment is exercised in these questions, the spending of money is wasted.

Such were the differences that marked the sisters in character. In personal appearance there was an even greater divergence. The elder was naturally more plump, although she was not strikingly tall. Her eyes were large, set wide apart, with imposing eyebrows. Her nose was inclined to be aquiline without being altogether so. She had golden hair, and her whole body was radiant with the whiteness of her skin. There were few signs of age in her; in fact, if you marked well the perfect harmony of her limbs, not knowing who she was, you would have said that here was a young woman, for no part of her skin was wrinkled, but all smooth and taut, and no furrows anywhere. Theodora, on the other hand, was taller, more taper of form. Her head was small, and out of proportion with the rest of her body. She was more ready with her tongue than Zoe, as I have said, and quicker in her movements. There was nothing stern in her glance: on the contrary, she was cheerful and smiling, eager to find any opportunity for talk.

So much for the character and physical appearance of the two empresses. I will return to the government. In those days, it seems to me, a peculiar magnificence, and an added prestige, attached to the executive power. The majority of the officials underwent a sudden change, as if they were playing parts on a stage and had been promoted to a role more glorious than any they had acted before. Largess was poured out as never in the past. Zoe, in particular, opened the coffers of the imperial treasury. Any trifles hidden away there were distributed by her with generous abandon. These monies had not been contributed by volunteers, but were the fruit of robbery and plunder. In fact, all this squandering, together with the high standard of living, was the beginning of the utter decline in our national affairs and the cause of our subsequent humiliation. But that was clear only to the prophets; only the wise saw what was really happening.

The prize-money for the soldiers and the revenues devoted

to army expenditure were quite unnecessarily diverted and
put aside for the use of other persons – a crowd of sycophants
and those who at that time were deputed to guard the empresses – as if the Emperor Basil had filled the treasuries with
riches for this very purpose.

Most men are convinced that the nations around us have
made their sudden incursions against our borders, these wild
unexpected inroads, for the first time in our day, but I myself
hold a different view. I believe the house is doomed when the
mortar that binds its bricks together becomes loose, and,
although the start of the trouble passed unnoticed by the
majority, there is no doubt that it developed and gathered
strength from that first cause. In fact, the gathering of the
clouds in those days presaged the mighty deluge we are
suffering today. But I must not speak of that yet.

THE AUGUSTA ZOE DELIBERATES WHOM TO PROMOTE TO THE IMPERIAL THRONE

In the description of the events that follow I will speak with
greater authority and more personal knowledge. The affairs
of State urgently demanded vigorous and skilful direction,
and the country needed a man's supervision – a man at once
strong-handed and very experienced in government, one
who not only understood the present situation, but also any
mistakes that had been made in the past, with their probable
results. We wanted a man who would make provision for the
future and prepare long beforehand against all possible attacks
or likely invasions from abroad. But the love of power, or the
lack of power, the apparent freedom and the absence of supervision, and the desire for ever greater power – these were the
things that made the emperor's apartment into a *gynaeconitis*.

Even so, most people had no settled convictions. One
rumour after another was bruited about, either favourable or
otherwise to Zoe (for there were some who thought that

Theodora should rightly be empress, on the ground that she had championed the cause of the people; moreover, they said, she had never married; others, again, believed the elder sister was more suited to rule, because she had had previous experience of power, and power exercised a peculiar fascination on her). While these rumours were spreading, first one way, then another, among the people, Zoe anticipated their decision and seized all power for herself a second time. The next move was to search for and find a man of the most illustrious descent and of the most distinguished fortune, whether he held a seat in the senate or served in the army.

Among others who were living at that time was a native of Dalassa (a most celebrated place) whose name was Constantine. He was an extraordinarily handsome man, and it seemed that Nature herself had prepared him for the supreme position in the Empire. Even before his tenth birthday rumour had it that he was destined for the highest honours. It was inevitable, of course, that the emperors should fear such a man, and all of them refused him access to the palace. In fact, Michael the Paphlagonian even committed him to prison, not so much through fear of him personally as for dread of the people acting on his behalf, for there was great excitement in the city when he was seen, and the people were so agitated that a revolution seemed imminent. However, Michael shut him up in a castle and he was closely watched. Michael's nephew, who succeeded him, was no sooner seated on the throne than he put an end to the young man's hopes of promotion by compelling him to enter the Church. Constantine's spiritual welfare meant nothing to the emperor, and his admission to a monastery was designed only to prevent him from achieving his secret ambitions. But Constantine was too enamoured of life to attempt resistance. Opportunity still held out the prospect of power, and he had an example near at hand where another had changed her profession, for the empress had once suffered the same fate and yet had given

up her nun's habit. Actually, it was some other business that
called him to the palace, but while there he was presented to
the empress. At this interview he spoke with more than usual
abruptness, expressing rather bold ideas on the subject of the
Empire and showing himself ready to compromise on
nothing. In fact, he adopted a lofty attitude of condescension.
The result was that most people found him rather unpleasant
and a somewhat overwhelming person to deal with: they
suspected his motives and took care to frustrate him.

So once again the votes were cast. In this case, the man was
not particularly distinguished in fortune, but blessed with a
commanding and dignified presence.[1] He was secretary once
to the Emperor Romanus, and not only succeeded in im-
pressing the great man with his administrative ability, but
also by his charming manners won the approval of Zoe.
Indeed, she was accused of meeting him secretly. Romanus,
however, was not a very jealous man and he turned a deaf ear
to all such talk. Michael, on the other hand, expelled him
from the palace. Under the pretence of giving him a more
important office, he was posted away from the capital. That
biased the empress in his favour and, after his recall from exile,
he cultivated her friendship, deliberately effacing himself in
order to please her. By this time everybody, up to a point, was
inclined to support his claims, but he was suddenly carried off
by an illness, and their hopes were never realized.[2]

Fate, indeed, decreed that the new master of the Empire
should be Constantine, the son of Theodosius.[3] He was the
last scion of the ancient family of the Monomachi in the male

1. Constantine Catepanus, surnamed Artoclinas.
2. Possibly poisoned by his wife, who, as Cedrenus says (753C, p.
542), could not bear to lose him.
3. Cedrenus, who is not without some humour, suggests that Zoe
decided to marry Monomachus because one Constantine was as good
as another: Catepanus had been murdered, another of the same name
should take his place. At the start of the reign he was recalled from exile
in Mitylene and given a post in Greece.

line. A long account of him will be given by me later, when I launch out into the history of his reign – a long account, because he was emperor for more years than any of Basil's successors, and because there was more to relate. Constantine was more active than his predecessors, although it must be admitted that he was not uniformly more fortunate. Indeed, in some ways he was greatly inferior. There is no reason why I should not be candid about this and tell the true story. Immediately after his accession I entered his service, served throughout his reign, was promoted to the Senate, entrusted with the most honourable duties. Thus there was nothing that I did not know, no overt act, no secret diplomacy. Naturally, therefore, I shall devote more space to him than to the other emperors.

THE MANNER IN WHICH THE AUGUSTA INTRODUCED THE EMPEROR CONSTANTINE INTO THE PALACE

But this is not the time to speak of those things. Our present task is to describe how, and for what reasons, and by what turn of fate, he came to power. Because of his family this man held very high rank in the Empire. He had the additional advantage of great wealth, and his personal appearance was singularly charming. Beyond all doubt he seemed a fit person to marry into the most illustrious families. In the first place he became son-in-law to the outstanding member of court society, but his wife fell ill and died. He was forced into a second alliance. At the time, Romanus, the future emperor, was still a private citizen, although high hopes were entertained that he would eventually be promoted and the people treated him with the greatest respect because of his position. Romanus had conceived a deep affection for Constantine – a young man in the flower of his manhood and scion of a most noble family – and he grafted this fine young cutting on his own rich fertile olive. The lady in question was none other than the daughter of his sister Pulcheria, who in the past had been married to Basil Sclerus (he had the misfortune later to be deprived of his sight) and had become the mother of this one child, a daughter. Alliance with this family conferred on the young man extraordinary brilliance, but he still held no important office. Basil's advisers, because of the hatred they nursed for the father, vented their spite on the son, and Sclerus's revolutionary designs had an unhappy effect on the emperor's relations with Constantine. That was the reason why neither Basil nor his brother Constantine ever promoted him to any responsible post in the government. They did him no actual harm, but he was slighted, and they certainly never dreamed that the man had a glorious future.

Even the accession of Romanus did little to help Constantine in his career, so mistaken was the new emperor in his estimate of the young man's qualities. However, Romanus did at least keep him at the imperial court, and, if for no other cause, he was very much in the public eye through his near relationship with the emperor. His fresh complexion (to the men of our generation he was as unspoiled as spring fruit) and his graceful manners and his conversation, in which he excelled all others, were the things that won the heart of the empress. She delighted in his company again and again. He for his part made himself thoroughly agreeable to her, and by cleverly adapting himself to please her on all occasions, he captivated her completely; by these arts he obtained favours from her, but at the same time both he and she were assailed with calumny from the court. There were times when their clandestine meetings were not much to the liking of most courtiers.

At any rate, these activities made him a likely candidate for promotion to the throne, and Michael (Romanus's successor) viewed him with suspicion. In fact, Michael, even after his own accession, remained stubbornly jealous, although not unfriendly at first. Later he trumped up false accusations, suborning witnesses unjustly, and Constantine was driven from the city. His punishment was relegation to a certain determined area, in this case the island of Mitylene (Lesbos), and there for seven years – the exact length of Michael's reign – he endured his misfortune. Michael Calaphates, like Paphlagon, inherited the emperors' hatred of the young man.

Zoe's first reaction, when for the second time she found herself at the head of the Empire, was, as I have already said, to protect herself against any sudden reversal of her good luck in the future. To strengthen her position she proceeded to look for a husband – not a man from abroad, but someone in the court circle. However, as one had been discredited through his calamity, another rejected because of his ignoble lineage, a third suspected as dangerous, and stories had been invented one after another to bring into disrepute her various suitors, she renounced all of them and again considered the claims of Constantine. She spoke openly on the subject to her personal bodyguard and household staff, and when she saw that they were unanimous in their support of him as the future emperor – their agreement seemed almost preconcerted – she informed the Senate also of her plans. These were greeted as an inspiration from God. So Constantine was recalled from his exile, and he set out, still a private citizen and without the paraphernalia of his new dignity.

When he drew near the city, however, a more sumptuous lodging was prepared for him and an imperial tent was pitched, surrounded by an imperial guard. In front of the palace there met his eyes a vision of magnificent splendour. People of all ages and conditions poured out in a flood to meet him. There were salutations and addresses of congratulation and good wishes. The city wore all the appearance of a popular festival; perhaps it would be nearer the mark to say that there were two cities, for beside the Queen of Cities there had been hastily erected a second city, and the townsfolk had poured out right up to the walls, with markets and fairs. When all was ready and the arrangements for the official entry had been completed, the signal to go forward was given, and with great pomp Constantine entered the courts of the palace.

Since the common laws respecting marriage[1] could hardly be flouted, the Patriarch Alexius settled the question of the wedding. He made concessions to expediency – or shall we say that he bowed to the will of God in the whole affair? Certainly he did not himself lay his hands upon them in blessing at the coronation, but he did embrace them after the marriage ceremony and the act of crowning had been performed.[2] Whether this was done in accordance with priestly tradition, or was a bit of flattery and done to suit the occasion, I do not know.

For the empresses these events marked the end of their authority and personal intervention in the affairs of State; for Constantine, the beginning of his reign. His power was now for the first time established. So, after a joint rule of three months, the sisters retired from public life and the emperor – but we must not speak of him yet. First I have some brief remarks to make, for the benefit of those who may be interested.

Several persons, on more than one occasion, have urged me to write this history. Among them were not only men of authority and leaders in the Senate, but also students of theology, who interpret the mysteries of Holy Writ, and men of great sanctity and holiness. Through the passing of time the historical evidence has already proved inadequate for the writing of a proper record. There is a danger that events may be hidden in the remote past, so forgotten that our knowledge of bygone days rests on no sure foundation. These gentlemen,

1. The Byzantine Church forbade a third marriage.
2. The ceremony was performed by the priest Stypes on 11 June 1042.

therefore, asked me to do what I could to remedy those deficiencies: it was not right, they argued, that our own contemporary history should be concealed and utterly obscured, while events that took place before our time should be thought worthy of record by succeeding generations. Such was the pressure and such the arguments with which they urged me to take up this task, but for myself I was not particularly enthusiastic for the undertaking. It was not that I was lazy, but I was afraid of two alternatives, neither of which could be disregarded: I might pass over, for reasons which I will explain later, things done by certain individuals, or distort my account of them, and so be convicted not of writing a history but of mere fabrication, as if I were composing a play; or I might go to extreme lengths in hunting down the truth, and so become a laughing-stock to the critics. They would think me, not a lover of history, but a scandalmonger.

For these reasons I was not very eager to tackle the history of our times, especially as I knew that in many things I should clash with the Emperor Constantine, and I should be ashamed of myself if I did not seize every opportunity of commending him. I should be ungrateful and altogether unreasonable if I did not make some return, however small, for his generosity to me, a generosity which showed itself not only in positive acts, but in the indirect ways in which he helped me to better my condition. It would be shameful if I did not prove my gratitude in my writings. It was therefore because of this man that I consistently refused to compose the history. I was most anxious to avoid imputing any blame to him. I did not want to reveal by my words any actions not to his credit and things it is better to keep dark. I was loath to put before the public a dishonest story, yet at the same time I was unwilling to defame the hero of my former eulogy. In my opinion it was wrong to exercise literary talents, which I had perfected because of his encouragement, to do him harm.

Philosophers will tell you that the vain and superfluous are

of all things on earth the most despicable. For them the object
of life is to understand those things that are necessary to their
nature. All else is regarded as merely so many external
attributes. However that may be, I cannot use such an argument as an excuse for ingratitude, especially to one who
honoured me above my deserts and raised me over my fellows.
What I would like, therefore, is either to commemorate him
in a panegyric or to pass over in silence those actions in his life
which did not spring from worthy motives. If, having set
out to eulogize his career, I then rejected those deeds which
were the fit object of praise, and gave the impression that I
had lumped together all that was reprehensible, I should be
the worst scoundrel on earth, like the son of Lyxes, who
selected the worst deeds of the Greeks for his history.[1]

On the other hand, suppose I set aside this project for the
moment and undertake to write a history of the lives of the
emperors, how, when I leave unsaid things which belong to
the province of history, am I to deal with those which are the
proper object of eulogy? It would look as if I had forgotten
my purpose, or was caricaturing the art of history, by failing
to distinguish its subject-matter and by confusing the role of
two forms of literature whose aims are incompatible. Actually
I had composed many panegyrics in honour of Constantine
before I undertook this work, not without commendation
from the public. The high praises I lavished on him were not
undeserved, but other writers have failed to understand my
methods of composition. The truth is, the actions of emperors
are a conglomerate patchwork of bad and good, and these
other writers find themselves able neither to condemn without

1. Herodotus is said to have been the son of Lyxes and Dryo, and was
born at Halicarnassus in 484 B.C. Several Greek writers are known to
have attacked him on the ground that he was biased in favour of the
Persians *vis-à-vis* his own countrymen. Judging by the work *De Maligni-
tate Herodoti*, usually ascribed to Plutarch, one would say their arguments were futile.

reservation nor to commend with sincerity, because they
are overmuch impressed by the close conjunction of opposite
qualities. In my own case, I do offer criticism, but only for
form's sake or in dramatic passages where the prose is affected.
In the composition of a eulogy, in fact, my subject-matter is
not chosen usually with complete indifference to good or bad:
the latter I reject, the former I set on one side, afterwards
putting it in proper order. So a homogeneous pattern is
worked out, a tapestry of the finest cloth.

Such is the method I have adopted in composing eulogies of
Constantine, but now that I have undertaken to write a
history, this plan becomes impossible, for I cannot bring
myself to distort the facts of history, where truth is of more
importance than anything else, in order to escape the re-
proaches of my contemporaries. They may accuse me of
blaming where in their opinion I should praise, but I prefer
to ignore such imputations. What I am writing now is not
an indictment, not a speech for the prosecution, but a true
history. Then again, had I seen other emperors pursuing an
uninterrupted, invariable course of noble action, on all
occasions displaying an admirable character, whereas the
reign of Constantine alone was marked by deeds of the opposite kind, then I would have said nothing about him at all.
Yet no one on earth is faultless, and we judge a man by the
trait which chiefly distinguishes him from everyone else. So
why should I feel ashamed to declare openly whatever injustice or indiscretion this man, in common with the rest,
may have committed?

Most men who have set themselves to record the history of
the emperors have found it surprising that none of them kept
his reputation untarnished in every particular. Some won
greater praise for their conduct in early life, others impressed
more in their later years, and while some preferred a life of
pleasure, others dabbled in philosophy, only to confound
the principles they had elected to follow and end in muddle.

For my own part I find such inconsistency nothing to marvel at; on the contrary, it would be extraordinary if someone were always unalterable. Of course, it is possible that you may discover some private citizen who pursued the same un-deviating path throughout life, from the very beginning to the very end (although there cannot be many examples of such consistency), but an emperor, one who inherited from God supreme power, especially if he lived longer than most, would never be able to maintain the highest standards all through his reign. In the case of the private citizen, his own nature, plus a good start in life, may be sufficient to ensure virtuous behaviour, for the simple reason that he is not over-much troubled by outside affairs, nor do external events have any effect on his private disposition. How different it is with an emperor, whose private life is never, even in its most inti-mate detail, allowed respite from trouble! Consider how brief are the moments when the sea is calm and peaceful, and how at other times it is swollen, or lashed by waves, as Boreas,[1] or Aparktias,[2] or some other storm-wind disturbs its rest – a sight I have seen myself again and again. An emperor's life is like that. If he seeks recreation, at once he incurs the dis-pleasure of the critics. If he gives rein to kindly sentiments, he is accused of ignorance, and when he rouses himself to show interest, they blame him for being meddlesome. If he defends himself or takes blunt reprisals, everyone levels abuse at his 'wrath' or his 'quick temper'. And as for trying to do anything in secret – Athos would be more likely to hide itself from human gaze than an emperor's deeds to escape the notice of his subjects. No wonder then that no sovereign's life has been blameless.

Naturally I would have wished that my favourite emperor had been perfect, even if such a compliment was impossible for all the others, but the events of history do not accommo-

1. The north wind (Latin, *Aquilo*).
2. A north wind (Latin, *Septentrio*).

date themselves to our desires. So, divine soul,[1] forgive me, and if sometimes in describing your reign I speak immoderately, concealing nothing and telling the truth, pardon me for it. Not one of your nobler deeds shall be passed over in silence. They shall all be revealed. Likewise, whatever derives not from the same nobility, that too shall be made manifest in my history. And there we must leave the matter and return to our narrative.

At the start of his reign Constantine ruled neither with vigour nor with discretion. Apparently, before his accession, he had imagined that being an emperor was to confer on him undreamed-of happiness, something he had never experienced in his life. He had visions, quite unreasonably, of a sudden and complete reversal of his fortunes, and no sooner had he ascended the throne than he attempted to realize these ambitions. Now two things in particular contribute to the hegemony of the Romans, namely, our system of honours and our wealth, to which one might add a third: the wise control of the other two, and prudence in their distribution. Unfortunately Constantine's idea was to exhaust the treasury of its money, so that not a single *obol* was to be left there, and as for the honours, they were conferred indiscriminately on a multitude of persons who had no right to them, especially on the more vulgar sort who pestered the man, and on those who amused him by their witticisms. It is well known, of course, that there is in the political world a proper scale of honours, with an invariable rule governing promotion to a higher office, but Constantine reduced this *cursus honorum*[2] to mere confusion and abolished all rules of advancement. The doors of the Senate were thrown open to nearly all the rascally vagabonds of the market, and the honour was bestowed not on two or three, nor on a mere handful, but the whole gang was elevated to the highest offices of state by a

1. Psellus here apostrophizes the emperor.
2. The Roman term for the proper sequence of magistracies.

single decree, immediately after he became emperor.[1] Inevitably this provided occasion for rites and solemn ceremonies, with all the city overjoyed at the thought that their new sovereign was a person of such generosity. The new state of affairs seemed incomparably better than that to which they had been accustomed, for the truth is, folk who live in the luxury of a city have little conception of government, and those who do understand such matters neglect their duties, so long as their desires are satisfied.

Gradually the error of this policy became apparent when privileges, much coveted in the old days, were now distributed with a generous abandon that knew no limits, with the consequence that the recipients lost distinction. At the time, though, most people had not yet recognized the implications of all this profusion, and so the squandering and waste went on, all to no purpose. Nevertheless, I know that some later historians will find in this trait of Constantine something laudable. My own custom, one that I have always followed, is to examine nothing in itself alone, whether apparently good or reputedly evil, but to search out the causes and probable results of each occurrence as well, particularly where my informants are also interested in such hypothetical arguments. Experience has proved that this systematic treatment is better than my successors may perhaps be prepared to admit.

The emperor's first act, therefore, was the result of what I may call youthful folly, but there was another side to his character which I confess met with my approval at the time; in fact, even today I am no less convinced of its nobility. I

1. Not altogether fair. Constantine relied on the advice and judgement of such eminent men as Michael Cerularius, who became patriarch in 1043, Constantine Lichudes, and Psellus himself. His elevation of Romanus Sclerus was perhaps not so wise, but he could hardly be expected to foresee the rebellion of Maniaces to which Romanus directly contributed the cause. There were personal reasons why this grandson of Bardas Sclerus was promoted: he was the brother of the new emperor's mistress, Sclerena.

refer to the man's utter lack of boastfulness and false pride; the fact that no haughty or bombastic words ever fell from his lips; that he bore no malice towards those who had treated him none too kindly in the past and who had offered him little help in his fight for power. Not only were all his former accusers forgiven, but he took especial care to conciliate ⸜those who might reasonably expect his vengeance before all others.

No man was better endowed by Nature with qualities that endeared him to his subjects. He was a good mixer, winning everyone's affections by an art that was conscious, yet unaffected. In his efforts to charm there was no trace of insincerity, only a genuine desire to cultivate friendship, by deliberately setting out to please.

Listening to the emperor's conversation was a real delight. He was always ready to smile and his expression was cheerful, not merely in moments of recreation when a smiling face is normal, but even when he was obviously engaged in serious business. His favourite companions were simple persons, the type that did not stand greatly in awe of himself, and he hated to see anybody approach him with a worried look. He had the lowest opinion of these latter individuals, with their air of superiority, their preoccupation with affairs of national importance, and their anxiety to discuss these matters with himself. They must, he thought, have a mental outlook quite different from his own. Consequently those who lived with him accommodated their behaviour to please him. If someone had serious business to put before the emperor, he would be careful not to mention it at once, but to begin the conversation with some playful remark, or mix serious and playful together, like a man offering an invalid a purgative, with a dash of something to sweeten its bitter taste.

Constantine looked upon the palace as a harbour, in which he had taken refuge after much buffeting by the waves in a storm – the sufferings he had endured as an exile – and, to

recompense him for the past, he needed complete rest and
absolute tranquillity. The man who found favour with him
was one with a smooth brow, a man with a tongue always
ready to tell a diverting story and to utter the most benign
prophecies about the future.

Although he could scarcely be called an advanced student
of literature, or in any sense of the word an orator, yet he
admired men who were, and the finest speakers were invited
to the imperial court from all parts of the Empire, most of
them very old men.

At the time I was in my twenty-fifth year and engaged in
serious studies. My efforts were concentrated on two objects:
to train my tongue by rhetoric, so as to become a fine speaker,
and to refine my mind by a course of philosophy. I soon
mastered the rhetoric enough to be able to distinguish the
central theme of an argument and logically connect it with
my main and secondary points. I also learnt not to stand in
complete awe of the art, nor to follow its precepts in everything like a child, and I even made certain contributions of a
minor character myself. Then I applied myself to the study of
philosophy, and having acquainted myself thoroughly with
the art of reasoning, both *deductive*, from cause to immediate
effect, and *inductive*, tracing causes from all manner of effects,
I turned to natural science and aspired to a knowledge of the
fundamental principles of philosophy through mathematics.

If the reader does not find me boring in this and will allow
me to go on, I will add to what I have already said concerning
my own activities. The fact to which I am about to refer will
undoubtedly win for me high approval among men of learning, quite apart from all other considerations. And you, who
read my history today, will bear witness to the truth of my
words. Philosophy, when I first studied it, was moribund as
far as its professors were concerned, and I alone revived it,
untutored by any masters worthy of mention, and despite my
thorough search finding no germ of philosophy either in

Greece or in the barbarian world. I had heard that the Greeks had a great reputation for philosophy, expressed in simple words and simple propositions, and their work in this field set a standard and criterion for the future. There were some who belittled the simplicity of the Greeks, but I sought to learn more, and, as I met some of the experts in the art, I was instructed by them how to pursue my studies in a methodical way. One passed me to another for tuition, the lesser light to the greater, and he again recommended me to a third, and he to Aristotle and Plato. Doubtless my former teachers were well satisfied to take second place to these two.

Starting from these authors I completed a cycle, so to speak, by coming down to Plotinus,[1] Porphyry,[2] and Iamblichus.[3] Then, continuing my voyage, I put in at the mighty harbour of the admirable Proclus,[4] eagerly picking up there his doctrine of perception, both in its broad principles and in its exact interpretation. From Proclus I intended to proceed to more advanced studies – metaphysics, with an introduction to pure science – so I began with an examination of abstract conceptions in the so-called mathematics, which hold a position midway between the science of corporeal nature, with the external apprehension of these bodies, and the ideas themselves, the object of pure thought. I hoped from this study to apprehend something that was beyond the reach of mind, something that was not subject to the limitations of substance.

1. Plotinus (A.D. 205–69), the great neo-platonist. The facts of his life are known to us chiefly through the *Vita* of Porphyry prefixed to the *Enneads*, the series of essays in which Plotinus explains his doctrines.

2. Porphyry of Tyre (A.D. 232–*c.* 305) wrote voluminously on many subjects, but without originality.

3. Iamblichus was born at Chalcis, in Coele Syria, about A.D. 250. His main interest lay in thaumaturgy.

4. Proclus flourished in the fifth century after Christ. He was given the surname Diadochus, because it was commonly believed that he inherited the mantle of Plato.

It was therefore consonant with this plan that I should pay especial attention to systems of number and examine geometrical proofs, which some call 'logical necessities'. Moreover, I devoted time to the study of music and astronomy, as well as to their various subsidiary arts. First I would concentrate on each study by itself, then synthesize my knowledge, in the belief that the several branches of learning would by their individual contributions lead me to one simple goal, according to the teaching of Plato's *Epinomis*.[1] So, thanks to these sciences, I was able to launch out into the more advanced studies.

I had heard it said by the most learned philosophers that there is a wisdom which is beyond all demonstration, apprehensible only by the intellect of a wise man, in moments of inspiration. Even here my resolution did not falter. I read some of the mystic books and grasped their meaning (as far as human nature allowed, of course, for I myself could never claim that I had an accurate understanding of these things, nor would I believe anyone else who said he had). On the other hand, it is by no means beyond our natural capacity to dwell on one science, as a special subject, and for sake of research to make excursions, as it were, into other branches of learning in a general survey, returning later to one's original starting-point.

Literature has two branches. One comprises the works of the orators, and the philosophers have arrogated the other. The first, knowing nothing of the deeper things, issues forth merely in a mighty torrent of noisy words; it concerns itself with the composition of speeches, sets forth certain rules for the arrangement of arguments on political subjects and for the various divisions of political orations, lends distinction to the spoken word, and in general beautifies the language of

1. The *Epinomis* is actually of doubtful origin. Diogenes Laertius (iii, 37) hints that the author was Philip of Opus, who is said to have transcribed the *De Legibus* of Plato.

politics. Philosophy is less concerned with the embellishments of words. Its aim is rather to explore the nature of
the universe, to unravel its secrets. Its lofty dictums are not
even confined to the visible world, for with great subtlety it
praises the glory of that realm, whatever it be, that lies beyond the heaven. Now I had no mind to follow the example
of most other men, and emulate their experiences – men who
study the art of the orator while despising the science of the
philosopher, or else engross themselves in philosophy and
enjoy the riches to be found in the marvels of thought, but
contemn the glories of rhetoric and the skill required to
arrange and divide the various parts of a speech. Thus, from
time to time, when I compose an oration, I introduce some
scientific proof, not without some elegance. Many persons
have reproached me for this and they dislike the way I
brighten a philosophic discourse with the graceful arts of
rhetoric. My purpose in this is to assist the reader when he
finds it difficult to absorb some deep thought, and so to prevent
his losing the thread of philosophic argument.

But there is a new philosophy, based on the mystery of our
Christian religion, which transcends the ancient systems. This
mystery, too, has a dual aspect, in nature (human and divine),
and in time (finite and infinite), not to mention a further
dualism when one considers how it is capable of proof and
yet the object of faith and divinely inspired into men's con-
sciousness. It was this philosophy rather than the profane
which became the object of my special study. In some
respects I agreed with the doctrine of the great Fathers of the
Church, but I also made some contribution to the corpus of
divine teaching on my own account. I say this in all sincerity
and without boastfulness: if any man should feel constrained
to praise my literary works, I would beg him not to commend
my researches in the field of religion, not to extol my exten-
sive reading (I am not deluded by a false impression of my
own importance, nor am I ignorant of my own limitations:

my capacity is very small when compared with the ability of the orators and philosophers who have surpassed me). No, if anyone praises my efforts, let it be rather because I drew my small measure of wisdom from no living fount: the sources I discovered were choked up, and I had to open and cleanse them myself. Their waters, too, were hidden in the depths and only brought to the surface after I had expended much energy.

Today, in fact, neither Athens, nor Nicomedia, nor Alexandria in Egypt, nor Phoenicia, nor even the two Romes (the ancient and lesser Rome, and the later, more powerful city), nor any other State glories any longer in literary achievement. The golden streams of the past, and baser silver, and streams of metal more worthless still, all are blocked and choked up: their damming is complete. So, since I was unable to reach the living sources themselves, I perforce studied their images. These second-hand imitations I greedily devoured in my mind, and, having collected the knowledge, I grudged no one else a share of what I myself had acquired at the cost of much labour. Everybody was welcome to learn from me, and far from demanding a fee for my lessons, I was even prepared to help keen students with money from my own purse. But that story must wait until later.

In my career, even before the fruit was ripe, the blossom gave promise of a brilliant future. Certainly the emperor did not know me yet, but I was well known to all his bodyguard and they spoke of me in his presence, some recounting one quality, and others stressing another. They told him, moreover, that I was an eloquent orator. I would like to say something on this subject here. At the time of our birth, we are endowed with certain natural virtues, or their opposites. When I use the word 'virtue' in this connexion, I am not referring to moral virtue, nor to political virtue, nor to the virtue which excels these others and attains to the pattern or perfection of the Creator; but just as some bodies, from the moment of birth, are endowed with beauty, while on others nature from their very beginning bestows blemishes and wrinkles, so with souls too, some are distinguished at once with extreme grace and attractiveness, while others leave a trail of sombre and deep gloom. As time goes on, the innate graces of the first sort become more and more apparent, but in the second everything goes wrong and even the reason functions poorly.

However that may be, even in simple utterances I have been told that my language is peculiarly graceful, and though I do not strive after effect, there is in my words a certain natural beauty. Of course, I would not know this myself, had not many folk told me so in the course of conversation and had they not listened with rapt attention while I talked with them. Anyhow, it was this characteristic that first won me access to the emperor, and it was the eloquence of my tongue that, so to speak, proved to be my forerunner, giving him a foretaste of the spirit deep-hidden within me.

At that first interview, my words were distinguished neither by their fluency nor by their elegance, but I told him about my family and the sort of education I had received in literature. As for Constantine, he was affected by a strange feeling of pleasure, as inexplicable as the divinely-inspired utterance of men in a trance. So influenced was he at the first sound of my voice that he almost embraced me. Other men had the right of access to him at set times and for a limited period, but to me his heart's doors were now thrown wide open, and gradually, as I became more intimate with him, he shared with me all his secrets. Please do not blame me if I have wandered somewhat from the main theme of my history, and please do not imagine that this digression is mere self-advertisement. If I have indulged in a certain amount of personal reminiscence, at least it is all directly concerned with the central thread of the story. Without disclosing the reason for it, it would have been impossible for me to speak of that first interview; and, of course, if I wished to explain the reason, it was essential to introduce some remarks on my own career. My history must be written in a methodical way: first the reference to my source, then the sifting of evidence, and finally the account of subsequent events. That is why so long a preface was necessary. Now that I have introduced myself with such a wealth of detail into this part of the history, I can assure you that my evidence will avoid all falsehood; whatever is not said, will remain hidden, but none of the things I am going to say will be of doubtful veracity.

Constantine had no very clear conception of the nature of monarchy. He failed to realize that it entailed responsibility for the well-being of his subjects, and that an emperor must always watch over the administration of his realm and ensure its development on sound lines. To him the exercise of power meant rest from his labours, fulfilment of desire, relaxation from strife. He had entered the harbour of the palace, so to speak, to enjoy the advantages of a calm retreat and to avoid the duties of helmsman in the future. As for the administration of public affairs, and the privilege of dispensing justice, and the superintendence of the armed forces, they were delegated to others. Only a fraction of these duties was reserved for himself. Instead, he chose a life of pleasure and luxury, as if it were his natural right (not without some justification, for he had inherited an innate predilection for such things). Now, having acquired supreme power, he had greater opportunity for pleasure, and he indulged himself more than ever.

A healthy animal, with a thoroughly strong constitution, is not altered in a moment at the first symptoms of illness. So with the Empire in the reign of Constantine: it was by no means moribund and its breathing was still energetic; the neglect from which it was suffering seemed an insignificant item, until, by slow degrees, the malady grew, and reaching a crisis threw the patient into utter confusion, complete disorder.

This later stage, however, had not yet been approached, and the emperor, taking little share in the anxieties of power, but seeking recreation in a multitude of pleasures, was preparing the then healthy body of his empire for a thousand maladies destined to attack it in the years to come.

What contributed in no moderate fashion to such immoderation was the weak character of the two empresses, and Constantine's willing acquiescence in their luxurious, laughter-loving habits. Participation in these revels he regarded as a service to them; and far from wishing in any way to oppose their desires, he took care to provide them with every amusement. When a certain trouble did arise, he would soon have clashed with them, had his wife not agreed with his point of view. Whether she merely concealed her jealousy on this occasion, or had become devoid of it because of her age, I know not.

DESCRIBING HOW AND BY WHAT MEANS THE AUGUSTA SCLERENA¹ WAS BROUGHT TO THE CAPITAL

It all came about in the following way. Constantine's second wife, a member of the famous Sclerus family, died, and, since he was at that time an ordinary citizen, he was prevented from marrying a third time, on conscientious grounds (by Roman law such marriages were illegal). But he substituted a less reputable condition for the marriage – a secret *affaire*. The lady in question was the niece of his late wife, a beautiful and normally a discreet woman. He induced her to share in this highly improper association. He may have bribed her;

1. Niece of Pulcheria, sister of Romanus Sclerus, and grand-daughter of Bardas, she had shared Constantine's exile on Lesbos. She was unpopular with the people and because of her there was a riot during the emperor's procession to the Church of the Holy Martyrs (9 March 1044) and he barely escaped with his life.

possibly he charmed her with words of love; or he may have used other methods of persuasion to achieve his purpose.

Whatever the reason, they were so much in love with each other that both found separation intolerable, even when they were threatened with misery, for when Constantine went into exile (as I have remarked in a previous chapter) this woman still remained at his side. With loving care she tended his wants, put at his disposal all her possessions, gave him all manner of comfort, and lightened the bitter load of his affliction. The truth is, she, no less than himself, was sustained by hopes of power; nothing else mattered if only in the future she might share the throne with her husband. I say 'husband' because at that time she was convinced that their marriage would be legally sanctioned, and all her desires fulfilled when Constantine, as emperor, overruled the laws. When one of these ambitions was realized (his elevation to the throne), but circumstances did not permit the realization of the second, because the Empress Zoe seized all power for herself, she despaired altogether, not only of her cherished hopes, but even of life itself. The empress filled her with dread, and she anticipated grievous retribution.

Nevertheless, the emperor did not forget his beloved, even after his accession. With his physical eyes he beheld Zoe, but in his mind's eye was the image of his mistress; while he folded the empress in his arms, it was the other woman whom he clasped in the imagination of his heart. Regardless of the consequences, regardless of Zoe's jealousy, turning a deaf ear to all entreaty, he brushed aside every counsel that would frustrate his wishes. Prominent among those who differed with him was his own sister Pulcheria, one of the cleverest women of our generation. She gave him excellent advice, but in vain, for he despised all opposition, and at his very first meeting with the empress spoke to her of this woman. He referred to her, not as a wife, nor as a prospective mistress, but as one who had suffered much at the hands of the imperial family. Moreover, she had endured, he said, much for his sake, and he begged Zoe to recall her from exile and grant her reasonable privileges.

The empress at once gave her consent. The fact is, Zoe was no longer jealous. She had had her own fill of trouble, and in any case she was now too old to harbour such resentment. Meanwhile, the emperor's beloved was expecting the worst, when suddenly there arrived messengers with an imperial bodyguard, summoning her back to Byzantium. They gave her letters, one from the emperor, the other from Zoe herself, promising a friendly reception and encouraging her to return. Such were the circumstances in which she arrived in the Queen of Cities.

At first it was considered proper that she should live in a modest house, with a bodyguard of no particular distinction. However, in order that he might have an excuse for going there often, Constantine treated it as a private residence of his own. Then, to give it an imposing appearance and make it a place fit to receive an emperor, he laid down new foundations for an annexe, with grand projects for the future.

He always had a pretext for these visits – that he was supervising some detail of the building – and several times a month he would go there, nominally to watch the progress of the work, but in reality to be with his mistress. He used to be accompanied by certain individuals of Zoe's faction, and lest they should busy themselves too much with his private affairs, he would see that a table loaded with delicacies was ready for them outside the house. They were invited to join in the banquet. The menu was chosen by themselves beforehand, and all their demands were satisfied. They were well aware of the real cause of these arrangements, but, for all their indignation at the way he treated their empress, it could not outweigh the pleasure they felt in the fulfilment of their own desires. Thus, if they knew Constantine was debating whether to visit his lady-love, but hesitating to set out and actually ashamed to go (and he usually was), they smoothed the path for him, each suggesting a different pretext. It was a singularly effective way of winning his favour.

At first, Constantine kept his assignations a secret, by visiting her in the way I have described, and he was still careful to avoid an open scandal. But gradually he lost all sense of impropriety and his real plans were revealed. All pretence of the lady's 'apartment' in his house was abandoned. From now on he accompanied her quite openly, as often as he wished, and lived with her. If I may sum up the whole story before I continue, the liaison had a strange air of unreality about it. Whether one saw what was going on with one's own eyes or merely heard of it from others, it was hard to believe, for Constantine no longer visited the woman as a mistress, but as if she were in truth his wife.

He wasted the imperial treasures in satisfying her every whim. For example, he found in the palace a bronze casket, ornamented with figures carved in relief, and having filled it with money, sent it as a gift to her. Nor was this an occasional present, for there was a constant stream of such offerings to his beloved.

HOW THE AUGUSTA WAS INTRODUCED INTO THE PALACE

So far, however, the love-affair was carried on in semi-secrecy. Yet efforts at concealment proved less and less effective as time went on, and eventually the emperor admitted publicly that he loved her. There followed an interview with Zoe, at which he proposed very plausibly that she should consent to live with his mistress. Even when Zoe agreed he was still not satisfied. A treaty of friendship was set out in a document and an imperial pavilion built for the ceremony of ratification. In front sat Zoe, Constantine, and Sclerena, while the Senate filed in to witness this extraordinary contract,

blushing and for the most part talking in undertones.
Despite their embarrassment, the senators still praised the
agreement as if it were a document sent down from heaven.
They called it a 'loving-cup' and lavished on it all the other
flattering epithets that deceive and cajole frivolous and empty-
headed persons.

The contract being signed and the oaths administered, she
who had hitherto been only a lover, was now introduced to
the private apartments of the palace, no longer called
'mistress', but 'My Lady' and 'Empress', officially. What
was most astounding was the fact that, although most people
were greatly distressed at the way in which Zoe had been
deceived and neglected and despised, she herself evinced no
emotion whatever, except that she smiled on everyone and
apparently was quite pleased with the arrangement. At all
events, she embraced her new partner with unusual warmth,
and both of them accompanied the emperor. Both, too, discussed with him the same problems. Constantine weighed the
judgement of each woman with equal impartiality, although
it must be admitted that occasionally he allowed himself to be
more readily influenced by his junior consort.

In appearance Sclerena was not specially remarkable. On
the other hand, she was certainly no easy target for insult or
raillery. As for her character and intellectual ability, she could
charm a heart of stone, and she was amazingly adept in her
interpretation of any matter whatever. Her speech was
wonderful. It had a delicate beauty of expression, the rhythmic
perfection of a scholar. There was in her conversation an
unaffected sweetness of diction, an inexpressible grace in her
manner of telling a story. She bewitched me, at any rate,
when, as often happened, she would ply me with questions
about the Greek myths and add a point here and there herself
which she had learnt from some expert on the subject. No
woman ever had a more sensitive ear, although I imagine
this was not a natural accomplishment, but acquired because

she knew that everyone was talking about her. She could hear a soft whisper quite clearly, and a word muttered under one's breath was readily understood by her.

I will give an example of this. One day, when we, the imperial secretaries, were all together, the empress's retinue was taking part in a procession. Zoe herself and her sister Theodora walked in this procession, followed by the Augusta (a new title granted her by the empresses, at the instigation of Constantine). As they were on their way – the route led them to the Theatre, and this was the first time the ordinary people had seen Sclerena in company with Zoe and Theodora – one of the subtle flatterers softly quoted Homer's 'It were no shame ...'[1] but did not complete the lines. At the time Sclerena gave no sign of having heard these words, but when the ceremony was over, she sought out the man who had uttered them and asked him what they meant. She repeated his quotation without a single mistake, pronouncing the words exactly as he had whispered them. As soon as he told her the story in detail, and the crowd showed its approval of his interpretation of the anecdote, as well as of the Homeric reference, she was filled with pride and her flatterer was rewarded for his compliment. The presents she gave him were not a few, nor were they paltry trifles, but such as she was used to receiving and giving in her own circle. As a matter of fact, the emperor had given her a private fund for presents to individuals of either sex, in order to win the sympathies of the court, and especially of the two empresses.

Now the elder of the two sisters (Zoe) had a passion for gold – not for the sake of mere possession or hoarding of it, but so that she could satisfy her instinct for generosity. She was also fond of sweet herbs, the purest Indian kind, in particular those that still retained their natural moisture,

1. Homer. *Iliad*, iii, 156–7, where the Trojans speak of Helen: 'It were no shame that Trojans and well-greaved Achaeans should suffer pain long time for a woman such as she.'

dwarf olives and the whitest sort of bays. The younger sister daily gloated over her collection of *darics*, for which she had had bronze coffers made. Knowing their hobbies, therefore, the Augusta won the gratitude of them both by giving the presents they liked best. It was no difficult matter, for Zoe no longer felt jealous of her rival (she was past the age for that) and there was no ill-will on her side. As the years passed, too, she had lost her capacity for vehement hatred. And as for Theodora, since her own desires were satisfied, she showed even less resentment than her sister.

Thus the wealth which the Emperor Basil had accumulated in the imperial treasury, at the cost of much sweat and labour, became the plaything of these women, to be expended on their pleasures. Presents were exchanged or given as rewards one after another. Some of the money was even paid out to strangers, and soon all was spent and exhausted. However, that is a subject which I must deal with later. Now I must finish the present story. When Constantine and the women had decided which apartments each was to occupy in the palace, the emperor had the room in the centre, with the sisters on either side of him, but it was Sclerena who had the most private quarters. And Zoe never visited the emperor's room, unless she had first made sure that he was alone and his lady-love far away. Otherwise she occupied herself with her own affairs. I must now explain what these activities were.

The tasks that women normally perform had no appeal whatever for Zoe. Her hands never busied themselves with a distaff, nor did she ever work at a loom or any other feminine occupation. Still more surprising, she affected scorn for the beautiful dresses of her rank, though I cannot tell whether she was so negligent in the prime of life. Certainly in her old age she lost all desire to charm. Her one and only concern at this time, the thing on which she spent all her energy, was the development of new species of perfumes, or the preparation of unguents. Some she would invent, others she improved.

Her own private bedroom was no more impressive than the workshops in the market where the artisans and the black-smiths toil, for all round the room were burning braziers, a host of them. Each of her servants had a particular task to perform: one was allotted the duty of bottling the perfumes, another of mixing them, while a third had some other task of the same kind. In winter, of course, these operations were demonstrably of some benefit, as the great heat from the fires served to warm the cold air, but in the summer-time the others found the temperature near the braziers almost un-bearable. Zoe herself, however, surrounded by a whole bodyguard of these fires, was apparently unaffected by the scorching heat. In fact, both she and her sister seemed to be by nature perverse. They despised fresh air, fine houses, meadows, gardens; the charm of all such things meant nothing to them. On the other hand, once they were inside their own private rooms, one sealing off the flow of the golden stream, the other cleaning out the channels to make it flow faster, then they really enjoyed themselves.

With regard to Zoe's other peculiarities – I must speak of her at rather greater length, while the emperor is still taking his ease with the beloved Augusta – there is not much that I can commend, but one trait never fails to excite my admira-tion: her piety. In this she surpassed all others, both women and men. Some men lose themselves in the contemplation of God; their whole being is directed to one perfect object, and on that object they depend entirely. Others, with still greater devotion, and truly inspired with the Divine Spirit, are even more identified with the object of their worship. So it was with Zoe. Her passionate veneration for the things of God had really brought her into contact, so to speak, with the First and Purest Light. Certainly there was no moment when the Name of God was not on her lips.

CONCERNING THE *ANTIPHONETUS*

I will give an example of this piety of hers. She had made for
herself an image of Jesus, fashioning it with as much accuracy
as she could (if such a thing were possible). The little figure,
embellished with bright metal, appeared to be almost living.
By changes of colour it answered questions put to it, and by
its various tints foretold coming events. Anyway, Zoe made
several prophecies with regard to the future from a study of
this image. So, when she had met with some good fortune,
or when some trouble had befallen her, she would at once consult her image, in the one case to acknowledge her gratitude,
in the other to beg its favour. I myself have often seen her, in
moments of great distress, clasp the sacred object in her hands,
contemplate it, talk to it as though it were indeed alive, and
address it with one sweet term of endearment after another.
Then at other times I have seen her lying on the ground, her
tears bathing the earth, while she beat her breasts over and
over again, tearing at them with her hands. If she saw the
image turn pale, she would go away crestfallen, but if it
took on a fiery red colour, its halo lustrous with a beautiful
radiant light, she would lose no time in telling the emperor
and prophesying what the future was to bring forth.

From my reading of Greek literature, I know that perfumes
give off a vapour which drives away evil spirits and which at
the same time invokes the spirits of the just, attracting them
by its very nature. The same property is found in other
substances: precious stones and certain herbs and magic
ceremonies have the power of invoking deities. The theories
of that sort expounded in Greek books made no impression
on me when I first read them, and far from believing in magic
rites, I rejected them with scorn. Zoe's religious ceremonies,
however, for all their attention to detail, were not conducted
after the Greek or any other style. She worshipped God in
her own way, making no secret of her heart's deep longing

and consecrating to Him the things which we regard as most precious and most sacred.

Having reached this point in our account of the empress, let us return once more to the Augusta and Constantine. Perhaps it may be the reader's wish that we rouse them from their slumbers, and separate them. The emperor we will keep for a later description, but Sclerena's life-history we will finish now.

CONCERNING THE AUGUSTA'S DEATH[1]

It is possible that the emperor intended to found an empire for her in the future – at least there was much talk of it. How it was to be done I do not know, but he certainly cherished ambitions in that direction. Whatever his plans, they were cut short, together with her hopes, by a sudden illness which resisted all the skill and attention of the doctors. Sclerena was afflicted with chest pains and suffered terribly from asthma. Despite all their efforts to cure her, she made no progress and death carried her off before her desires could be brought to fruition – she who till then had imagined for herself such a glorious future.

It would be superfluous to interrupt the main thread of my history at this point, by dilating on the tremendous effect her death produced on the emperor, his lamentations, and the way he behaved. It would be of no real value to describe how, overcome by his sorrow, he expressed the grief he felt like a child. It is no part of the historian's duty to give a minute account of all that is said or done, nor is he required to write on what are comparative trifles. Where details are of little consequence, they belong to the province of the critic; where they give occasion for praise, it is the panegyrist who

1. The exact date is unknown, but she probably died in 1044. She was buried in the monastery of Mangana and eleven years later Constantine was interred beside her.

must use them. If I have a few times made use of details my-self – the sort which I am advising historians to shun – that need cause no surprise, for the province of history has no positive, clearly-defined boundaries. There may be places where it is even right to indulge in digression or parenthesis. For all that, the historian should waste no time in returning to his narrative. The important thing is to concentrate on the subject, and treat everything else with reserve.

So I think I am justified in passing over the details in this case, and as for the chief thing that resulted from his mourning – the tomb that he built to commemorate her – I will not refer to that yet. It shall be dealt with in the proper place, after I have first given an account of all the matters that preceded her death. The fact is, in touching on the subject of Sclerena and in priding myself that her story had been told in its entirety, I have omitted many remarkable things that happened before she died. The reason why I did this was to avoid the necessity of referring to her on separate occasions and so breaking up the continuous narrative. Anyhow, as far as she is concerned, the story ends at the moment when she departed this life. We will return once more to the emperor, the hero of this part of my history.

More than once already I have remarked that Constantine was like a man who fought the waves in a great storm, and then put in to a shore where all was peace, the calm waters of an imperial harbour, and he had no intention of sailing the high seas a second time. In other words, he wanted to rule his empire in peace, and not fight any wars, exactly like most of the emperors before him. Unfortunately affairs do not usually follow the course we would prefer. A stronger power, beyond our control, presides over human destiny and guides it according to *His* plans. Sometimes the path is smooth, often strangely rough. So with Constantine, affairs did not go as he had hoped. Waves of trouble, one after another, descended upon him. At one time the Empire was gravely perturbed by civil wars, at another by the incursions of barbaric tribes, who plundered most of our provinces and returned to their own countries laden with useful articles of all kinds and with booty to their hearts' content.

It would require much time and many words to describe minutely all these things in order as they occurred, to give an accurate account of the causes and results of every single event, to tell of the armies and camps, the skirmishes and battles, and all the other minor points in which the careful historian is accustomed to indulge. For the moment I must defer such a plan, for it was your declared wish, my dearest friend,[1] that I should produce a history which was more a summary than an elaborate treatise. To meet your wishes I have passed over in this work many facts worthy of mention. The years have not been numbered by Olympiads nor divided into seasons (as Thucydides divided his), but I have simply drawn attention to the most important facts and all the things which I have been able to recollect as I was writing this book. As I say, I am not making any attempt at the moment to investigate the special circumstances of each event. My object is rather to pursue a middle course between those who recorded the imperial acts of ancient Rome on the one hand, and our modern chroniclers on the other. I have neither aspired to the diffuseness of the former, nor sought to imitate the extreme brevity of the latter, for fear lest my own composition should be over-burdened, or else omit what was essential.

I will say no more on that subject now. To return to Constantine: I will describe the events of his reign in chronological order, beginning with the very first war in which he was engaged as emperor. But first I will go back a little further still, putting the head, as it were, on the body I am creating. 'Goodness,' say the epigrammatists, 'is scarce.'[2] True enough, but even the few are not immune from the creeping paralysis

1. Probably Constantine Lichudes.
2. Proverb ascribed to Solon.

of envy. It is universally true that wherever the fine bloom of natural fertility, or of stoutheartedness and courage, or of any other good quality, wherever such a bloom appears, there straightway stands the pruner ready with his knife, and that part of the plant is cut off. But the shoots that run to wood and produce no flowers at all, these are encouraged to spread, while the thorns grow apace. It is not surprising that those who are less endowed with admirable qualities should normally envy persons of outstanding character, but I do regard it as strange that emperors also are not exempt from this failing. It is not enough, forsooth, that they should have their diadems and their purple, for unless they are wiser than the wise, cleverer than the experts – in short, if they are not placed on the highest summit of all the virtues – they consider themselves grievously maltreated. Either they must rule over us like gods, or they refuse to govern at all. I have seen some of them myself who would have died, with the greatest of pleasure, rather than accept help from certain individuals, rather than owe their position of power to any assistance these persons might render them. Just when they should have rejoiced that God had raised up for them a helping hand, they chose rather to cut it off, simply because of the quarter from which that help was coming.

I have written this long preface with an eye on one who flourished in our time, a man who proved the worth of good generalship, who, no less by his boldness as a soldier than by his great skill, thwarted the hostile expeditions of the barbarians, and who assured for the Romans a liberty that was freed from danger.[1]

THE REVOLT OF MANIACES

This George Maniaces did not rise to the rank of army commander from the baggage-men all at once. It was not a case

1. George Maniaces. See Appendix III.

of blowing a trumpet and acting as herald one day and on the next being entrusted with the leadership of a legion. Actually his progress was gradual, and he held successive ranks until he attained the highest position open to a soldier. No sooner did he win some success, however, than he was again thrown into prison, even in the hour of his triumph. He returned to the emperors a conqueror, and for a home he was given – the public gaol! He was sent forth as general, with supreme command over all the armed forces, with a staff of senior officers to help him. They were young men and they urged him to take a road he should never have traversed – but here things will go wrong both for him and for us. Edessa was captured and he was accused; he was sent to conquer Sicily, and then, to prevent him from winning that honour, he was recalled once more, in disgrace.

I have seen this man myself and I wondered at him, for nature had bestowed on him all the attributes of a man destined to command. He stood ten feet high and men who saw him had to look up as if at a hill or the summit of a mountain. There was nothing soft or agreeable about the appearance of Maniaces. As a matter of fact, he was more like a fiery whirlwind, with a voice of thunder and hands strong enough to make walls totter and shake gates of brass. He had the quick movement of a lion and the scowl on his face was terrible to behold. Everything else about the man was in harmony with these traits and just what you would expect. Rumour exaggerated his appearance and the barbarians, to a man, lived in dread of him, some because they had seen and marvelled, others because they had heard frightful tales of his prowess.

When we were despoiled of Italy and the noblest part of our Empire was lost, the second Michael sent this man to make war on the enemy who had seized it. He was ordered to recover this province for the Romans. When I speak of Italy here, I am referring not to the whole coast-line, but only to

that part which lies opposite us and has appropriated the name
of the whole peninsula. Maniaces descended on those districts in full force. No military stratagem was left untried,
and it was clear that he would drive out the conquerors and
check their inroads – if all else failed, then he would do it
with his own hands.

Now when Michael was forced to abdicate and the present
emperor succeeded him, the latter should have lost no time
in loading Maniaces with honours; he should have dispatched
all manner of letters to recommend him, decorated him with
ten thousand crowns, done anything in the world to win his
favour. Instead, the emperor affected utter contempt for such
things, and thereby sowed the seeds of distrust in Maniaces
and laid the foundations of trouble destined to fall on the
Empire long afterwards. When he did eventually notice the
man, although Maniaces' evil intentions were by then recognized and he was known to be contemplating revolt, even
then Constantine failed to handle the affair with diplomacy.
Instead of pretending to be ignorant of what, even at that
stage, was still only a project, he burst out in anger against his
general as if he had already raised the standard of rebellion.

The envoys he sent out to him were intended neither to
flatter, nor simply to smooth out his troubles and bring him
back to the path of virtue. Their task, to put it bluntly, was
to kill him, or, less drastically, to chide him persistently
with his unfriendly attitude to the emperor. They could do
anything short of flogging him, casting him into prison, and
driving him out of the city. The leader of these ambassadors,
moreover, was not a man who had proved his worth in
missions of this kind before; he had not even had previous
experience over any considerable period in civil or military
affairs. He was, in fact, a parvenu off the streets who had
wormed his way into the palace.[1]

By the time he had sailed to Maniaces, the latter had already

1. The *protospatharius* Pardus.

decided on open revolt, and he was now in command of an army and awaiting his arrival with suspicion. The envoy gave him no definite assurance, before he actually arrived, that his errand was a peaceful one. Indeed he gave no previous intimation of his arrival at all. Instead, he suddenly rode up to him on horseback, as if he were about to attack him, and without one word of appeasement, without any introduction such as would put his conversation with the man on a proper footing, he promptly struck out at him with violent abuse, in a haughty manner, and threatened him with the most dreadful punishment. Maniaces, now quite convinced that his distrust was excusable, and nervous too of other secret intentions of which he knew nothing, flared up into a rage and lifted his hand against the ambassador, not intending to strike, but only to scare him. The other, as if from that moment he had caught him in the very act of rebellion, called the bystanders to witness his audacity. He added that Maniaces would not escape the consequences, for it was a serious matter to be caught in such an act. Naturally Maniaces, and his army with him, was impressed by the desperate position. With one accord they fell upon the envoy and killed him. Believing that the emperor would, in any case, refuse to negotiate, they there and then broke into open defiance.

It was not surprising that multitudes flocked to join a man so brave and such a master of strategy as Maniaces, not only men of military age but youths and old men. He knew that victories are won not by mere numbers, but by skill and experience, and so he picked out for his army those who had the most practical acquaintance with war, men with whom he had sacked many cities and gained possession of much treasure and many prisoners. Then with his army he crossed over to the opposite mainland, after avoiding the attention of all the coastguards. None of his adversaries dared to attack him; without exception, they retired to a safe distance, so terrified were they.

Meanwhile the emperor, having heard of the envoy's assassination and of Maniaces' foolish conduct, levied an enormous army to fight him. Then came the problem: who was to command this force? Constantine was afraid that the defeat of the enemy might be the signal for another revolt; his own general might turn against himself, the very person who had put him in command, and a second pretender might well prove more dangerous than the first, with a considerable army already mobilized and fresh laurels of victory. The man appointed, therefore, was not a distinguished soldier, but was a loyal servant of the emperor, a eunuch in fact and a person who inspired no respect whatever in his troops.[1] Setting out from the capital, this man advanced on the rebels with his huge army. Information reached Maniaces that the whole Roman army was on the march, but the news did not alarm him; neither the enemy's superior numbers nor their strategic change of position could divert him from his plan. His object was to catch his opponents off their guard, and before they expected him he launched an attack with his light-armed troops.

The imperial forces were slow in drawing up their line of battle, and once they were in position, they were much more concerned to watch Maniaces himself than take part in actual fighting, although most of them never had a chance of seeing him because he moved too fast. Thundering out words of command, riding up and down his ranks, he struck terror at once into the hearts of everyone who saw him, and his proud bearing overwhelmed our vast numbers from the very start. Nevertheless he met his downfall. It was one of those acts of God, the reasons for which are beyond our ken. He was circling round our legions, spreading confusion everywhere: he had only to attack, and the serried ranks gave way, the

1. Stephanus. The battle took place near Ostrovo. Maniaces was saluted as emperor on the field of battle by his men, but fell mortally wounded (1043) (Cedrenus, 757B, p. 549).

solid wall of troops withdrew. Indeed, our whole army was
being broken up into groups and destroyed. Then, suddenly,
he was hit in the right side. It was not a superficial wound,
and the blood flowed freely at once from the deep gash. Apparently he was unaware of the blow at first, but when he
saw the trickle of blood, he tried to staunch it with his hand.
He realized that he had been mortally wounded and in sheer
desperation tried to regain his own lines. He did, in fact, get
some little way from our army, but as he was now unable to
turn his horse's head – his body had lost all strength and he was
fainting – he gave a gentle moan, a last gesture, dropped his
reins and slid out of his saddle to the ground, a pitiable sight.

Even when our men saw him lying there, they did not recover their bravery. They still reined in their chargers, for
fear lest the enemy were planning an ambush. However, as
Maniaces' attendant squire was some distance away and his
horse, free to roam now, cantered up and down the space
between the two armies, all of them, in one great mob,
rushed up to the body. The sight that met their eyes was
astounding, so great was the area of ground covered by that
sprawling corpse. The head they cut off and brought it back
to their own general, whereupon a host of men claimed to
have killed him. Descriptions of the murder were supplied
as invention or imagination dictated, but since it was impossible to demonstrate the truth of these stories, they invented another, to the effect that certain unknown horsemen
had fallen upon him and cut off his head. Many such accounts
were fabricated, without any convincing evidence. On the
other hand, they did claim, from the fact that he was wounded
in the side, that the weapon must have been a lance. Yet the
man who inflicted the wound was still unknown, right up to
the day when I wrote this history.

That, at all events, was the manner of his death. Maniaces
had undoubtedly suffered injustice in his life, although one
cannot commend all that he did. As for his army, some got

away to their native countries without attracting the enemy's attention, but the majority deserted. The emperor was presented with the rebel's head before his army actually returned to the capital, and he had it impaled at the top of the Great Theatre, suspended in mid-air for all men to see, even at a distance. Then, with the air of a man who has been delivered from some wave that was about to overwhelm him, like a man who has won some respite from danger, he gave thanks to God.

When the army came back, most of the soldiers were decorated with crowns in honour of the victory. They were now encamped near the walls, in front of the city, and Constantine decided that he must celebrate their success with a Triumph. He had a genius for organizing shows on a grand scale. The procession, worthy of its author, was arranged as follows: the light-armed troops were ordered to lead, armed with shields, bows, and spears, but with ranks broken, in one conglomerate multitude; behind them were to come the picked knights in full defensive armour, men who inspired fear, not only because of their forbidding appearance, but by their fine military bearing; next came the rebel army, not marching in ranks, nor in fine uniforms, but seated on asses, faces to the rear, their heads shaven and their necks covered with heaps of shameful refuse. Then followed the pretender's head, borne in triumph a second time, and immediately after it some of his personal belongings; next came certain men armed with swords, men carrying rods, men brandishing in their right hands the *rhomphaia* – a great host of warriors preceding the army commander – and, in the rear of them all, the general himself on a magnificent charger, dressed in magnificent robes and accompanied by the whole of the Imperial Guard.

Such was the order of march. The emperor, meanwhile, very distinguished and proud, was seated in front of the so-called Chalke Phylake, in the actual precinct of the sacred

church built by John, the great emperor who succeeded
Nicephorus Phocas. Seated with him, on his left and right,
were the empresses, also watching the Triumph. When the
procession, as I have described it, was finished, he returned to
the palace wearing his crown, the object of extraordinary
tributes. It was characteristic of the man that he should celebrate his victory with one glorious Triumph and then
return to his usual moderate habits.

This part of the emperor's life was indeed brilliant, and yet,
despite all the hero-worship, he never exulted in his victories
nor did he make vainglorious speeches. He got a natural
pleasure when he triumphed, but he still kept his head. It
was normal for him to live moderately. Nevertheless, he was
lacking in circumspection: like a man who needs rest after
great exertions, he was in the habit of easing off – a custom
which involved him in wave after wave of misfortune.

THE RUSSIAN UPHEAVAL AND THE REVOLT
OF TORNICIUS

This lack of vigilance was the cause of the war against the
barbarians, the war which followed the crushing of Maniaces'
revolt. Russian vessels, almost too numerous to count, either
slipping past the intercepting squadrons that had long kept
them at bay, or forcing their way in, occupied the Propontis.
It was like a mighty cloud that came up from the sea and en-
veloped the city in darkness. At this stage of my history I
would like to explain the reasons for this naval expedition on
the part of the Russians, quite unprovoked by the emperor.

This barbarian nation had consistently cherished an insane
hatred for the Roman Empire, and on every possible occasion,
first on one imaginary pretext, then on another, they waged
war against us. After the Emperor Basil died (he really
frightened the Russians) and after his brother Constantine,
his successor, had fulfilled the allotted span of life too (an

event that marked the end of a noble dynasty), they once more revived their ancient antagonism and little by little trained themselves for future struggles. Some traces of glory and distinction in Romanus's reign impressed them – their preparations were in any case still incomplete – but when he died, soon after his accession, and when power fell into the hands of some obscure person called Michael, they proceeded to mobilize all their forces. Recognizing the necessity of a sea-borne invasion, if any attack was to be launched against us, they cut down trees in the interior and made boats large and small. Step by step their preparations were made in secret until they were ready for war. A great fleet was, in fact, on the point of sailing against Michael, but while they were making the final adjustments and war hung in the balance, this emperor, too, died before the assault was begun. His successor, without making any notable contribution to national affairs, also departed this life, and the Empire passed into the safe keeping of Constantine. There was no complaint, as far as he was concerned, that the barbarians could make to justify the war, but lest their efforts should seem to be wasted, they attacked him fiercely and without provocation. Such was the cause then – the unjustifiable cause – of their assault on the emperor.

Having escaped detection, they were already inside the Propontis when they made their first proposals for peace, conditional on the payment of an enormous sum for reparations. They mentioned the actual amount, a thousand *staters* for each ship, on the understanding that this money should be counted out to them in one way only – on one of the ships in their own fleet. Such were the proposals they put forward, either because they imagined that there were springs of gold in our domains, or simply because they had decided to fight in any case.[1] The terms were impossible, purposely so, in

1. The Russians had long been friendly with the Byzantine emperors (cf. Cedrenus, 758, p. 551). Trade between them was cultivated and

order that they could have a plausible excuse for going to war. So, as their envoys were not even considered worthy of an answer, both sides prepared for combat. The enemy were so confident in their own overwhelming numbers that they thought the city, with all its inhabitants, would surrender.

At the time our naval forces were below strength and the fireships were scattered at various naval stations, some here and some there, on guard duty. The emperor therefore gathered together some hulks of the old fleet and strengthened them with new thwarts, added some transport vessels used in the imperial service, and got ready for sea a few triremes, on which he embarked a certain number of fighting men. After a generous supply of Greek Fire[1] had been put aboard these ships, he ranged them in the opposite harbour to face the Russian vessels. He himself, with a picked body of senators, spent the night at anchor in the actual harbour, not far from the shore. A clear declaration of war at sea was made to the barbarians by a herald, and when day broke Constantine set his fleet in battle-array. The enemy also put to sea from the port on the other side. They sailed out as if they were leaving a military camp, complete with fortified rampart. When they were well out from the land, they arranged all their ships in line, so that they formed a continuous chain stretching across the water from the harbour on one side to the harbour on the other. They were now ready to attack us, or, if we made the first assault, to repel us. It was a sight that produced the most alarming effect on every man who saw it. For my own part,

---

merchants travelled freely. The immediate *casus belli* was said to be the death of some Scythian nobleman in a brawl at Constantinople. Vladimir, son of the Russian king, collected a force of some 100,000 men and despite the efforts of Constantine to avert war refused to accept compensation for the outrage (according to Cedrenus the sum mentioned was three pounds of gold for each sailor).

1. The secret weapon of the Byzantine emperors, the invention of a Syrian (Callinicus) in the seventh century. See Appendix IV, p. 387.

I was standing at the emperor's side. He was seated on a hill which sloped gently down to the sea, watching the engagement from a distance.

Such then was the order of battle on their side and on ours. No attempt was made to join combat, however, for each fleet remained motionless, with line intact. A considerable part of the day had already passed when the emperor signalled two of our ships, big vessels, to advance slowly on the enemy. They sailed forward abreast, moving beautifully, with the pikemen and stone-throwers cheering aloft and the hurlers of Greek Fire standing by in good order ready to shoot. At this, several of the Russian ships left their line and bore down on our vessels at full speed. Then, dividing in two, they circled round each of the triremes and hemmed them in, while they tried to hole them below deck with long poles. Our men, meantime, engaged them with stones from above and fought them off with their cutlasses. Greek Fire, too, was hurled at them, and the Russians, being unable to see now, threw themselves into the water, trying to swim back to their comrades, or else, at a loss what to do, gave up all hope of escape.

Thereupon a second signal was given and more triremes put out to sea. Other ships followed or sailed alongside. It was our fleet now that took courage, while the barbarians hove-to in amazement. When the triremes neared the enemy, the latter lost all coherence and their line broke. Some had the fortitude to stay where they were, but the majority fled. Suddenly the sun attracted a mist off the low-lying land (most of the horizon consisted of high ground) and the weather changed. A strong breeze blew from east to west, ploughed up the sea with a hurricane, and rolled waves down on the Russians. Some of their ships were overwhelmed on the spot under the weight of tremendous seas; others were driven far away and hurled on to rocks and precipitous coasts. A certain number of these latter were hunted down by our triremes. Some they sank in deep water, with the crews still aboard. The

fighting men in the triremes cut others in half and towed
them, partially submerged, to nearby beaches. So a great
massacre of barbarians took place and a veritable stream of
blood reddened the sea; one might well believe it came down
the rivers off the mainland.[1]

After this notable victory over his enemies, the emperor
returned to the palace in triumph. As a matter of fact, there
was a widespread legend – despite a thorough examination of
these stories I myself discovered no real foundation for the
prophecy – however, it was *said* that although the emperor
was destined to meet with a host of dangers, some arising from
abroad and the barbarian world, others engineered in territories then under Roman domination, all of them would come
to nothing. Some special fortune, it was said, favoured the
emperor, and because of it he would stamp out every revolt
with the greatest ease. It is a fact, too, that Constantine himself used to refer proudly to certain prophecies and auguries
connected with his reign. He recalled extraordinary visions
and dreams, some that he had experienced himself, others
that he had heard of from soothsayers. On this subject he had
some wonderful things to say. So it came about that when
danger was imminent and while other men were alarmed and
filled with dread for the future, he himself was confident of
ultimate victory. He would comfort the faint-hearted and
face disaster with a self-composure that gave no indication of
the perils threatening him.

Personally, I know of no power of divination possessed by
the man. I attribute the phenomenon to an easy-going and
carefree disposition. Men who have an eye for trouble, men
who know that tiny causes have often given birth to very

1. There were no less than 15,000 enemy corpses washed up on the
shore of the Bosphorus (Cedrenus, 759D, p. 553). The commander of
the Roman fleet was Basil Theodorocanus. After the battle the Russians
retreated by land up the west coast of the Black Sea, harassed constantly
by the victors.

great disasters, are full of worry at every unusual event, and, when their troubles are at the zenith, they fear for the outcome and tremble at every harassing rumour. Even if their luck turns, they still cannot believe it. On the other hand, there are the simple-minded folk, who neither suspect the origin of future troubles nor bestir themselves to deal with the cause of their woes. They have an inclination for pleasures and they desire to revel in them for ever. What is more, they like to convert strangers to the same way of thinking. In order to live a peaceful existence, to follow their peaceful pursuits, they tell the rest of the world, with the air of soothsayers, that they will find swift relief from their grievous misfortunes. There is also a third class of people, with a finer temperament. If trouble should come upon *them* surreptitiously, it does not catch them unprepared. Certainly their ears are not dinned with the crashes and noise around and outside them. Trouble does not scare them, cannot cow them into surrender. On the contrary, when all others have given up in despair, these persons stand imperturbable in the face of peril, relying for support not on material things, but on the soundness of reason and on their own superior judgement. I must admit, though, that so far I have not met with men of that sort in my lifetime. In our generation it is considered a fine thing if a man, believing trouble to be at hand, braces himself to meet the blow and, when it has fallen, tries to the last gasp to repel it. In the emperor's case, the people were convinced that some supernatural power foretold him the future: because of this he had more than once shown himself undaunted in time of calamity. Hence, they argued, his contempt of danger and his utter nonchalance.

The reason why I have made such a long preliminary explanation is to prevent the majority of my readers from thinking the man was possessed of prophetic powers. They might believe he had such powers when I tell them in the course of my history that he predicted or repudiated this or that result.

They must realize that his words were merely in harmony with his general character. The outcome of events must, of course, be ascribed to the Will of God. At this stage I would like to describe a second revolt against the emperor, a revolt more terrible even than the first. Let me go back, therefore, to the beginning of the story. First I will explain the origin of this rebellion and what were its causes. Then I will give an account of the mutiny which preceded it, its character and background, the person responsible for both outbreaks, and what it was that encouraged him to make his attempt.

I will begin then where I left off the narrative. The emperor had a second cousin on the maternal side, a man called Leo, a member of the Tornician family.[1] He lived in Adrianopolis and reeked of Macedonian arrogance. The fellow was not insignificant as far as personal appearance went, but his disposition was crafty and his mind was perpetually open to revolutionary ideas. He had not yet grown up to manhood before a brilliant career – the usual kind of nonsense often talked of with regard to certain people – was predicted for him by a great number of persons. When he did become a man and showed some strength of character, the Macedonian party definitely attached itself to him. Daring attempts at mutiny, involving considerable danger, were made frequently, but they failed to make them at the right time; sometimes Leo was not available, because he was out of the country; sometimes the excuse for revolt was inadequate. However, the idea of rebellion was still cherished secretly in their hearts. Such was the state of affairs when the following event took place, an event that not only stirred them to secede

1. Leo was a patrician and traced descent from Armenian kings. He had in fact been governor of Iberia and, being charged with treason there, had been compelled to become a monk. He disapproved of imperial policy in Armenia (its king, Gagik II, had been dethroned and exiled) and of course he hated Constantine for breaking up the love-affair with Euprepia.

from the Empire, but to engage in active opposition to the emperor.

Constantine had two sisters, the elder called Helena, the younger Euprepia. Of Helena he took no notice, but in the case of the younger woman his treatment was quite different. In her youth she had no particular distinction to boast of: her fortunes had not then attained their subsequent splendour. She was a woman of great pride. In fact, of all the women I have seen, she was the most steadfast and the hardest to influence. Her brother, as I have already remarked, was cautious in his dealings with her – not unnaturally. He had no brotherly feelings for the lady, even when she acquiesced in his wishes; on the contrary, there was more fear than respect in his demeanour. She was therefore deceived of the proud hopes she had built up on her brother, and although she refrained from showing her chagrin by really eccentric behaviour – she never did that – yet she rarely approached him, and, when she did, she was not confident in his presence, as a sister should have been. If she condescended to talk with him at all, it was in a supercilious way. With old-fashioned arrogance she would find fault with most of his actions. She would find fresh causes for complaint and then, when she saw that he was angry, quietly withdrew with a glance of disdain, murmuring abuse under her breath. Now when she found that her brother was by no means favourably disposed, or rather downright hostile, to the aforesaid Tornicius, she welcomed the attentions of the latter and showed herself most amiable to him. She held frequent conversations with him, though in the past her relations had not been so friendly. Constantine was extremely angry about this, but he kept dark his intentions with regard to Tornicius; so far he had no fair pretext for doing him injury. However, in order to separate them, he sent him away from the city without for the moment disclosing his real purpose to Euprepia. The excuse was plausible enough – he was to be made governor of Iberia, and, although he did not say so, he was thereby condemned to an honourable exile.

Yet even when the man was abroad his reputation followed him. Perhaps I ought rather to say that most people seized on this reputation of his as an opportunity to accuse him. They invented stories to slander him, declaring that he was plotting a *coup*, and so persistent were they that Constantine was forced to anticipate the danger. He himself was not unduly upset at these rumours, but when he saw his sister taking the part of Tornicius, and when he heard her pass a remark on one occasion to the effect that her cousin would assuredly not come to any harm, for the Lord on High watched over him, he was really alarmed. Although no longer able to contain his wrath, he still made no attempt to destroy the man: his policy was rather to cut him off from all possibility of leading a revolt. He therefore sent men under orders to make Tornicius undergo tonsuration and garb him with all speed in a monkish habit. Thus was Tornicius bereft of his hopes. Once clothed in magnificent robes, he was now suddenly reduced to rags, and it was in this sorry plight that he returned to the city. Even under these circumstances Constantine had no word of sympathy for him, no pity for his fate, that destiny which had once buoyed him up with high expectations and then had suddenly cast him down. Many a time when Tornicius approached him he sent him away harshly, and then laughed at his pitiable condition. Only Euprepia, whether because of their kinship or for some other reason, befriended him and greeted him in a kindly way. Their relationship gave her an excellent pretext for this charity.

It happened that at that particular time there was a Macedonian colony living in the neighbourhood of the city. Prominent among them were people who had originally lived in Adrianopolis. They were crafty individuals, saying one thing and meaning another, only too willing to take up any ridiculous project and most energetic in carrying it out, very clever at hiding their thoughts, and absolutely loyal to the agreements they made among themselves. The emperor treated them with complete indifference. As far as he was concerned, the lion had already been sacrificed and his claws had been drawn. However that may be, the Macedonians thought that here at last was the oft-sought chance of revolution, and after a brief consultation between their leaders – they had long ago determined their aims – they stirred Tornicius to make his absurd attempt and encouraged themselves to give mutual undertakings to strike the daring blow. They got him out of the city by night, secretly, with the help of a few confederates – quite insignificant persons – and drove straight for Macedonia. To prevent horsemen riding out in pursuit and reaching the passes before them, or hunting them down by following their tracks, each time they stopped at a stage they killed the state horses. So, pressing on without respite, they crossed the Macedonian border, seized Hadrian's city as an acropolis, and at once set to work.

As they had to levy troops and no money was ready to hand, nor anything else likely to induce army commanders to join them and subscribe to their plan of campaign, their first move was to send out immediately a band of expert propagandists in all directions. These men approached individual soldiers wherever they chanced to be and deliberately confirmed that the emperor was dead. They told them that Theodora was now mistress of the Empire and had chosen as her partner, in preference to all others, Leo of Macedonia, a man distinguished for his wisdom, and a man of action, and descended from illustrious forebears. Thanks to this ruse and by inventing this lie, they assembled the armies of the West from all areas in a matter of days. It was not the lying story alone that effected this union: no doubt they nourished some hatred for the emperor on their own account. There were reasons for this: he had somewhat disparaged their military talents, and he suspected them (there had been some revolu-

tionary movement before this) and it was his intention to
punish them one by one. It was now a question of the first
blow.

The concentration of their forces was carried out with an
expedition which surprised even themselves. A common
policy was adopted and they chose Leo as emperor.[1] The
ceremony of proclamation was performed as far as circumstances allowed, with Leo dressed in magnificent robes and
raised on the shield. For his part, once he was garbed in an
emperor's apparel, he lorded it over his supporters in a
dictatorial and truly imperial fashion, as if he had already
won success in his rebellion. He forgot that he was merely a
kind of actor playing a role on the stage or striking a pose.
Admittedly his followers were quite content that he should
rule with a firm hand, and the mass of the people, since he was
neither able to distribute largess nor win them over by bribes,
became adherents when he remitted their taxes. They were
given the privilege, moreover, of going out to plunder and of
reckoning as their own undisputed property whatever they
could capture. With regard to the officials and members of the
senate, once he had made his selection, he appointed some to
command his armies, others he kept near his imperial throne,
others he constituted an inner council of state. In all cases he
conformed to their wishes as well as his own, and the administrative posts were divided among them to suit each man's
individual capacity. Then he set out without further delay for
the city. They hoped in this way to forestall the emperor's
plans by surprise and to throw themselves upon him before he
could move his eastern army to repel them. Besides, they were
under the impression that the inhabitants of Constantinople
would not remain loyal; they expected no opposition there,
because the emperor had made himself unpopular by introducing reforms which curbed the liberty of the citizens. The
people loathed him as a ruler and wanted to see a soldier-

1. In September 1047.

emperor, a man who would endanger his own life on their behalf and put an end to barbarian incursions.

Certainly, even before they drew near to the city walls, a considerable body did join them on the march and a host of soldiers came from the uplands too. The whole country as far as the city, in fact, was favourable to their enterprise and lent its support. Such was the state of their affairs. With the emperor it was altogether different. There was no national army; no auxiliary forces were concentrated anywhere in the district, with the exception of a small band of mercenaries whose duty was to act as escort in the imperial processions. As for the army of the east, it was not even encamped in its own provinces where, if the order was given, it could muster quickly and bring help to the emperor when danger threatened. These men had been quartered in the depths of Iberia, where they were busy driving out barbarian invaders. There was no hope of succour from abroad. Safety depended on one thing only – the circle of walls around him – and it was on the walls that he expended his efforts, building up the parts which had been allowed by negligence to fall into disrepair, and planting his stone-throwing machines thick on the ramparts.

By some chance it was precisely at this moment that his gout became worse. In fact, it became so distressing that his hands were completely dislocated, and his feet swollen, with terrible pains. Apart from that, he was quite incapable of walking. His stomach, too, was in a disordered condition with diarrhoea and general putrefaction. His whole body was being consumed and eaten away by a wasting illness, so that he could neither move nor come into contact with the people. It was natural, therefore, that the city populace should think he was dead, and mass meetings were held in different parts of the city where they debated whether to run away and join the pretender. To counter this, although it was against his inclination, Constantine was compelled from time to time to mix with the people, or allow himself to be seen from a distance and prove by his gestures that he still lived.

So much for the emperor. The pretender, meanwhile, running like the wind, encamped with all his army on a spot in front of the city. The operation was not war, nor a pitched battle, but a pure siege and simple wall-fighting. I heard some of the soldiers and some of the older men say that never before had any rebel been so daring as to make ready artillery in front of the city and bend his bows against its battlements, with an army encircling the whole outer circumference of the walls. Amazement and confusion reigned everywhere, and it seemed that the entire city would fall an easy prey to the enemy. The rebel had moved up to a position some little distance from the walls. Here he threw up a rampart and pitched camp in full view of the defenders. He bivouacked on his rampart for a short time that night, but the rest of the time he spent on horseback, encouraging his men to follow his own example and sleep on the fortifications. He arranged his light-armed troops and went forward himself on foot. At break of day they were all in position before the walls, not in a confused mob, nor massed together in one great body, but disposed in a soldier-like manner and giving every sign of readiness for battle. And in order to fill us with terror – we, forsooth, had no experience of war – every man wore armour. Some were completely armed, with greaves and breastplate, and their horses clad in mail at all points, but others were protected with whatever they could get.

The rebel himself, riding on a white horse, was in the exact centre of his army, together with the pick of his knights and the better part of his troops. He had surrounded himself also with light-armed soldiers, all of them good shots at long range, and lightly equipped and fast runners. The rest of the army stood on either flank in order of battle under their several commanders. Although the battalions preserved their formations, they had been divided into groups, not of sixteen men, but less. The object of this was to allow the whole body to deploy over a bigger area; thus congestion was avoided and the men were not in close order. Behind was a great multitude, which to those on the walls seemed countless, for they too had been divided into small groups. Nevertheless, as they charged on foot or on horseback, both groups at the same time, they gave the impression not so much of a strong army as of a disordered mob.

I will leave them and come back to the emperor. Besieged as he was inside the city walls, his immediate object was to prove to his enemies that he was still alive. So, dressed in his imperial robes, he sat together with the empresses on a balcony of one of the imperial apartments, breathing faintly and groaning in a feeble manner. The only part of the enemy's army that he saw was that straight in front of him and near. The rebels were, in fact, drawn up in good order close by the walls. Their first move was to remind the defenders on the wall of the dreadful things they had suffered at the emperor's hands. They brought to their notice the alleviation that would result from his capture, the torments that would follow his continued freedom. This information was proffered at different parts of the wall in turn. They begged the defenders to open the gates to them and receive within their city a sovereign who was kindly and merciful, one who would treat them with humanity and bring new glory to the Roman Empire by waging victorious wars against the barbarians.

As no favourable reply was forthcoming from the persons to whom these remarks had been addressed – actually they poured forth a torrent of abuse with all manner of disgraceful epithets, both on them and on their pretender – they definitely gave up hope of any support from the people of the city. Thereupon they began hurling insults at the emperor. They reviled him for his bodily weakness. They called him 'accursed', a 'degenerate seeker after unholy pleasures', 'the bane of the city', 'corrupter of the people', with a whole

stream of other disgusting and scurrilous invective. Most of
the Macedonians, being a folk who delight in arrogance and
insolent bearing, more accustomed to the buffoonery of
townsmen than the simplicity of the camp, most of them, I
say, dismounted from their horses and started choral dances,
where everyone could see them. They improvised comic
turns at the emperor's expense, stamping on the ground with
their feet in time to their music and dancing in triumph. Some
of these performances Constantine saw, others he only heard.
I was standing near him at the time, shocked at the things
that were being said, but still trying to comfort him. He did
not know what to do, put to shame as he was, not only by
their actions, but also by their insults.

However, some of the city-men went outside the wall and
stopped their cavalry as they were riding up and down, some
by hurling stones from their slings, others by shooting
arrows. The enemy feigned flight – a manoeuvre they had
rehearsed beforehand – and, having lured our men to pursue
them, they suddenly wheeled about, slaying with sword and
spear. One of the rebels, who knew how to shoot arrows
from horseback, came near the walls without our knowledge
and drawing his bow right opposite the emperor shot straight
at him. The arrow sped through the air at tremendous speed,
but Constantine moved slightly to one side and it missed him,
just grazing one of his chamberlains in the ribs, a young man
of some note. We ourselves were transfixed with terror. The
emperor shifted his seat and took up a position farther away
from the enemy's troops. They had risen early, as I have said,
and they stayed there right up to midday, talking, listening,
now flattering us, now uttering threats. Then they turned
their horses aside and made for their rampart. Machines of
war were prepared and the siege of the city was immediately
begun afresh.

The emperor, after he had recovered his self-composure,
thought it would be disgraceful if he did not get together

some soldiers to oppose them; they would have to be prevented from making attacks by a ditch, and cut off from entry into the city by a barricade. He must keep them at a distance, so as not to hear their remarks or have insults thrown in his teeth. That was his first bad mistake. The second was made when he referred his plan to certain persons who had no experience of war. Most of them were pleased with his scheme, so, first of all, a thorough search of the prisons was carried out to find if any soldiers had been shut up there. These men were liberated, armed with bows and spears, and equipped for battle. Constantine's next step was to enrol in what was left of his army a mob of ordinary citizens. They were quite numerous, volunteers who fooled at war as if it were just another of their games. Throughout that night the digging went on at a ditch to encircle the city, and a palisade was set up in front of it. At dawn, before the enemy presented themselves to our view, he drew up in order of battle the *élite* of our troops and got them into position exactly opposite the enemy. They were partly composed of squadrons of cavalry, partly of companies of light-armed soldiers, all protected by defensive armour. He arranged the whole force in battalions, and then, seating himself a second time on a high vantage-point, he decided to watch what happened from a distance.

The enemy knew nothing of these preparations. When they approached and found our battalions massed in their path, they immediately drew rein, judging it wise to find out first whence all this army of ours had been collected. What they feared was that some contingent from the east had come to our aid. However, when they discovered that the defenders were merely a pack of vagabonds and saw the ditch was shallow and easy to cross, they laughed the emperor to scorn for his folly. Here, they decided, was the chance they were seeking. So, in close order, shield to shield, and howling their war-cry, they made a concerted attack in full force on horseback. The ditch was cleared without the slightest difficulty and the defenders, who until that moment had kept their ranks, were at once put to flight. The enemy then worked round to their rear and wiped them out to a man, some by the sword, others with their spears. Actually the majority were jostled by their own comrades, slipped off their horses, and were trampled to death on the spot. Nor were those who had gone outside the city the only ones to run away: their example was followed by all those who chanced to be standing near the emperor. They believed the rebel was on the point of entering the city and all of them would be destroyed.

Apart from arguments suggested by prudence, there was nothing to prevent the enemy's getting inside the fortifications: the prize was there to be taken with impunity. The officers in charge at the wall-gates had already abandoned their guard, while they looked for some place to give them shelter. Throughout the city were men on the way back to their homes, or men who contemplated going over to the pretender. But Tornicius shirked the final entry. Perhaps it would be truer to say that he was confidently awaiting our invitation to make him emperor. He expected to be led up to the palace preceded by torches, in a procession worthy of a sovereign, and so he put off his entry to the morrow. For the moment he was content to ride on horseback to the several divisions of his army, shouting his orders. There was to be an end to the murder of their kinsmen; the massacre of the emperor's men must stop. He even set free intended victims and prevented any show of force.

Meanwhile the emperor had been deserted, and it was believed that he was about to die in a few moments. But when he heard Tornicius shouting these orders and saw him stopping the massacre, he turned to me. 'This is really serious,' he said. 'When a cruel fellow like this rebel turns to compassion and mercy, it may win him Divine approval.'

His sister was meanwhile lamenting bitterly (I am talking

now of the elder sister, for Euprepia had already been condemned to exile) and she urged him to flee and take refuge in
one of the churches. Constantine glared at her fiercely. 'Let
somebody lead her away,' he said, 'if we still have anyone left.
She can keep her dirges to herself. Besides, she may make me
soft as well.' Then he added, turning to me a second time,
'The enemy's good luck will end today. From now on his
fortunes will change. He might as well try to get foothold in a
quicksand.'

After completing his arrangements and taking a fair number
of prisoners, Tornicius retired to his own entrenchments in
good order. For his part, the emperor decided against any
fresh attempt at surprise. Instead, he repaired the breaches in
the city walls, and proceeded to curry favour with the people.
He showed his appreciation of their loyalty in the past, and
promised them rewards, as if at the Games, if they continued
to be faithful in the future. The siege itself had little effect on
him. Meanwhile his opponent, after bivouacking just that
one night on the rampart, advanced at daybreak with his
army, apparently under the impression that the Empire was
his for the taking. With him he brought his prisoners, loaded
with chains, and set them before the walls. They had been
instructed what to say at the appointed moment. So they
stood there, some distance apart from one another, stirring
pity by their cries as well as by their gestures. To the emperor
they said nothing, but addressed their remarks to the people.
They begged them not to treat with contempt men of their
own race and their own families, nor bear to watch themselves, a pitiable sight, being hacked to pieces before their very
eyes, like victims at a sacrifice. They warned us not to tempt
Providence by making light of a sovereign such as the world
had never seen in the past, one whom they themselves knew
well by experience. He could have destroyed them even then,
they said, and he could have treated them as enemies, but no –
till that moment he had put off the massacre, sparing their

lives in order to do us a favour. Thereupon, by way of contrast, they gave a dramatic account of the terrible deeds of *our* ruler. They described how in the beginning of his reign he had raised very high the hopes of the city, only to bring us down from the clouds to the edge of a precipice. Such were the main points touched on by these prisoners. But the people's loyalty still did not waver.

The sequel to these events came about in the following way. The defenders kept throwing great masses of rock from inside the walls at their enemies, but no one was hit, for the missiles fell short. Then those who were working the machine pulled back the sling farther than usual and shot one of the biggest stones at Tornicius himself. They missed him, but so frightened him and his staff that they took to their heels. The panic and confusion caused among them by this one incident not only broke their ranks but made them retire to their own rampart.

That event marked the change in their fortunes. After being buoyed up by their hopes for a brief interval, and (it must be admitted) by the serious condition of our own affairs, their expectations swiftly declined and vanished away. At all events, they never came near the walls again, but after bivouacking a few days in their camp they returned whence they had come, most of them in disorder, with all the appearance of an army on the run. At that stage, no doubt, if only sixteen or seventeen knights had come in sight of their rearguard, not even a *pyrphorus*[1] would have been left in that scattered undisciplined mob. The emperor expected them to retreat, but no attempt was made to pursue, for he was held back by memories of his previous shock, and so the opportunity was lost.

Nevertheless, to us, even the withdrawal from their

1. In the Spartan army the *pyrphorus* was the priest who kept the sacrificial fire. Hence to say that not even a *pyrphorus* was left is equivalent to admitting total defeat (cf. Herodotus, viii, 6, and Dio Cassius, 39, 45).

entrenchments seemed a most glorious triumph, and the populace of the city poured out to see them. They found great quantities of supplies left in the encampment, abandoned because the enemy had no time to load them on their baggage-animals. They had been more concerned with their own retreat from the lines, without attracting attention, than with getting away loaded with riches and full equipment. Despite this precaution, the rebels no sooner got away than they vented their wrath on Tornicius. Everyone was eager to desert him, for they all dreaded the future. On the other hand, mutual suspicion, as well as the difficulty of escape, forced them to stay together. Meanwhile, when opportunities of leaving did occur they seized them, and made off to the emperor and Byzantium with all speed. Not only was this the case with the ordinary soldiers, but with the officials and commanding officers too. The rebel suffered a chain of misfortunes, one after the other. He attacked the fortresses in the West, which for several reasons were easy to capture: in particular the ground favoured the assailants, and the disposition of the walls; it was a long time since they had been a prospective line of defence. Yet he failed to reduce any of them. The storming-party, in fact, was more intent on running off home than on pressing a siege, and they made it very plain to the beleaguered enemy that they had no stomach for fighting, except in mock battles.

Such was the shameful withdrawal from the Great City of the man who had once contested its throne. Still more shameful was his repulse before the castles which he attacked in succession. The emperor, meanwhile, was summoning the armies of the east, and as soon as they arrived, he dispatched them westwards, where the rebel forces were composed of national and barbarian troops alike. When Tornicius heard of their advance, the question of war or peace was debated no more. The rebels at once dispersed, with maledictions on their leader. Some returned home, but the greater part came over to Constantine, forgetful of the many oaths they had sworn, ignoring the fact that they had promised by the Holy Relics to die, united in one common cause, side by side under the eyes of their rebel general. Now, frozen with fear, they had little thought for those professions of loyalty.

One man, of all that number, remained faithful to Tornicius to the end – an old comrade-in-arms, John by name, with the surname Vatatzes, a man who in physique and strength rivalled the famous heroes of old. So when Tornicius fled and sought refuge in a sacred building, this man fled with him and together they asked for sanctuary, although Vatatzes could have left him and won great honours for himself. Yet he refused to break his pledged word: nothing else mattered. They fled then to a certain holy church, and, drawing their swords, threatened to kill themselves if anyone dared to drag them away by force. Being assured on oath that they would be safe, they finally left the sanctuary and surrendered to the person who had given the promise. At this stage the erstwhile pretender lost his courage. Not only did he emit pitiable cries, but turned to begging for his life. Nor were these the only proofs of his cowardice. Vatatzes, on the contrary, even in these dreadful circumstances, never forgot his pride. He still assumed an air of lofty disdain, and his undaunted bravery was evident in all he did.

At that time it was the emperor's intention to grant a general amnesty. None of the rebels was to be punished, and he made this promise before God, calling down on his head the most fearful curses if he failed to show clemency and grant forgiveness to all who had raised a hand against him. However, when these two (Tornicius and Vatatzes) arrived at the walls, he at once recalled their previous effrontery. Without a moment's hesitation, with no thought for reason, he condemned them to blinding on the spot. At that the pretender emitted a cry of anguish and basely lamented his fate; his comrade merely remarked that the Roman Empire was losing a valorous soldier, straightway lay down on the ground, face upwards, and nobly submitted to his punishment. Afterwards the emperor celebrated a triumph greater than any of those which won renown in the past, and, having vented his spite on them so far, made peace with the rebels, apparently content with this vengeance.

There is one thing that I forgot to mention before, namely, the state of his bodily health at the beginning of his reign, the quality of that manliness and vigorous strength which later suffered such complete degeneration, and the manner in which, so far from preserving the freshness of his youth unspoiled to the end, he exhibited to all beholders his natural glory dimmed, like a sun obscured by the clouds. I will describe these things now, beginning with his youthful excellence.

THE EMPEROR'S PERSONAL APPEARANCE

It was a marvel of beauty that Nature brought into being in the person of this man, so justly proportioned, so harmoniously fashioned, that there was no one in our time to compare with him. To this symmetry she added a robust vigour, as though she were laying firm foundations for a beautiful house. This strength that she gave him was not manifest in long hands or the great size of his limbs or other parts of his body; rather, I fancy, she hid it deep in his heart, for it was not revealed in the parts that were visible. They, in fact, were more distinguished for their beauty and proportion than for any unusual size. Indeed, his hands were only moderately big, and the same can be said of his fingers: their medium size was most noticeable, but they were endowed with more than ordinary strength, for there was no object, however hard and solid, which he could not very easily crush with his hands and break in pieces. An arm gripped by the man was painful for days. They do say that he rode very well too and was an extremely fast runner, supple and light, and absolutely without a rival in the pentathlon, so strong was he and agile and swift of foot.

His beauty, we are told, was that of Achilles or Nireus.[1] But whereas, in the case of these heroes the poet's language, having in imagination endowed them with a body compounded of all manner of beauties, barely sufficed for their description, with Constantine it was different, for Nature, having formed him in reality and brought him to perfection, with the fine skill of the sculptor shaped him and made him beautiful, surpassing with her own peculiar art the imaginative effort of the poet. And when she had made each limb proportioned to the rest of his body, his head and the parts that go with it, his hands and the parts that go with them, his thighs and his feet, she shed over each of them severally the colour that befitted them. His head she made ruddy as the sun, but all his breast, and his lower parts down to his feet, together with their corresponding back parts, she coloured the purest white all over, with exquisite accuracy. When he was in his prime, before his limbs lost their virility, anyone who cared to look at him closely would assuredly have likened his head to the sun in its glory, so radiant was it, and his hair to the rays of the sun, while in the rest of his body he would have seen the purest and most translucent crystal. His personal characteristics, too, contributed to the general harmony of the man, his refined speech, his charming conversation, and a singularly attractive smile which exercised an immediate fascination over those who saw him.

CONCERNING THE EMPEROR'S ILLNESS

Such was the beauty with which the emperor was endowed when he ascended the throne, but a year had not gone by

1. Nireus was said to have been, next to Achilles, the handsomest of the Greeks who fought at Troy.

before Nature, in her efforts to glorify him, seemed to falter before such wonder and delight; it was as if she gave up the task in exhaustion, and then destroyed his strength and ruined his manhood. At all events there can be no doubt that a radical change took place in the disposition of the primary substances in his body (that is, the basic humours) and they accumulated, in proportions that made harmony impossible, in his feet and the cavities of his joints, then in his hands. Later they descended in great waves on the muscles themselves, and the bones in his back, shaking him through and through, like sea-currents converging on a ship of burthen which had started its voyage in calm water.

The symptoms of his disease were not all immediately apparent. The humours first flowed into his feet, and at once he was compelled to take to his bed. If he had to walk at all, he did so with the help of other people. The illness was recurrent, and it was evident that the flux continued for a certain number of days, followed by an equal period of rest. Later on, the intervals between these attacks diminished and his relief became short-lived. As this condition developed, the flux gradually approached his hands, then with a kind of upward flow, the humours attacked his shoulders, and finally occupied the whole of his body. The result was that every one of his members, swamped by this terrible flux, lost the ability to perform its natural functions. His muscles and ligaments were out of place, his limbs ceased to work in harmony, with consequent lack of general equilibrium and a development of nervous exhaustion. I myself saw his fingers, once so beautifully formed, completely altered from their natural shape, warped and twisted with hollows here and projections there, so that they were incapable of grasping anything at all. His feet were bent and his knees, crooked like the point of a man's elbow, were swollen, making it impossible for him to walk steadily or to stand upright for any length of time. Mostly he lay on his bed, and, whenever he wished to give audience, others had to prop him up and make him comfortable.

For the sake of the city populace he considered it his unavoidable duty to attend the imperial processions, and it was on these occasions that he complained most bitterly. However, through the skill of his equerry he was arranged and settled in the saddle, and since he found breathing difficult once he was mounted, and as the bridle hung useless, attendants, tall, strong men, used to hold him up on either side as he rode. So, keeping him steady on right and left, like some heavy load, they would convey him to his intended destination. Yet, even in these distressing conditions he never entirely forgot his normal habits. He would assume an expression of great benevolence, and even moved and changed his position (the only time he ever did so unaided) so that the spectators were not really sure that he was in pain, or that his body was suffering from paralysis. Such were the arrangements made for him at the processions. Even the stones of the pavements were covered with carpets, to prevent his horse slipping on a smooth surface. Of course it was different in his palace, for there he was carried on a litter, and he used to pass from one apartment to another and be conveyed wherever he wished. But if the flux came on – what awful agonies he endured!

Even while I write this history I am still absolutely amazed to think how the man was able to bear the excruciating pain of those attacks during that period of his life. Paralysis followed paralysis in rapid succession, impairing the parts still untouched by the disease and dislocating what was still coherent. He did not know how to lie on his bed so as to enjoy a proper rest: every position was uncomfortable. His valets would hold up and support his poor body on either side until after much experiment they discovered the posture which afforded some relief to him. Then they would arrange him and make him comfortable, with cushions so placed that he might be kept firm in that position. But change of posture was not the only thing that caused him pain: even his tongue hurt him when he was speaking, and the slightest movement of the eyes set the humours in motion. Thus he remained absolutely still, never turning in either direction.

While on the subject of this illness, I solemnly declare, and I call on God to witness the truth of my words, that Constantine, despite the dreadful troubles that exhausted and overwhelmed him, despite the altogether pitiable condition in which he found himself, never once allowed a word of blasphemy against God to escape his lips. In fact, if he saw anyone else dismayed at his own sufferings, he sent him from his presence with more than usual severity. The misfortune, he said, was laid upon him as a punishment. More often he referred to it as a 'curb on his nature'. Indeed, he was afraid of his instincts, and he used to say, 'When they refuse to give way to reason, they yield to bodily pain. My body is afflicted, but at least the unruly desires of my heart are now repressed.' So he argued about his sufferings like a philosopher, and, if one set aside all else that he did, and considered him in this matter only, surely one would say that here was a godly man.

He had another good quality, one that I myself do not wholly approve of, but he held it in high esteem. However, I will leave my readers to judge for themselves. He completely neglected to take precautions for his own safety. When he was sleeping the doors were left open and no guard kept watch outside his bedchamber. Indeed, the chamberlains often left him altogether and it was possible for anyone to walk past his door, and pass it again on the way back, without the slightest interference from others. If one took the liberty of rebuking him for this laxity, Constantine was not vexed about it, but he dismissed the reproach as unnecessary. It was due, he said, to wrong ideas about God. What he meant by this was that he occupied the throne by the grace of

God and by Him alone he was protected. Being defended by
the Perfect Guard, he saw no need of human sentinels who fell
short of perfection.

On several occasions I tried myself to convince him of the
danger. I quoted the case of builders and helmsmen, and
finally of captains and generals. 'Not one of these men,' I
argued, 'undertakes his particular task without placing his
trust in God. Yet the one levels off his building with a rule,
the other guides his ship with a rudder, and everyone who
goes to war carries a shield and sword. The soldier's head is
protected by a helmet, while a breastplate covers the rest of
his body.' Having got so far, I developed the theme: these
safeguards were even more appropriate in the case of an
emperor – but all my attempts to persuade him were in vain.
It does credit to the man's noble character, but his obstinacy
made things easy for would-be assassins.

THE PLOT AGAINST THE EMPEROR'S LIFE

There is no doubt that it brought about a host of calamities.
One or two of them I will describe, and leave my readers to
deduce from them the nature of the rest. Here I will deviate
somewhat from the main narrative for one moment. In well-
governed cities there are inscribed on the citizen-rolls the
names not only of the best persons and men of noble birth,
but also of people whose origin is obscure, and military
authorities observe this custom no less than civil magistrates.
That, anyway, was the system followed by the Athenians
and in all those cities which emulated their form of democracy. In our polity, however, this excellent practice has been
contemptuously abandoned, and nobility counts for nothing.
The process of corruption has been going on in the Senate
for a long time; it is, in fact, a heritage of the past, for Romulus
was the first to encourage the kind of confusion we see now.
Today the citizenship is open to all. No doubt you would find

not a few wearing civilized clothes, who formerly covered themselves in a goat's-hair cloak. Many of our governors are, I am sure, ex-slaves whom we bought from barbarians, and our great offices of state are entrusted not to men of the stamp of Pericles, or Themistocles, but to worthless scamps like Spartacus.

There was a fellow in my time, a filthy barbarian scoundrel who far outdid the Romans in arrogance, and was so brazen that he took advantage of his exalted position and physically maltreated some who afterwards became emperors and then, when they had actually ascended the throne, proudly boasted of it in public. 'With this hand,' he would say, showing his right hand, 'with this I have many a time struck Roman emperors!' I once heard him utter those words myself and I was terribly upset. I almost strangled the insolent foreigner with my own two hands; the shock of that boast was more than I could bear.

However, this remark caused no more offence than his promotion to our Senate, the noble members of which had been polluted by his presence shortly before the incident. In the first place he had done the emperor some service, then he wormed his way into favour with the magistrates, and his name appeared on the roll of the Senate. He was, as I have said, a person of obscure origin. To be more explicit, he was a common worthless rogue. Having once drunk of the Roman streams, and found them good to the taste, he thought it would be a pity if he missed the chance of becoming master of their source – emperor, in fact, with Romans of the noblest families his subjects, and he a slave bought at a price! When the rascal conceived this idea, he saw in the emperor's un-guarded state a godsend for his venture. Meanwhile he kept his design secret, informing none of his colleagues, and smoothed the path to the realization of his dreams. When the emperor was in procession from the Theatre to the Palace, he mingled with the ranks in the rear of the guard and marched with them. Once inside the palace he lay in wait somewhere near the kitchens, everyone who met him believing that the emperor had told him to stay there, and so nobody whatever threw him out. Later, under cross-examination, he disclosed his secret intentions, and it appears that his idea was to fall upon Constantine in his sleep, kill him with a sword (which he had concealed in his clothes), and make himself supreme ruler.

Such was his plan. When the emperor went to rest, lying there, as I have already said, quite unguarded, the desperado proceeded to carry out his plot. However, after advancing a few paces his nerve gave way and he faltered, overcome with faintness. He was caught, running hither and thither in an aimless fashion, quite bewildered. The emperor was at once roused from sleep. Meanwhile the guards had collected and were questioning the barbarian with some severity. Naturally, Constantine was annoyed at the fellow's daring; what offended him most was the thought that such a man could bring himself to treat an emperor with impudence so brazen. He put him in chains at once, and on the next day he himself sat as judge at the trial – a very stern judge too. The man was interrogated about the attempted assassination. Constantine asked if he had accomplices in the plot, if there was a ringleader of the conspiracy, if someone else had instigated him to dare it. These preliminary investigations having produced no useful reply, the prisoner was put to the cruellest tortures. He was stripped, hoisted up to a wooden beam and suspended from it by his feet, then flogged till he was half dead. This punishment had a crushing effect on him, I fancy, for he denounced certain high-ranking officials as his accomplices, and among his victims the barbarian madman numbered some gentlemen whose loyalty and honour were quite undeniable. Nevertheless, time has restored them to their original place of honour, while he, as the years go by, is still numbered among the greatest scoundrels of history.

For a while the emperor did take precautions for his safety, but later the vigil was relaxed again – a negligence which very nearly cost him his own life and involved the city in troubles even greater and more terrible still. I will set forth the causes of this calamity, the extent to which it prevailed, and the manner of the emperor's deliverance from peril a second time, after all had despaired of his salvation. Constantine had a cheerful disposition; any kind of pastime appealed to him and he required constant amusement. But he had no taste for organ music, or the melody of flutes, or a fine voice, or dancing, or mimes, or anything of that sort. On the other hand, if anyone had an impediment in his speech and was unable to pronounce his words correctly, or if a man simply talked nonsense, uttering any word that chanced to come into his head, the emperor thought it highly diverting. Generally speaking, in fact, nothing was more calculated to please him than a wrong use of words.

Now at that time there used to visit the palace a certain scallawag[1] afflicted with just that kind of impediment in his speech. When he spoke his tongue would stop functioning altogether, or when he made special efforts, just glide over the words. This fellow, moreover, exaggerated the natural defect, and the resulting jumble of syllables was no more effective than the noises of a mute. Indeed, in both cases, whether he spoke normally or affected dumbness, the audience was quite incapable of understanding what he meant.

At first the emperor treated the man with indifference. In fact, he only appeared at court every now and then after the ceremony of ablution. It was typical of the emperor, though, that as time passed he should take more pleasure in his babblings, till he reached a point where he found himself unable to be parted from the fellow. Consequently there was

1. Romanus Boïlas rose to high rank about 1049. Cedrenus (788B, p. 605) speaks of him as a person of some accomplishments.

a time set apart for his foolery; even when Constantine was holding audience, appointing magistrates, or carrying out any of his other public duties, the man was there with him, showing off his natural defect and generally acting the clown. Indeed, there can be no doubt but that the emperor encouraged him. He went further: he made a new man of him, an imitation of the great men of the realm, and this street-lounger was translated to the centre of Roman government. He was rapidly promoted to positions of honour, took his place with the chief officers of State, had permission to go anywhere, and was appointed captain of the emperor's bodyguard. With characteristic lack of courtesy he did not confine his visits to any fixed time, but suited his own convenience. He would go up to Constantine, kiss him on breast and face alike, speak to him without first being addressed himself, and then, breaking into a wide grin, sit down on the same couch and squeeze the emperor's feeble hands between his own, an action that pained him yet at the same time gave him pleasure.

For my own part I did not know at whom to wonder the more, this fellow who had been transformed to suit the whim and fancy of the emperor, or the sovereign who brought himself down to the other's level, for each was desirous of pleasing the other, and they were devoted friends. What the master wanted the comedian did; what he did the master wanted. So it came about that although Constantine understood the general drift of his clowning, he was still content to be the object of buffoonery, and the actor made merry over his ruler's stupidity, making joke after joke admirably suited to the other's simple nature.

It went so far that the emperor refused to be parted from him at all. The clown, on the other hand, became bored with this constant attendance. He longed for freedom, to pass the time as he wished. Now it chanced on a certain occasion that he lost a particularly good polo pony. At that time he used to sleep beside the emperor. Suddenly, in the middle of the night, he got up, roused him (Constantine) from a deep sleep, and gave way to uncontrollable demonstrations of joy. The emperor, who was by no means displeased at being awakened in this manner, asked him what was the matter and why he was so exultant. The clown put his arms round the emperor's neck and kissed him, over and over again, on the face. 'Sir,' said he, 'he's been found – the horse that I lost! A eunuch rides him now, a wrinkled old chap, too old for riding. Please let me take a horse from the palace now and bring him here to you, and the mount as well.' At these words the emperor laughed gaily. 'Ah well,' he replied, 'you have my permission to go – but mind you come back as soon as possible, and tell me all about it when you find him.' So off he went, without wasting a moment, to enjoy the pleasures he had in mind. After his feasting was done, back he came in the evening, panting and puffing, trailing behind him a eunuch. 'Here he is, Sir,' he said, 'the fellow who stole my horse. He has it for sure, but he won't give it up. What's more, he swears he never stole it in the first place.' At this, the poor old man appeared to be weeping. He seemed to be at a loss for words to answer the clown's abuse. The emperor meanwhile did not know how to refrain from laughing.

To settle the matter, he consoled the one with a fresh horse, a better one too, while he dried the counterfeit tears of the eunuch with gifts that surpassed his wildest dreams. Actually, this eunuch was one of the comedian's most fervid admirers, and the object of his flattery had long desired him to benefit from the emperor's generosity. Since, however, he could hardly petition Constantine on behalf of a man unknown to him, he devised the play-acting about his dream. The emperor was duped, tricked with the story of the old man and the imaginary vision – a deceit made easier because of his somewhat dull wit. What made it even more deplorable was the fact that we were all aware of the duplicity, but we never dared to complain. We were merely victims, compelled to witness

the emperor's stupidity and the other's public miming, forced
to laugh at things which should have made us weep. Indeed, if
I had not promised to write on serious matters, and if I cared
to record foolish trifles, my history could be augmented with a
vast collection of such anecdotes. This is only one of many
and it must serve as an example of the rest. I will return to my
narrative of events as they happened.

Well, this clown of ours not only took possession of the
men's apartments in the palace, but having wormed his way
into the imperial *gynaeconitis* (women's quarters) as well, he
won the favour of both empresses. Indulging in all kinds of
silly talk, he maintained he had been born of the elder sister.
Further than that, he swore most solemnly that the younger
sister, too, had given birth to a child. His own birth, he said,
had taken place thus – and then, as if recalling how he had
been brought into the world, he gave a description of her
labour, with shameless details. His most witty anecdotes,
however, concerned Theodora's accouchement, the conversations she had during the pregnancy, and the manner of
her delivery. These foolish women, captivated by the clown's
stories, allowed him to come and go as he pleased by secret
doors. It would not, indeed, be easy to enumerate all the
privileges that were showered on him, both in the men's and
women's apartments in the palace.

For some time his foolery was confined merely to play-
acting of this sort, but when the empress died (an event which
I will describe shortly) the simpleton began to commit
crimes, crimes which eventually caused great trouble. I will
tell part of the story, but first I will anticipate my history by
touching on a subject which will be dealt with later. The
emperor had a mistress, a girl who was held as a hostage by
us from a country of no great importance. She was not distinguished in any way, but being of royal blood she was
respected by the emperor and treated with great honour.
Our clown conceived a deep love for this girl. Whether she

returned his affection I cannot say with any certainty, but it appeared that the love was mutual. Maybe she moderated her passion, but in his case concealment became impossible – it was the only time his acting failed him. Certainly he gazed at her quite brazenly and they met frequently. He was undoubtedly on fire with love. However, since it was beyond his power to master the affection or win his beloved princess for himself, he made up his mind to become supreme ruler of the Roman Empire. The idea, of course, sounds utterly absurd and quite incredible, but he determined to carry it out. Perhaps he had been influenced by the advice of ill-disposed persons, or maybe the plot originated in his own mind; I do not know, but in any case he thought his plan would be extremely easy to put into practice, for two reasons. He calculated that there was no difficulty in murdering the emperor, and, secondly, he himself had the keys to the secret entrances: he had power to open or shut all doors as he wished. Unfortunately for him, he had been led to believe that his success would be popular, and it simply was not true. The fact is, he listened to the not inconsiderable mob of sycophants who fed at his table, and one of the leaders of that chorus, a man who had complete ascendancy over him, happened to be commander of the mercenaries.

Well, to begin with, he kept this plan to himself, and no one at all had an idea that he was considering any such scheme. But when his crazy infatuation proved altogether too much for him, he threw caution to the winds and revealed his intentions to quite a number of other people, a move which led rapidly to his downfall. In fact his arrest came none too soon – less than an hour before he was to commit his horrible crime. When evening came and the emperor, following his normal custom, lay down to rest, he was probably engaged in sharpening his dagger ready for the murder, but one of his confidants arrived suddenly at the palace, saying he had a message for Constantine. Still panting hard, he entered the imperial bed-chamber, and without waiting to get his breath, gave warning: 'He will kill you, Sir! At once – your dearest friend' (mentioning the man by name). 'Find some way of escaping instant death!' The emperor could not believe it. The clown, meanwhile, realizing what had happened, threw away his dagger, made for the church which was near there, and took refuge at the Holy Altar. He confessed his plot and all the deception he had practised in order to carry it out; he admitted the preparations he had made and acknowledged that he had intended to kill the emperor outright.

Constantine, instead of returning thanks to God for his deliverance, was very angry with the messenger, because, forsooth, his beloved friend had been caught. Already, before he even heard the charges brought against him, he was defending the prisoner. However, as the plot could not be hushed up in any way (for everyone knew of it) he decided to hold a semblance of trial the next day. The culprit was led into court, in chains, to hear sentence pronounced. At the sight of his friend's hands bound thus (it was a strange and unusual spectacle) the emperor could hardly help showing his sorrow openly. His eyes filled with tears. 'Be good enough to set him free,' he said, 'for my heart melts with pity when I look at him thus.' And when those who had been ordered to do so had loosed him from his chains, Constantine gently urged him to make his defence; the charges were dismissed at once. 'You have a most ingenuous character,' he said. 'I know your sincerity and frankness. But tell me, who pushed you into this ridiculous plot? Who has deceived your simple soul? Who led you astray from the path of innocence? Tell me again, which of my possessions do you covet? What is it that pleases you most? I assure you, you shall have all your heart's desire.'

Thus spoke the emperor, his eyes all swollen with weeping and his cheeks wet with tears. As for the clown, he ignored the first questions as if they had never been asked; in fact, he offered no explanation whatever. To the later queries, which referred to his desires, he did reply, and a wonderful exhibition of play-acting it was. Kissing the emperor's hands and laying his head on the emperor's knees, 'Seat me on the imperial throne,' he said, 'and adorn me with a crown of pearls. Give me this collar too' (pointing to the ornament Constantine wore round his neck) 'and let me share in the acclamation with you. I longed for this before, and now it is my greatest desire.'

The effect of these words on the emperor was extraordinary. He was really delighted. What he wanted was to find some reasonable excuse for acquitting the fellow of making this absurd attempt on his own life. If it could be shown that he was simple and honest, then he would be completely free of suspicion, and condemnation would be unnecessary. 'I will put a diadem on your head as well,' he said, 'and clothe you in a robe of purple. One thing I beg of you: please be your old self and put an end to this trouble. Away with that dark look on your face and let me see there the old expression, the happiness that used to shine in your eyes!' Even the serious-minded smiled at these words, and the judges, without so much as a single question, left the court in a body, laughing. They did not even wait to see the end of the comedy. As for the emperor, he made a thank-offering to God for his safety and rendered prayers of gratitude, as if he himself had been the accused and had himself been acquitted. This was followed by a feast more sumptuous than usual, the emperor giving the banquet and presiding over it, and the guest of honour was none other than this clown, the very man who had plotted against him.

When the Empress Theodora and his sister Euprepia, like the goddesses in the poem,[1] expressed severe disapproval of these proceedings, and instead of being agreeable constantly criticized the emperor's stupidity, his composure was ruffled, and to please them he condemned the culprit to exile. The

1. Athena and Hera (Homer, *Iliad*, iv, 20).

place was not far away; in fact, he ordered him to reside quite near, on one of the islands lying off the city, advising him to enjoy the bathing there and amuse himself in any way he wished. Less than ten days afterwards he recalled him with every mark of honour. He was to be granted more licence than ever: greater favours should be conferred on him. In a history such as this I have passed over in silence many remarkable facts, things which not only injure the reputation of an author, but bore his readers. In the case of this particular incident I have not told the whole story. To complete it I shall have to digress at some length and insert here another anecdote, in order to make the record free from obscurity. After this digression I will return to my original story and finish it.

The Empress Zoe was already past the age for sexual relations, but the emperor's desires were still feverish. His Augusta had died some time ago, and his conversations on the subject of love tended to become involved in a mass of strange and fanciful ideas. He was naturally inclined to sexual indulgence, but he could find no satisfaction in cheap harlotry. Yet memories of his early amours were always rousing in him fresh waves of desire, and eventually he fell in love with a young girl, one of our hostages from Alania (I have already mentioned this earlier in my history). The kingdom of Alania was not particularly distinguished in itself, nor had it any great prestige, but it regularly supplied pledges of its loyalty to the Roman Empire. This girl was the daughter of the king there. She was not outstandingly beautiful, and few suitors asked for her hand in marriage. Only two attributes lent her especial charm – the whiteness of her skin and the brilliance of her very beautiful eyes. Yet when the emperor once came under her influence, he forsook all his other paramours. He lived with this girl alone and conceived for her a most violent passion.

As long as the empress was alive his intrigues were more or

less clandestine; he preferred to go and come unseen, under a cloak of mystery. When she was dead, he flaunted his passion and openly fanned the flame of desire. He very nearly had a bridal chamber furnished and escorted his lady-love there, as if she were indeed his wife. Her appearance was suddenly transformed in an extraordinary way; her head was garlanded in strange decorations, her neck was resplendent with gold, bracelets of gold, fashioned like snakes, twined round her arms, and heavy pearls were suspended from her ears. As for her girdle, it was made of gold, adorned with a chain of pearls. The woman was a veritable Proteus, with all his changes and variations.[1]

Really he wanted to crown her with the diadem of an empress, but two things restrained him: the law limiting the number of marriages, and the Empress Theodora, who would neither tolerate this insult, nor agree to be both ruler and ruled. So the lady was not permitted to wear the imperial robes, but Constantine did allow her to share his title, for he called her Augusta. An imperial bodyguard was also provided for her. Every door that led to her desires was thrown wide open, rivers flowing with gold were diverted for her pleasure, streams of wealth, endless floods of opulence. So once more all our treasures were wasted away and squandered. Some were scattered inside the walls of the city, others carried off to the barbarian world. For the first time in its history the land of the Alanians was surfeited with good things that came to it from our Rome. Ships sailed into harbour, and when they once more put to sea, they were all loaded with precious things that belonged to us, things that in the old days made the Roman Empire the object of envy.

It used to grieve me then, seeing all our possessions thrown away like that, and I am just as distressed at the thought of it today, for no one ever admired the Romans or loved his

1. The legendary old man of the sea who had power to change his shape.

country more than I do. I still blush for my master and emperor. Two or three times every year envoys used to come from her father in Alania to this girl Augusta, and Constantine would show her off to them (like an exhibition on a stage), proclaiming that she was his consort and empress, and actually calling her by those names. He himself gave them some gifts, others he encouraged his beautiful 'wife' to present to them.

The actor fellow, of whom I spoke some time ago, had been in love with this princess before, and he was successful in his wooing. So he plotted against the emperor, but the plot went awry. When he returned from exile, he was more passionately in love than ever. I was well aware of this, but I thought Constantine knew nothing of it. Really, I was rather doubtful. However, it was he himself who settled the question for me. On a certain occasion when I was accompanying him on one of his visits to the lady (he was being carried on a litter), her lover was also one of the party. At the time she was in her private apartment in the palace, standing by some latticed gates. Before embracing her the emperor stopped, thinking of something, and while he was concentrating on the matter in question, the clown cast his eyes in the direction of his beloved. Seeing her, he smiled gently and then showed other signs of his love for her. Again and again his eyes turned towards her. While this was going on, the emperor gently nudged me in the ribs. 'See the rascal,' he said, 'still in love. His past punishment hasn't done him the least good.' Immediately I heard him I was covered in confusion, but he went on to see the lady, while the other, by no means abashed, looked at her with more insolence than ever. However, it all came to nothing, for the emperor died, as I shall tell you later in my history, and of the other two the Augusta was again considered a mere hostage, and the lover saw his passion end in nothing but empty dreams.

It must be clear that in this account I have repeatedly passed over many events that occurred during this period, so I will return to the emperor. But first I will devote some pages to the Empress Zoe, ending with her death, and then I will take up my main story again. What she was like in her youth I cannot say with any certainty; I have already given some description of her earlier in this book, but what I wrote depended on hearsay.

THE PHYSICAL ATTRIBUTES OF THE EMPRESS ZOE

When she had grown old, she was somewhat lacking in stability. I do not wish to convey the impression that she was deranged or out of her right mind, but she was absolutely ignorant of public affairs and her judgement was completely warped by the vulgar extravagance that prevailed in the palace. Whatever intellectual advantages she may have enjoyed in the past, her character did not suffer her to preserve even them free from insincerity, for a perverse delight in displaying her knowledge showed her for what she was – not intellectually honest, but lacking in taste. We will not speak of her reverence for God: I cannot find fault with immoderation in that. Surely nobody could surpass her in that good quality, for she depended wholly on God, ascribed all events to His influence, thought all things were determined by Him. I have duly commended her for this earlier in my book. For the rest, she was characterized not only by tenderness and laxity, but also by extreme harshness and tension, and these two aspects would interchange for no reason at all in a single moment. She could be both things to the same person. For instance, if one saw her unexpectedly and made pretence to fall down as if struck by lightning (many played this trick on her), he was at once presented with chains of gold, but if he expressed his gratitude with too much effusion, he would promptly find himself in chains of iron. Again, perceiving that her father was somewhat indiscriminate in the infliction of blinding as a punishment, she would put to a similar torture anyone who committed even the slightest error, without any hesitation. Had not the emperor frowned on this, many a man would have lost his eyes for no reason at all.

She was the most generous of women, and this virtue of generosity, which in her case knew no bounds, led her to pour out all her wealth regardless of all economy. With one hand she would pay out the money, and at the same time raise the other in supplication to God for blessings on the head of her beneficiary. Any enthusiastic account of the glorious deeds of her family, especially those of her uncle Basil, filled her with delight; the effect on her spirits was instantaneous. Although she had already passed her seventieth year, there was not a wrinkle on her face. She was just as fresh as she had been in the prime of her beauty. It must be admitted, though, that her hands were unsteady; she was subject to tremors too, and her back was bent. As for ornaments about her person, she absolutely despised them: she wore neither cloth of gold, nor diadems, nor lovely things about her neck. Her garments were not of the heavy sort: in fact she clothed herself in thin dresses.

She left the administration of the Empire entirely in the hands of Constantine, preferring to be relieved of all responsibilities in that direction. Nor was she interested in the things that appeal to women – looms, distaffs, wool, or weaving. One thing above all claimed her attention, and on this she expended all her enthusiasm – the offering of sacrifices to God. I am not referring so much to the sacrifice of praise, or of thanksgiving, or of penitence, but to the offering of spices and sweet herbs, the products of India and Egypt.

As her life drew to its appointed close, when she was on the point of dying, slight changes made their appearance in her normal state of health, signs that the end was near. She lost her appetite, and, as the lack of nourishment made itself felt more and more, she caught a fever, which proved fatal. It was obvious from the pining away of her body – one might almost say its decay – that death was at hand. Her first thought was for those in prison. Debts were remitted, and an amnesty granted to condemned criminals. She opened up the imperial treasury and allowed the gold kept there to pour forth like a river. So the gold was squandered with all the uncontrolled profusion of a flood, and Zoe, after a short and painful illness, but little change in her outward appearance, departed this life at the age of seventy-two.[1]

Having completed my account of the empress, I will return to Constantine. First, however, I have this observation to make: it was not my desire to write a history, nor to acquire a reputation for veracity in that sphere; what I wanted to do was to compose a panegyric in honour of this ruler. Certainly I should have been able to contribute a host of compliments to my eulogy, for he afforded abundant justification for them. The encomiast, you see, passes over all that is unworthy in his hero, and concentrates on his nobler deeds. Where the bad deeds are in the majority, the *orator* needs to find only one incident where his subject conducted himself in a noble fashion, and he will produce a passable eulogy. By clever handling even mean exploits can be misinterpreted so that they become an excuse for praise. But the man who writes a *history* is like a judge, no respecter of persons and incorruptible. In his description of events he is biased in favour of neither side, but adopts in his account a policy of strict impartiality. He brings forward no subtle arguments on behalf of the good, or of the bad, but purely and simply tells what happened. Where two persons are involved in the history, and of them one (a virtuous man) had previously treated the author with boundless contempt, while the other (a man of quite different stamp) used to confer on him certain favours, the historian will not be influenced by the behaviour of either

1. Zoe died in 1050.

man towards himself, and each will be represented in his true character. Suppose the historian *were* allowed to return favour for favour, in the case of someone who had been friendly to him in the past, and suppose he *were* granted the privilege of perverting the truth for that purpose, all because of some act of friendship or generosity, is there any man more entitled than I to eulogize this particular emperor in his writings? Indeed, Constantine never set eyes on me before he ascended the throne, and yet, once he had seen me, he was so charmed with my eloquence that he seemed to 'hang on my lips by his ears', as the proverb says.

My difficulty is this – how am I to preserve the true story, and at the same time give him the credit that he deserves? If I am unduly particular in writing a true history, at least I preserve his great reputation in one respect, for when I make a thorough and candid examination of his career, even where his actions are apparently bad, if we still see the light of virtue shining through his good deeds, and if we find that the good scale on the balance, carrying a fairly heavy weight of good deeds, outweighs the bad, then surely Constantine will be considered a greater man than all those emperors whose panegyrics appear to be suspect, plausible rather than true. Was there ever a man (here I am trying to justify his mistakes), above all, was there ever an emperor who won the crown of praise for *all* his deeds, without exception?

When we look at the great leaders of men, persons renowned for their characters and their words and deeds, men such as Alexander the Macedonian, the two Caesars,[1] Pyrrhus of Epirus, Epaminondas the Theban, Agesilaus the Spartan, not to speak of others who won brief commendation from their admirers, when we look at these men, we do not find in their lives an equal balance of virtue and vice, as we know from their biographers, but generally they incline somewhat to the worse. What then can one say of those who imitated

1. Psellus is referring to Julius Caesar and Augustus.

them, if they seemed inferior to them in some small degree –
I do not mean in all aspects of virtue, but in those where
these great men have succeeded above all others?

When I compare this very great emperor with them, I am
aware that he is their inferior in bravery, but he is a finer
man than they when one considers the other good qualities –
and his superiority here is just as marked as theirs in the first
case, where he had to yield them the palm. He was impetuous by nature, gifted with remarkable shrewdness and a
most retentive memory, but he exercised such control over
this lively temperament that he, more than all the others,
seems to have been endowed with kindliness. I was not
deceived by appearances myself though, and I knew that he
had a temper, and that he held it in check, as a charioteer
holds back a spirited horse. So, when the blood rushed to his
face and his body was suddenly moved with anger, he would
calm down more quickly still and give way at once to reason.
If, by any chance, in the course of his duties as emperor he
spoke rather sharply or threatened anyone with punishment,
he would blush immediately afterwards, as if he were ashamed
of uttering words which were, to him, unusual.

When he acted as judge, it was impossible for an onlooker
to distinguish either the successful litigant, or the defeated
party, by their behaviour after he had given the verdict. To
put it more clearly, the party that obtained the white pebble
(won the case) naturally went away radiant with joy; his
opponent, on the other hand, even before he knew that he
had lost the case, had no hopes of success, but, meeting with
treatment more lenient than he had expected, he too went
away in triumph, more privileged than he had dared to
anticipate.

Numerous conspiracies were formed against him, and in
the majority of them the rebels even went so far as to attempt
assassination. Yet he preferred to draw a veil over their recklessness and talk with them in his normal manner, as if he

knew nothing of these attempts, or had at once forgotten
their impudence. And when those who surrounded the
throne, and who had not been deprived of the right to speak
freely in his presence, tried to provoke him to anger against
them, saying that he would very soon be killed if he did not
take steps to defend himself against these adventurers, he
was more concerned to score a verbal triumph over them in
court than to submit them to a regular trial. He appointed
judges to hear them, and himself discussed their daring
efforts in a speech full of bombast – and what a clever speaker
he was, with what range of expression! Then, as he saw them
cowering in fear, he would conclude his speech with a brief
defence, conducting even that in frivolous vein – and straightway sent them away unpunished.

With regard to his public acts, I will leave the recording of
them to many other writers who like to chronicle those
things. But I will disclose a small number of intimate facts
about him, things which are the common topic of conversation, the kind of deeds likely to be either praised or blamed.
Of the qualities which have built up his good reputation I
choose one for special commendation: his clemency. He
knew that he was by temperament a kindly and merciful
man, and he never bore malice against any of the individuals
who vented their spite on him. This gentleness was most
obvious in his dealings with moderate offenders – I mean by
'moderate' those who did no great harm to others. But if he
discovered men going so far as to utter blasphemies against
the Lord Himself, he punished them by exile, or restricted
their movements to a circumscribed area, or kept them in
close confinement in prison, and he used to bind himself by
secret oaths never to release them.

I once remarked that he would not find it easy to keep this
resolve, and he understood me to mean that that was the
only way he could keep evil-doers in check. For a few
days, anyhow, he stood by his original decision – righteous

indignation was still fresh in his mind – but as soon as his anger began to die (the inevitable result of hearing someone praise his kindness, or speak highly of some predecessor of his for the same virtue), he immediately recalled the culprits in prison. He burst into tears, quite at a loss how to deal best with them. He asked for my advice on such a problem, and I suggested that it was better to err on the side of humanity. He did so, too, appeasing God in some other way.

In all my past experience, I have never seen a man more sensitive to the feelings of others. In my opinion, none of the present generation can compare with him in that respect. What is more, I know of nobody more generous, nor one who in his behaviour more resembled the ideal emperor. He was persuaded that his power had been inherited for this very purpose, that he might exhibit these qualities. Any day, therefore, that passed without some kindly deed on his part, any day in which he did not exercise in some way his generous instincts, marked a failure to fulfil his duties as a sovereign. Nor did he sow the seeds of well-doing in what I may call *fertile* hearts, in order to reap the harvest of gratitude at once, and certainly the recipients were not more eager to show forth the fruits of thankfulness than he to sow 'the earth, rich-clodded and fat'.[1]

For the sake of those who appreciate such anecdotes, I will give a brief example of this characteristic virtue. A certain man was caught stealing military funds, and was condemned to pay a heavy fine, far beyond his means. He was actually one of the moneyed class and a nobleman. The collector of fines was unrelenting in his demands, for the imperial treasury, as well as the public funds, was concerned in the case. The debtor thereupon demanded an audience of the emperor, with the idea of getting him to pass judgement in his favour. The public tribunal would thus be prevented from enforcing the verdict against him. Both parties to the suit were granted

1. Homeric epithets (cf. *Odyssey*, ii, 328, and v, 34).

the right of appeal to Constantine, and the trial attracted a
large audience in court. I was there myself, in the important
role of secretary, to record the decisions of Themis.[1] When
the two parties came into court, the person who had committed the theft – or apparently had done so – defended himself in a straightforward and most pathetic manner. He
pleaded that restitution to the public funds should be made
from his own personal property alone: he did not want to
leave the obligation to meet debts incurred by himself as a
heritage to his children. At this point he began to strip off his
clothes, as if he could meet his liabilities in only one way – by
divesting himself of all his possessions.

Here Constantine interrupted him, his eyes full of tears.
'Wait, my dear fellow! Surely you would be ashamed to
bring dishonour on your family? You mustn't reduce yourself to such sudden and extreme poverty that even food and
clothing depend on others' generosity!' – 'But, Sir,' replied
the man, 'with all the good will in the world, I could not
possibly provide the money they ask for.' And the emperor's
answer to this? 'If someone were to pay off a part of this
debt, would you be satisfied that justice had been done?' –
'It would be a godsend,' said the other, 'but, so far as I can
see, no angel or divine being has come down from heaven to
watch over human justice and busy itself with the affairs of
this world's cities.' – 'Never mind,' answered Constantine,
'I will act the part and relieve you of a third of the debt.'

At these words the nobleman could restrain himself no
longer, but fell on his knees on the ground and almost expired
with joy. Constantine, deeply impressed by his gratitude,
went on: 'I will do more. I will pay off two-thirds.' And
then, before the other could really understand what he had
said, he added: 'And the rest!' The debtor had never dreamed
that the emperor could be so generous, and now, all his

1. In the Homeric poems Themis is the personification of Law and
Justice.

245

worries solved, like a man who has won a great victory, he clothed himself in his finest robes and with a garland on his head offered thanksgiving to God.

I could, if I wished, tell you other anecdotes of this sort about Constantine. There are things which a historian would probably reject, but which a really convincing orator would not disdain to use as the legitimate material for a panegyric. I will give a few examples. The emperor devoted some time to amusements, and while to other men 'amusement', however they regarded it, had only one connotation, to him it was a serious business, invested with dignity. If he wished to make a grove, or to fence a park, or to flatten a race-course, it was not sufficient to carry out the plan as he had first conceived it. New ideas at once occurred to him. As some men covered the meadows with soil, others were fencing them round (all with the greatest expedition); vines and trees were rooted up, but others immediately took their place, already loaded with fruit.

How was it done? Well, suppose the emperor wanted to transform a barren plain into a fertile, productive field. No time was lost. Trees which were growing elsewhere were transported to the plain, complete with their fruit, and planted in the earth there; clods of soil covered with grass, brought from mountain groves, were spread all over it. And if grass-hoppers were not soon chirruping among his blossoming trees, if nightingales were not soon singing everywhere in his grove, Constantine was a very disappointed man. He took the thing seriously and it was not long before he was enjoying all kinds of sounds to his heart's content.

These habits and the trouble they involved seem, to me at least, perhaps unworthy of a 'counsellor, one to whom the guidance of the people has been entrusted, one who has so many cares', to quote the poetic language of Calliope.[1] Another man, however, seeing the beauty of his works, may

1. The Muse of Epic Poetry. Psellus quotes Homer, *Iliad*, ii, 24-5.

admire the emperor for their magnificence, and he will use
every argument he can think of to persuade you that Constantine showed extraordinary acumen in dividing his life
between business and pleasure, so that neither interfered with
the other. No embellishments, he thought, were necessary
for the serious side of his life – that was already endowed with
a peculiar beauty of its own – but the pleasure he invested
with a most gracious charm, or rather with a rare dignity.
And as for his acumen, that was proved by the profits he made;
by the clever ways in which he saved labour; by the successful
and yet economical basis on which he ran his estates; by the
way he produced things from nothing, with their qualities
already developed, like the Creator in the beginning of the
world; by the way he forestalled the seasons in the development of his crops; by the ingenious inventions which enabled him to dispense with farm-workers; by the miracles of
improvisation he performed, so wonderful that most people
could not believe their own eyes when they saw a field today,
where yesterday they had seen a flat plain, and two days ago a
hill.

When I make statements like this, I am using my arts of
rhetoric and persuasion only to a minimum degree. If one
were willing to bring into play the *full* force of one's powers of
argument, it would be possible to convince any intelligent
audience of anything. To me, however, such feats are not to
be commended – I loathe the clever dialectic that perverts
the truth.

My object in this history is to stick to the truth, and in my
opinion these trifles are absolutely inconsistent with Constantine's good qualities. So was his puerile infatuation for an
extremely callow and foolish youth who, a year before, had
never used a pen and ink, a guttersnipe promoted to the
centre of an empire's government. Such an influence did this
scoundrel exert over Constantine that he almost put in his
hands supreme power. He used to call him 'his sweet boy',

and made him a leading member of the Senate. The 'sweet boy' was in reality a thorough rascal and good-for-nothing, but the emperor looked upon his every word and deed as divinely inspired. I will explain the reason for this sudden affection and for the youth's promotion, but first I must go back to events that happened before he obtained this power.

When Constantine acceded to the throne, he thought the time had come for a rest, like a man who has reached harbour after a long sea-voyage. So he handed over the administration of the Empire to someone else. The gentleman in question was of noble birth, a first-class scholar, a practised and witty speaker in all departments of oratory, and an experienced politician.[1] In addition to his study of rhetoric (an art on which he conferred greater distinction because of his unusual powers of persuasion) he had applied himself to civil law. This versatility enabled him to express in clear language the difficult points of legal interpretation. He had the ability to shed new light on any given law. Moreover, Providence had endowed him with an intelligence that was remarkably practical, with the result that he was most admirably adapted, by training and nature, to the intricate task of conducting public affairs. Although an ardent student of all branches of rhetoric, he devoted himself to forensic oratory in particular. When delivering a public speech, he cultivated a style both elegant and pure Attic, but in everyday business he spoke simply, in the direct language of the ordinary man. He had a distinguished presence and a fine figure; his voice, too, lent him dignity, for it had resonance and clarity – qualities that were much in evidence when he read the imperial decrees from the balcony in the palace.

The emperor, having entrusted his duties to this excellent man, indulged in some quiet recreation – a natural reaction

1. Constantine Lichudes, who was promoted to the high office of *protovestiarius* as successor to Michael Cerularius. The latter had become patriarch in 1043.

for a mariner who had but lately escaped a storm at sea and who was still spitting out the brine. Meanwhile affairs prospered, or were changing for the better, and his vice-regent gradually became more prominent, until he was playing the leading role in the state. Then the emperor became jealous. He was unable to bear the thought that power had been transferred to someone else. He wished to control matters himself, not that the Empire might be more efficiently governed, but in order to have his own way. At the moment he was nothing better than a puppet, and every time he tried to follow the example of his predecessors, his powerful minister restrained him.

I recognized what was going on – there were certain indications – and I warned the gentleman of the emperor's secret intentions. He, being a man of spirit, was by no means inclined to relax his hold, nor to hand over the reins to his master. With philosophic detachment, he remarked that he would not voluntarily stand by and watch the emperor crash, but, when he did climb down from the chariot and resign the whip, he would not envy Constantine his new position.

After one stormy scene the latter deprived him of his vice-regal power and turned a deaf ear to all remonstrance. One might, of course, argue that this act was to his credit. One could assert that the emperor was a highly intelligent man himself, quite capable of sustaining on his own shoulders the whole burden of government and in need of no outside assistance. Anyhow, he deposed him. But, by the will of God, he was promoted to a position even more important – no other than that of Interpreter of the Mysteries and of High Priest in the Church of St Sophia.[1] The story of that elevation I will tell in more detail later in my history.

These acts are of doubtful interpretation – it depends on your point of view – but there was nothing at all moderate about certain other activities which I propose to speak about:

1. Lichudes was made patriarch by Isaac Comnenus in 1059.

he put his whole heart and soul into them. It was typical of the man, for instance, that, where he loved, his love knew no bounds; and if he was angry with someone, he would recount his troubles most pathetically and with more than common bitterness, even letting his imagination run away with him. On the other hand, it was incredible how affectionate he could be, if he liked.

Again, when the Empress Zoe departed this life, in extreme old age, he was completely heart-broken at the loss. Not only did he mourn her and shed tears at her tomb and propitiate Heaven on her behalf, but he even wished to pay her divine honours. One of the little columns that surrounded her burial-place became somewhat moist in a spot where the precious metal had cracked (it was plated with silver) and by some trick of nature a mushroom sprang up there. At this phenomenon Constantine was like a man inspired and he proclaimed loudly in the palace that the Lord had worked a miracle at the empress's tomb, so that all men might know that her soul was numbered with the angels. Everyone knew, of course, what had really happened, but they all supported him in his ardent belief, some through fear and others because they saw in the lie some opportunity for enriching themselves.

Such was his attitude to Zoe, but his sister Helena's death passed almost unnoticed, and mention of it had not the least effect on him. If his other sister (the one about whom I wrote earlier in the history) had gone before him, he would have been equally unperturbed.

In this catalogue of the emperor's foolish excesses, I now come to the worst example of all – the building of the Church of St George the Martyr.[1] Constantine pulled down and completely destroyed the original church; the present one was erected on the site of its ruins. The first architect did not plan very well, and there is no need for me to write of the old

1. The Church of St George of Mangana.

building here, but it appears that it would have been of no
great dimensions, if the preliminary plans had been carried
out, for the foundations were moderate in extent and the rest
of the building proportionate, while the height was by no
means outstanding. However, as time went by, Constantine
was fired by an ambition to rival all the other buildings that
had ever been erected and to surpass them altogether. So the
area of the church and its precincts was much enlarged, and
the old foundations were raised and strengthened, or else sunk
deeper. On these latter, bigger and more ornate pillars were
set up. Everything was done on a more artistic scale, with
gold-leaf on the roof and precious green stones let into the
floor or encrusted in the walls. And these stones, set one above
the other, in patterns of the same hue or in designs of alternate
colours, looked like flowers. And as for the gold, it flowed
from the public treasury like a stream bubbling up from
inexhaustible springs.

The church was not yet finished, however, and once again
the whole plan was altered and new ideas incorporated in its
construction. The symmetrical arrangement of the stones
was broken up, the walls pulled down, and everything levelled
with the ground. And the reason for it? Constantine's efforts
to rival other churches had not met with the complete success
he hoped for: one church, above all, remained unsurpassed.[1]
So the foundations of another wall were laid and an exact
circle described with the third church in its centre (I must
admit that it certainly was more artistic). The whole conception was on a magnificent and lofty scale. The edifice itself
was decorated with golden stars throughout, like the vault of
heaven, but whereas the real heaven is adorned with its golden
stars only at intervals, the surface of this one was entirely
covered with gold, issuing forth from its centre as if in a never-
ending stream. On all sides there were buildings, some completely, others half surrounded by cloisters. The ground

1. St Sophia.

everywhere was levelled, like a race-course, stretching farther
than the eye could see, its bounds out of sight. Then came a
second circle of buildings, bigger than the first, and lawns full
of flowers, some on the circumference, others down the
centre. There were fountains which filled basins of water;
gardens, some hanging, others sloping down to the level
ground; a bath that was beautiful beyond description. To
criticize the enormous size of the church was impossible,
so dazzling was its loveliness. Beauty pervaded every part of
the vast creation, so that one could only wish it were even
greater and its gracefulness spread over an area still wider.
And as for the lawns that were bounded by the outer wall,
they were so numerous that it was difficult to see them in one
sweeping glance: even the mind could scarcely grasp their
extent.

It was not merely the exceptional beauty of the whole, composed as it was of most beautiful parts, but just as much the
individual details that attracted the spectator's attention, and,
although he could enjoy to his heart's content all its charms,
it was impossible to find one that palled. Every part of it took
the eye, and, what is more wonderful, even when you gazed
on the loveliest part of all, some small detail would delight
you as a fresh discovery. To attempt to place its various merits
in any order of preference was useless for, when all the parts
were so lovely, even the least attractive could not fail to give
pleasure inimitable. Its every detail excited the greatest admiration. People marvelled at the size of the church, its
beautiful symmetry, the harmony of its parts, the variety and
rhythm of its loveliness, the streams of water, the encircling
wall, the lawns covered with flowers, the dewy grass, always
sprinkled with moisture, the shade under the trees, the
gracefulness of the bath. It was as if a pilgrimage had ended,
and here was the vision perfect and unparalleled.

Yet to Constantine all this was but the prelude to the future.
There were new miracles to be devised, fresh additions to be

made. He lived in a dreamland, where past achievement, however won, however acclaimed, seemed to him at once despicable, and he neglected his masterpiece. But he had secret ambitions. These were his new incentives: it was they that fired him with a desire for paths hitherto untrodden.

He was moody and inconsistent, but he had one object above all others: to make his country great and famous. I must admit that in this respect he was not altogether unsuccessful, for the boundaries of the Empire were much extended in the east, and a considerable part of Armenia was annexed. Certain kings of that country were deposed and forced to acknowledge Roman suzerainty. On the other hand, when expediency demanded that he should address other rulers in terms of extreme arrogance, he dispatched envoys to them with letters that were abject, quite unworthy of an emperor – doubtless because he wished to win their friendship.

In the case of the Sultan of Egypt, for example, he was far too conciliatory – deliberately so, to all appearances – and the Sultan flattered himself because of Constantine's humility. Like a wrestler who is losing a fight, he changed his tactics. Instead of allowing his opponent to dictate the strategy of the contest, he introduced grips of his own – and won. He was proud of it too. Many a time the emperor entrusted to me secret dispatches and ordered me to write them for him (he recognized my patriotism and my love for the Romans), suggesting that I should voluntarily humiliate himself and glorify the Egyptian. Nevertheless, I conveyed exactly the opposite impression by subtle allusion: what I wrote had one meaning for Constantine and another for the Sultan. I had sly digs at the latter and hurt his dignity without being too overt. And that is why letters to the Egyptian were in future dictated by the emperor himself, my own efforts being ambiguous. Writing on states of bodily health, Hippocrates the Coan[1]

1. The well-known Greek physician and contemporary of Socrates.

points out that, when they have developed to their fullest extent, it is impossible for them to remain quiescent, owing to the constant changes going on in the body: they must, therefore, enter on a decline. Now Constantine did not suffer that experience himself, but he made his friends do so. He would quietly advance them to high office, then suddenly cast them down, his whole attitude completely altered. It is a fact, though, that some of them were reinstated in their former positions. It was all a gamble.

THE STORY OF PSELLUS'S TONSURE

The story I am about to tell will explain why I adopted the life of a monk. Most people have expressed astonishment that I should hurriedly abandon the brilliant reputation so painfully acquired, just at the moment when I had overcome the jealous machinations of my rivals, and turn to the Church. The change was due partly to an innate desire which I had experienced from my earliest years, a deep love for the meditative life, and partly to the complete metamorphosis in political affairs. The emperor's fickleness alarmed me. He was like a soldier in war, striking out at his foes indiscriminately. In order to trace the whole story, however, I will explain what happened from the very beginning.

Many persons had claims on my friendship, but two men in particular.[1] They came from other countries and migrated to our great capital. For these two I had the deepest affection. The reason for our mutual attachment was an interest in learning. They were both much older than I, and, lest I should be accused of perverting the truth, I must admit that, while they loved philosophy, I was more advanced in my studies.

1. John Xiphilinus, a native of Trebizond, who had been appointed Professor of Law (*Nomophylax*) in the University of Constantinople reorganized in 1045, and probably John Mauropous, a native of Paphlagonia, who was Psellus's old teacher.

When they met me, each of them saw in me something of a kindred spirit, and I, no less, recognized my own enthusiasms mirrored in them. We were complementary one to the other. Just as my studies were more advanced, so, if I may be allowed to say it, was my spiritual progress. My position at court, moreover, was higher than theirs. Since I could not bear to be separated from them in any way, I at once introduced one of them to the emperor. The other, who was not so willing to approach the sovereign, was presented later.

When we were all admitted to the imperial circle and enjoyed to the full what men call 'high life', we naturally got to know how affairs were conducted, and we were not very favourably impressed by this outward splendour. However, each of us was afraid to express his feelings: each waited for a suitable opportunity before revealing his inmost thoughts. The primary cause of our mutual revelations was provided by the emperor himself. It was he who set in motion the chariot of State, and of those who rode in it most were thrown overboard or struck down by him. As we, too, were aboard, there was every reason why we should fear some great jolt on the wheel: he might jerk us off, as well as the rest, for we were not very firmly seated.

Such was the reason for our common decision – it was the emperor's own character that made us choose the monastic life. Having once arrived at the same conclusion, each of us read the other's thoughts. We were agreed, therefore, on the action to be taken and we made an everlasting covenant, but seeing that any immediate or sudden alteration of status on the part of all together would be necessarily out of the question, we postponed it for the present. Nevertheless, we bound ourselves by solemn oaths to follow the example of the first one to become a monk.

First to lead along the path to God was he on whom Fortune had smiled most favourably. True to his character, having once made a decision on solid grounds and having once determined to serve God, he brought forward a pretext for his conversion. He pleaded ill-health. Bit by bit, with much panting and puffing, he informed the emperor of his trouble, and begged to be allowed to go. Constantine was much concerned over the matter, but he gave his permission. It grieved him exceedingly to lose so soon a man of such qualities.

The outcome of this interview reacted instantly on me. I could neither sleep nor rest because of it, and it was equally difficult to wait patiently for my own opportunity to go. I visited my friend and with many tears of protestation I promised that I would follow his example forthwith. And he, once again with a feigned excuse – this time that his health had miraculously improved since he had donned the monkish habit – without more ado retired to the holy monastery on Mount Olympus.

I decided to imitate him exactly and alleged, by way of excuse, that I was suffering from liver trouble and serious heartburn. I pretended to be delirious and talked to myself, as though the business of everyday life was too much for me. I went dumb and made signs with my fingers that I desired tonsuration. Messages soon reached the emperor that I was out of my senses. He was told that I was on the point of dying, that I was heartbroken by the terrible disaster that had overtaken me, but that whenever I did recover my wits, I longed for the chance to enter Holy Church. At the news of my 'illness' Constantine was greatly upset, far more than my position deserved. His first concern was that my life was in danger – a prospect that filled him with consternation and called forth bitter laments. The thought that he was about to lose me particularly worried him, for he loved my conversation immensely. There is no reason, surely, why I should not admit it. Perhaps I may be permitted to speak with some little pride of my own resourcefulness in dealing with him. My

life, as far as possible, was dedicated to the pursuit of philosophy, but I carefully accommodated myself to his every
mood. He was a man who soon tired of his enthusiasms. He
liked change – in musical parlance, he alternated the highest
treble with the deepest bass; sometimes he struck a chord of
both together. There were certain occasions, therefore, when I
would discourse to him in philosophic vein on the First Cause,
on the Universal Good, on Virtue, on the Soul. I would prove
to him how the soul can be visible in the body, and again,
how it can float above the body, like a cork, but still attached
to it; this phenomenon I compared to some object suspended
in the air, balancing itself lightly on the wing, relying entirely
on its own strength and altogether unaffected by the weight
of the bond that ties it to something else below it.[1] Then,
when I saw that he was becoming bored with these lectures,
and that he wanted to change the subject to something more
to his own taste, I would turn to the Muse of Rhetoric and
introduce him to another aspect of Excellence, delighting him
with word-harmonies and rhythmic cadences, composition
and figures of speech (which lend the art its peculiar force).
The function of Rhetoric is not merely to deceive by persuasive argument, or to deck itself out with ambiguous
sentiments: it is an exact science. On the one hand, it expresses
philosophic ideas; on the other, by means of its flowery
imagery, it beautifies them. The listener is equally charmed by
both. Rhetoric teaches a man to think clearly, undisturbed by
the *associations* of words; to classify, to analyse, to make one's
meaning plain without undue fuss. Its peculiar excellence
lies in its freedom from confusion, its clarity, the way it suits
itself to time or to circumstance, even when a man uses
simple diction, without recourse to periods or long sentences.
By dwelling on all these points I inspired him to a love of the
art. But if I perceived that he was growing weary, I would
alter my tactics and pretend that my memory was failing, or

1. A neo-platonic theory.

that my fire, after the manner of Hermogenes' Heat,[1] had
almost burnt itself out through its own excess.

Constantine, recalling these conversations, was by no means
willing to let me go to a monastery. To begin with, in his
eagerness to stop my design he sent me letters and deputations
of noblemen. He assured me that I would soon recover my
health, and promised me a brilliant future. Even to this day
I cannot read those letters without shedding tears, so great was
the affection he displayed in them. He called me 'the apple of
his eye', 'the comfort of his soul', 'his heart and light and life'.
He begged me not to 'leave him in darkness'. Despite this
I was deaf to all entreaties, for my friend, who had preceded me to the monastery, meant more to me than Constantine's letters. So, as gentle persuasion had failed, he
abandoned the fox for the lion, and brandished the big stick.
He swore that he would consign me, and my fellow-conspirators, to the flames with no more ado: he would bring
utter disaster, not only on myself, but on all my family.

I heard these threats with composure – they were an omen
of better things to come – and took refuge in the harbour of
Holy Church. There I surrendered that which covered my
head, and cut myself off from the life of this world. When he
heard that I had undergone the ceremony (of tonsuration), he
did not bear me a grudge. In fact, he sent me other messages,
of quite a different tenor, in which he congratulated me on
preferring the spiritual life and actually encouraged me in my
resolve. He criticized the courtier's brilliant coloured robes,
and praised the rough habit I was now wearing; he crowned
me with the victor's diadem – all because I had risen superior
to every enticement.

1. Hermogenes of Tarsus (*c.* A.D. 150) was a celebrated sophist and
rhetorician. He acquired a great reputation as an orator in his youth,
but apparently was afflicted with some disease that rendered him totally
unfit mentally, and although he lived to a great age he did nothing
worthy of note after he was twenty-five.

But enough about myself, for it was not my wish to figure in this history. Unfortunately, my plans were upset by these digressions. What compelled me to adopt a monastic life was the emperor's inconstancy. We were afraid of his whims, and therefore we preferred a monk's life to the inferior existence of a courtier, the untroubled calm of the Church to the confusion and disorder of the Palace.

Now that the emperor was deprived of our comforting presence, and now that he no longer had the lyre of rhetoric to charm him, he took refuge again in worldly pleasures. For instance, in the middle of a park, teeming with all kinds of fruit, he had a deep pond made. It was so constructed that the edge of it was level with the surrounding earth. Water was then directed into it by channels. The result was that, unless someone knew beforehand that the ground in the middle of the park had been excavated, he would walk about unsuspectingly to gather apples or pears, and fall into the pond. Getting into deep water he would bob up to the surface and swim for it – much to the amusement of our emperor. However, the pond was not made only for fun, and a pleasure-house was built near it, in most beautiful surroundings. Here Constantine would bathe several times a day in the warm water, and it was while going in and out on one of these occasions that he caught a chill. At the time he did not notice it, and, although not much troubled by it at first, he was affected later: the poison spread to his vital organs and attacked his lungs.

He thought he was going to die and lay on his bed like an expiring ox that has just been sacrificed. Yet he held no consultation with the Empress Theodora about a successor.[1]

1. Theodora had been in retirement and took no interest in state affairs. Her advisers showed great determination and energy at this crisis (Cedrenus, 791C, p. 610). Constantine consulted the leading men of his government and together they decided that the new emperor should be one Nicephorus, governor of Bulgaria. Theodora's faction

Instead he kept his designs secret and, without any reference to her, considered by himself who was to be the next occupant of the throne. Such an inquiry, of course, could not remain a secret, and Theodora was told of it. She at once embarked on one of the imperial galleys with her leading advisers, and, like a traveller returning home from a stormy voyage, took refuge in the courts of the palace. Having arrived she won over to her side the whole of the imperial bodyguard. There were certain factors that made her influence with them all-powerful: the fact that she had been 'born in the purple'; her gentle character; the sad circumstances of her former life. The emperor was seriously perturbed by this news and he became more ill than ever, but as a restoration to normal health and the making of any sensible plans were equally out of the question now, he plunged once more into deep meditation. His eyes closed; his mind and tongue wandered. He did rally for a brief interval, enough to realize the seriousness of his condition. Then he died, cursing his fate.[1]

So passed the Emperor Constantine Monomachus, after a reign of twelve years. In public life he had, for the most part, covered himself with glory; in his private habits, too, he had set a fine example to those who cultivate the good life. I say this, because apart from his quick temper, he was in other respects the mildest of men. His history appears to be somewhat inconsistent, on account of his moodiness: the changes in himself and the various phases of his character are reflected in the record of his reign. Mine is a true record, not a rhetorical exercise – a sympathetic picture of the emperor as he really was.

---

quickly cut short their plan; Nicephorus was detained at Salonica and deported.

1. He died on 11 January 1055 and was buried in the monastery of Mangana beside Sclerena.

THEODORA

THE REIGN OF THE EMPRESS THEODORA

WHEN he died, supreme power passed into the hands of
Theodora, the daughter of Constantine (VIII). Everybody
expected that she would entrust the government to one of
the leading noblemen, but, contrary to all belief and opinion,
she took on her own shoulders the duties of a Roman sovereign. The truth is, she knew that there is no man on earth so
ungrateful as one who finds himself emperor through the
generosity of someone else; his greatest benefactor, indeed, is
the last person to whom he shows his indebtedness. She had
good reason to believe this, not only from her own experience
but from that of her immediate predecessor, and she had before
her examples of it in the case of her sister. She had no desire,
then, to establish another on the throne. The Empire was hers
alone – she inherited it – and she superintended all the affairs
of State in person. She was supported in this resolution by her
retinue and palace officials, men who from long experience
understood imperial policy and knew how the administration
of the Empire functioned.

Convinced that she was doing what was right, the empress
proceeded to use her authority in all matters of government,
quite openly. Without the slightest embarrassment she assumed the duties of a man and she abandoned all pretence of
acting through her ministers. She herself appointed her
officials, dispensed justice from her throne with due solemnity, exercised her vote in the courts of law, issued decrees,
sometimes in writing, sometimes by word of mouth. She gave
orders, and her manner did not always show consideration

for the feelings of her subjects, for she was sometimes more than a little abrupt.

Now it was the custom among the Romans, at the accession of new emperors, that honours should be distributed both to civilians and to the soldiers, but this empress, while ignoring precedent, persuaded the people that she had not really broken with tradition. It was, in fact, generally admitted that this was not her first introduction to the government of the Empire. She was not succeeding to the throne now, but had inherited it long ago from her father, only to see it snatched away by outside powers; now she was again assuming her natural and rightful heritage. This explanation seemed plausible enough, and, although the people were ready to complain before, they were satisfied now.

Everyone was agreed that for the Roman Empire to be governed by a woman, instead of a man, was improper, and even if the people did not think so, it certainly seemed that they did. But if one removes this single objection, one must say that in everything else the Empire prospered and its glory increased. No conspiracy whatever was formed against the government:[1] nobody held in contempt the proclamations and orders issued by it. Throughout the Empire the seasons of the year went well, and the harvest was abundant. No Roman territory was plundered by marauding barbarians, and there was no open warfare. No section of the State was discontented; justice was maintained everywhere.

Most people expected her to live a long life, past the normal span. Well they might, for her body was in no way bent despite her exceptional height, and her mental powers were quite equal to more than usually long spells of work or of conversation. To some problems she would devote study before discussing them, but there were other occasions when she

1. Nevertheless, a revolt was imminent. Not only was Cerularius plotting, but Theodora's own parsimony alienated the sympathy of the people.

considered them without any previous deliberation, and her facility of expression enabled her perfectly to explain what she meant.

Nevertheless, the situation called for an energetic man, one who understood the functions of government, one thoroughly conversant with the imperial rescripts, but none of Theodora's courtiers was entrusted with this responsibility. She knew his downfall would quickly be brought about, for his companions at court would soon become jealous. Her search for the best man in the Senate resulted in an unfortunate choice; the person she placed at the head of affairs was not one with long-standing qualifications in the realm of literature or of oratory. His recommendations comprised an ability to hold his tongue and keep his eyes fixed on the ground, a certain gaucherie in society, a complete lack of all the other graces that normally characterize a politician. This was the man whom she promoted to the most important place in the state.[1] It is a fact, of course, that the emperors allot the higher offices to men whose fidelity is least likely to waver, provided that they are dignified in appearance, rather than to others who are eloquent and highly cultured individuals with an inherited aptitude for politics. In the case of this man, it has to be allowed that he did have a certain facility in speaking, but his oratory owed more to gestures than words, for, although he used neither tongue nor hand with any adroitness, he undoubtedly was more successful with the latter – indeed, it was the one thing in which he showed any natural ability, for, if he tried to demonstrate his knowledge in words, the impression produced in his audience was just the opposite of what he intended – his style was so crabbed and obscure.

At any rate, this man took upon his shoulders the burden of imperial administration. Most people found him intolerable, for he was, as I have said, completely lacking in political

1. Leo Paraspondylus, the *protosyncellus* (the patriarch's confidential adviser). Psellus is biased in his judgement of him.

temperament. There was nothing very gracious about him: his conversation in society was awkward, and invariably, in whatever company he happened to be, he gave the impression of habitual rudeness. He avoided all intercourse with others and made himself generally unpopular because of his fits of rage and ill-humour. He indulged in these displays of temper when someone failed to go straight to the point of his subject and made remarks by way of preface. Nobody was willing to approach him, unless compelled by absolute necessity. I myself admire the inflexibility of such a mind, but its proper place, in my opinion, lies not in time, but in eternity; not in this present life, but in the existence hereafter. The absolutely unemotional and the completely inexorable, I believe, are above all the spheres, outside the circumference of the universe. But human life, just because it is lived in the wider circle of society, is better fitted to encounter the vicissitudes of its present existence – in other words, the emotional element in the soul reacts harmoniously to the physical stimuli in the body.

According to my observations, I distinguish three kinds of soul, each having a character of its own. The first type is that which lives in isolation, by itself, freed from the body, unbending and altogether incapable of compromise; the other two I have examined in the light of their coexistence with the body. For instance, if the soul, despite the deep and numerous emotions to which it is subject, chooses to live the life of moderation, as though it were the exact centre of a circle, then it brings into being the man who plays his part in public affairs. Such a soul is neither really divine nor entirely concerned with the apprehension of spiritual things, nor yet over-prone to indulge the body, nor subject to passion. On the other hand, if the soul turns aside from this middle course and marches on the path that leads to low, base passions, then it produces the voluptuous and the sensual man. Suppose then that someone were able to step outside the bounds of all

things pertaining to the body, and take up his position at the
height of spiritual perfection, what would he have in common with the world around him? 'I have put off my tunic,'
says the Scripture, 'and how shall I put it on again?'[1] By all
means let him go up his high and lofty mountain: let him
stand with the angels, so that unearthly light may be shed
upon him: let him separate himself from men and avoid their
society. No one on earth has ever triumphed over the force
of nature to such an extent, but, if this imaginary person were
by any chance entrusted with the direction of state affairs,
I would counsel him to take matters in hand like a man dealing with his fellow-men, not to pretend that he was endowed
with the unerring straightness of a ruler, for not all have been
made equally perfect. If he renounces all deviation from the
path of moral rectitude, it naturally follows that he at once
rejects also those who traverse the crooked path.

This will explain why the gentleman I was talking about,
by acting the philosopher in matters that were not the proper
object of philosophy, earned the reputation, not of being a
philosopher, but a mimic of one. However, in order to consider all aspects of the man, it has to be allowed that he was
quite different in private life, for he lived on a magnificent,
sumptuous scale, was generous and incorruptible. If someone
dining with him assumed a smiling gaiety and, to quote from
the poet, 'stretched forth his hands to the food that was
ready',[2] he would eat with more gusto than usual, chatter
away with his guest, and follow his mood with all kinds of
pleasantry. Afterwards he would change again, returning to
his normal habits, in no way modified. Nobody else, if he
had his way, would share with him the duties of government
– but that word reminds me: I must digress once more and
introduce myself again to this history.

Not long before Theodora's accession, I had adopted the

1. Septuagint, Song of Songs, v, 3.
2. Homer, *Odyssey*, i, 149.

monk's cowl. Owing to the fact that I took this step shortly before Monomachus died, many persons surmised that I had previous knowledge of the event. According to them, I knew he was going to die and for this reason changed my manner of life. It is a fact that most people give me credit for more learning than I possess. Because I have dabbled in geometry, they imagine that I am capable of measuring the whole heavens, and, since I have devoted a certain amount of study to the phenomena of the celestial sphere, they insist that I must also be acquainted with the phases, the obliquity of the ecliptic, full moons, cycles and epicycles. They even claim that I can predict the future, despite my repudiation of books written on these subjects.

Another thing in which I have been interested is Horoscopy, enough to learn something of the nonsense that derives from it. The truth is, my education was so wide and the questions of those who consulted me so diverse, that there is no science which I was not induced to study. Because of this interest in horoscopes, I find myself inevitably subjected to troublesome inquiries about them. That I have applied myself to the science in all its aspects I admit, but at the same time none of these studies, forbidden by the leaders of the Church, has been put to improper use. I know the theory about the lottery of Fortune and about a presiding Evil Genius, but I certainly do not believe that the positions or the appearance of stars affect what goes on in the sublunary world. To blazes with all those who tell us that there is a spiritual life, and who then declare that its direction lies in the hands of their new-fangled gods! These are the folk who deny the unity of human life, for while according to them life owes its origin and birth to the Creator in Heaven, and derives from Him alone, they also insist that the stars, which have no power of reasoning, are living beings, and they give them a dwelling-place in every part of the human body before it lives, grafting on to it, so to speak, the power of thought afterwards.

Nobody with any sense would find fault with a man who knew these theories, but gave them no credence. On the other hand, where a man rejects Christian Doctrine, and turns to such hypotheses, his studies are useless and may well be regretted. For my own part – and this is the truth – it was no scientific reason that made me give up these ideas, but rather was I restrained by some divine force. It is not a matter of logical argument – and I certainly pay no attention to other methods of proof. But the same cause which, in the case of greater and more learned scholars than I am, has brought them down to a level where they accept Hellenic culture, in my case exercises a compulsion upwards, to a sure faith in the truth of our Christian theology. If then my deeds have not always harmonized with what I profess, may I find mercy with the Mother of the Word, and with the Son born of no earthly father, with the sufferings He endured, with the crown of thorns about His Head, the reed and the hyssop, the Cross on which He stretched out His Hands, my pride and my glory!

But I must return to the original subject that I was discussing and carry on my narrative. As I was saying, shortly before the emperor's death I renounced the worldly life I had been living and became a monk. But when Theodora ascended the throne, she at once sent for me. After a tragic account of the treatment she had received at the hands of her brother-in-law, she told me of her own secret plans and encouraged me to visit her frequently. If I had any information I was on no account to conceal it from her. This was not the first occasion on which I had an interview with her. In fact, even during the lifetime of Monomachus, if she wished to write confidential dispatches or conduct any other private business, it was her habit to consult me about her letters and plans.

My visits, made at her invitation, excited jealousy, and, when those who had got there before me were unable to injure my reputation with malicious tales, they proceeded to criticize my monastic robes and the way I lived apart from the others. Theodora listened to their complaints and in future she was careful to treat them with the same friendly regard as myself. However, I saw how things stood, and my visits became less frequent, with the result that she again turned to me for advice. She reproached me for lack of initiative and accused me of neglecting her orders altogether.

This typifies her tenacity of purpose and the way she would set her heart on some course of action, regardless of consequences. The truth is, she had little faith in her own opinions, and this led her to fear for the Empire's future welfare. So she came to rely more on the counsel of others than on herself. There is no doubt that she had a great respect for the emperor who preceded her, even after his death. Not only did she keep alive the memory of his noble deeds, but no decision made by him, so far as she was concerned, could be looked on as worthless. Despite this determination to follow his example, she failed, with the result that most of his measures were rendered invalid. As a matter of fact, the person to whom she entrusted the general supervision of the government – the man I was speaking of just now – having failed to obtain high honours in the reign of the last emperor, and having been denied the privilege of standing beside him in council, as he always had done in the case of the sovereigns before him, grumbled at Constantine during his lifetime, and now that he was dead bore him malice for past slights. Of course, there was some justification for what he did, as well as for the attitude of the empress, and for the feelings of others who had been ill-disposed towards Monomachus. What was indefensible was the way she forgot that she was only a *temporary* dweller on this earth, and her failure to make proper provision for the future. Her councillors, moreover, should have impressed this on her, instead of imagining that she would live for ever, always at the same age, or even that she was freed from the influence of time altogether and had blossomed afresh, like some young plant. They thought their fortunes were secured for ever, refused to consider the appointment of an emperor, made no effort to ensure a smooth transfer of power. Surely no one could excuse, either in her or in them, such extreme and such disgraceful folly.

When I saw her actually installing certain persons in positions of authority in the Church, and explaining her actions in endless, wearisome discourse, I could contain myself no longer. I expressed my dissatisfaction in private, complaining of her behaviour to trusted friends. Her conduct surprised me, because I knew she was most careful in matters concerned with religion. Desire for absolute power had led her even to break the law: at all events, it altered her pious attitude towards Heavenly things, and she was not so inclined to be sympathetic as she had been before. Whether she was reverting to her real character, to show that her past life had been merely a sham, or whether this lack of sympathy was deliberately cultivated, to avoid being imposed on by her courtiers, or to discourage attempts to win her over by sudden outbursts of emotion, I am unable to say.

The Oecumenical Patriarch (the customary title of the Patriarch of Constantinople) was at that time Michael, the successor of the divine Alexius on the Holy Throne.[1] Although she had been most friendly to him in the time before she became empress, and had treated him with marked respect, once she was firmly established in power she abominated the man, refusing even to meet him. There was a reason for this: the patriarch was vexed because the Roman Empire was being governed by a woman. Characteristically he was filled with wrath at this state of affairs, and he spoke his mind freely. It is not improbable that she would have deposed him from his office, had her mortal life been somewhat prolonged.

The extremely generous persons who surpassed all bounds of liberality, with their munificent gifts, were not angels

1. Michael Cerularius.

carrying messages to her from God, but *men*, who imitated the
angelic beings in outward appearance, and at heart were hypo-
crites. I am referring to the Naziraeans of our time.¹ These
men model themselves on the Divine, or rather they have a
code of laws which is, superficially, based on the imitation
of the Divine. While still subject to the limitations of human
nature, they behave as though they were demi-gods among
us. For the other attributes of Divinity they affect utter contempt. There is no effort to harmonize the soul with Heavenly
things, no repression of the human desires, no attempt by the
use of oratory to hold in check some men and goad on others.
These things they regard as of minor importance. Some of
them utter prophecies with the assurance of an oracle,
solemnly declaring the will of God. Others profess to change
natural laws, cancelling some altogether and extending the
scope of others: they claim to make immortal the dissoluble
human body and to arrest the natural changes which affect
it. To prove these assertions they say that they always wear
armour, like the ancient Acarnanians,² and for long periods of
time walk on air – descending very rapidly when they smell
savoury meat on earth! I know their kind and I have often
seen them. Well, these were the men who led the empress
astray, telling her that she would live for ever, and through
their deceit she very nearly came to grief herself and brought
ruin on the whole Empire as well.

They predicted for her a life going on for centuries without
end. In fact, she was already nearing the day which Fate had
decreed should be her last. I ought not to use such an expression – what I mean is that she had nearly finished her life and

1. To the Byzantines 'Naziraean' was synonymous with 'monk'
(derived from Hebrew *nazir*, 'separate'). Psellus has nothing but contempt for these fighting monks.
2. Psellus knew his Thucydides well. We are told by the Greek historian that the Acarnanians, being semi-civilized, still went about armed
in his time (i, 5).

the end was at hand. As a matter of fact, she was assailed by a very terrible illness. Her excretory processes broke down, and this was followed by loss of appetite and vomiting. Later she was afflicted with violent diarrhoea, and an almost total evacuation of the intestines left her at death's door. Everyone (I am talking now of her intimate friends) despaired of her life, quite naturally, and they at once began to consider what was to become of the Empire and also of themselves. They started to make plans. I am not making this statement from hearsay, for I was present myself when these projects were discussed and made, seeing with my own eyes and hearing with my own ears how they played fast and loose with the Empire, like men playing at dice.

It was not yet midday, the empress was breathing with difficulty, and appeared to be on the point of dying. The councillors were gathered together round the throne, their leader in the midst, deciding whom they should elect as the new emperor in preference to all others, a man likely to favour themselves, one who would be reliable and would protect their own interests. It is not my purpose at the moment to describe the object of their choice, but I will say that the man chosen was pretty well the best candidate, except that he was the sort of person less qualified to rule than to be ruled by others. He was already in the autumn of his years, verging on old age, and his hair was completely grey.

This was the man, therefore, that they persuaded her to nominate as their future sovereign. There was no hesitation on her part and she at once crowned him as her successor. She lingered on for a little while, still as empress, and died four months before the year's end.[1] So Michael ascended the imperial throne, only to be deprived of power soon after. Before I enter on any description of him as a man, however, I will give a brief introduction to his reign.

1. Theodora died on 31 August 1056, at the age of seventy-six.

BOOK SEVEN

MICHAEL VI

ISAAC COMNENUS

1057-9

BEGINNING OF THE REIGN OF MICHAEL THE
AGED, WHO HELD POWER FOR ONE YEAR

APPARENTLY the last few emperors were convinced that they
were firmly established once the civil element acclaimed
them. Indeed, their close relations with these persons were
such that the emperors believed the throne was safely ensured
beyond all dispute if the civilians were well-disposed. Naturally, therefore, as soon as they took up the sceptre it was to
the civil party that they granted the right to speak in their
presence before all others. If they evinced pleasure, if they
uttered flattering speeches and gave vent to a little nonsensical
clap-trap, then the emperors needed no further assistance. It
was as if they had the sanction of God. Really, of course, their
power rested on three factors: the people, the Senate, and the
army. Yet while they minimized the influence of the military,
imperial favours were granted to the other two as soon as a
new sovereign acceded.

In the case of the aged Michael, the conferring of honours
surpassed the bounds of propriety. He promoted individuals,
not to the position immediately superior to that they already
occupied, but elevated them to the next rank and the one
above that. In fact, the emperor's courtiers had only to put
themselves forward as candidates for a fourth promotion and
he would readily consider their claims. Thereupon another,
standing at his other side and plucking at his other sleeve,

so to speak, would ask for and get a fifth. His generosity led
to a state of absolute chaos.

THE GENERALS' DEPUTATION TO THE
EMPEROR MICHAEL

When this came to the ears of the soldiers, and among them
those who held positions of command and were crack troops,[1]
they came to Byzantium too, with the object of winning
equal honours for themselves, or even greater ones. A day
was therefore fixed for them to have audience with the emperor and I myself was present on the occasion, standing
beside him. The men who came into his presence were noble
warriors, men of fine reputation. After bowing to him and
making the usual acclamation, they stood, at the emperor's
command, awaiting their turn. Now at this juncture he
should have taken them aside individually. He should have
begun his conversation with generous words, in a manner
worthy of his high rank.[2] Instead, he started by finding fault
with them *en bloc* – a mean thing to do. Then, having made
their leader stand forth in the centre of the group, together
with his second-in-command – Isaac Comnenus[3] was the chief
man in the deputation and Cecaumenos, from Colonus, was
the other – he poured out a torrent of abuse on Isaac. He

1. The deputation, headed by Catacalon Cecaumenos, Isaac Comnenus, Michael Burtzes, Constantine and John Ducas, met the emperor
on Easter Day, 1057.

2. According to Cedrenus (794, p. 615) Michael did meet them
privately and commended their services to the Empire, but obstinately
refused their demands.

3. The Comneni came originally from Comne, near Hadrianople,
and had estates in the Castamon district of Asia Minor. Isaac was the son
of Manuel Eroticus, a distinguished prefect under Basil II. He had
married the daughter of a king of Bulgaria and had a son who died
young and a daughter who became a nun some time after 1057. Both
Isaac and his brother John had already held high office.

charged him with all but losing Antioch and with corrupting
his army; he had shown no sign of gallantry or leadership;
on the contrary, he had levied the people's money for his own
use, and, instead of using his command to win glory, he had
made it a pretext for satisfying his personal greed. In the face
of these sudden blows Isaac stood transfixed. He had come expecting promotion; instead he had been grossly insulted.
When his fellow-generals tried to defend him, the emperor
forbade them even to speak. If he despised the others, he
should have considered Isaac, at least, worthy of an honour-
able hearing. Yet he, like the others, was denied that favour.

THE REVOLT OF COMNENUS

All this made an enormous impression on the soldiers, and
their rebellion against Michael dates from this interview.
Indeed, the effect produced by this tragic event on their morale was nothing less than shattering. Nevertheless, although
the seeds of disaffection were sowed there, no immediate
attempt was made to seize power. A second interview was
tried first, in the hope that the emperor might prove more
friendly.[1] But when they asked him for bread he offered them
stones; when they protested, even the stones were refused.
They were repelled and rejected. The others were all for immediate action – they were almost prepared to lay violent
hands upon him there and then, and to tear him down from
his throne – but Isaac restrained them. There was need, he said,
for wiser counsel. However, from that moment the conspiracy was afoot and they began the search for a leader, some
man capable of governing the Empire.[2]

1. Leo Paraspondylus tried to intercede for the generals, but without
success.
2. Psellus does not mention Bryennius and Hervé Francopullus. The
former, commander of the Macedonian army in Cappadocia, was denounced by one Opsaras, an agent of the emperor, and lost his eyes.

Despite Isaac's persistent refusal to press his own claims to the throne, and despite his assertion that all of them were equal to the task, it was unanimously decided that the honour was his. He was in fact pre-eminent, not only by birth but in his kingly appearance; his nobility of mind and firmness of character, too, were outstanding. One look at the man was enough to inspire respect. However, I must describe his qualities in a later chapter. After the conspirators had agreed on their aims, there was another brief encounter with the emperor and they all went away to their homes. By the early morning, however, when the sun was just rising, they were within easy call of one another. So, after waiting a few days, they assembled in one place[1] and concerted their plans. Even so, their deliberations were not completed before a gallant army was already flocking to their standard. A host of warriors joined them, adding fresh strength to their confidence. The news spread that a valiant general was the new emperor, and that he had won over to his side the most powerful families, persons whom they knew by name. Without the least hesitation recruits poured in, every man, like a good runner, trying to get there before his comrades.

Even before this time it had been the ambition of the military to subjugate the whole of the Roman Empire, to serve a soldier-emperor and break down the civil succession to the Principate, but hitherto these designs were kept secret. Their plans were cherished only in private – for the simple reason that nobody seemed competent to rule. Not even in their wildest dreams had they expected Isaac to entertain ambitions for sovereignty, because of the difficulties of such an enterprise. Now the position was altogether changed. They saw

---

Hervé was an Armenian and demanded the rank of *magister*; when Michael refused, he joined the Turks. The fate of these men caused the other generals to proclaim Isaac emperor without delay.

1. On the plain of Gunaria where, on 8 June 1057, Isaac was acclaimed emperor.

Isaac at the head of a revolutionary party; they saw him
personally taking decisions necessary to its success. The time
for compromise was now over. Without more ado men rallied
to his side, strongly equipped and provided for the exigencies
of war.[1]

Considering that this was the first time he had commanded
such an expedition, one must say that Isaac's conduct of the
revolt showed more wisdom than boldness. Being aware of
the supreme importance of great wealth in managing his
army, he began by barricading off all the roads into the city
and leaving an adequate guard at each obstruction. Permission to go in or out was refused unless Isaac himself had first
been informed and had already agreed to movement in either
direction. His next move was to exact the public taxes. This
was not done in any hurried or confused manner, but rolls
were drawn up, honest tax-gatherers appointed, and separate
entries made in the accounts, so that when he was officially
made emperor he might have accurate records of the revenues.
Now you will understand what I meant when I said that he
showed more prudence than audacity. And here we may note
another admirable provision. After dividing the great force
that had joined him into appropriate ranks, he set on one side
the braver men and soldiers known to be cool and steady
under fire. These men were then distributed among the various companies and regiments. Actually the segregated men
were in the majority, and the others proved themselves in no
way inferior to them in valour.

Isaac's first order was that they should keep to their own
separate groups and avoid any disorderly mingling and confusion. They were to advance in silence, preserving the ranks
and companies in which he had arranged them, and the same
discipline was to be observed when they encamped. Next he

1. The rebel H.Q. was at Nicaea. Isaac hoped that the enemy would
desert the emperor, but only the rank and file came over to him
(Cedrenus, 800B, p. 627).

settled the amount of rations required for the campaign by each soldier, and the equipment sufficient for a military expedition. Promotions were made, the higher ranks being assigned to the better soldiers and the lower to the rest. His own safety was made the special care of men chosen from his own family. So, with his bodyguard about him, he advanced fearlessly and again pitched camp. The nights he spent in ceaseless vigil over the affairs of State, while in the daytime his brilliant direction was more evident still. There was stern resolve in the manner of his advance, but since many things are wont to befall armies, and since most soldiers are more distinguished for boldness than for wisdom, Isaac refrained from disciplinary action against defaulters, at least for the moment. One look from him was enough to terrify them and a scowl on his face was as good as any corporal punishment.

Thus the army was strictly disciplined. Meanwhile he was already at the gates of the city. The emperor's jurisdiction was confined to Byzantium alone, yet he took no counter-measures to check his daring opponents, nor did his former advisers make any effort to stop the rebels. You would have believed no state of emergency existed at all. What is more, no attempt was made to pit against the enemy what forces were still left to the emperor. No action whatever was taken to break up the revolutionary army. Some of the court did indeed jerk Michael out of his apathy by insisting on the need for consultation and a good supply of money. They urged him to collect an army. A council was thereupon summoned, and besides some other public-spirited gentlemen – they were very numerous, but until that moment their advice had been completely disregarded – he also called in myself. He treated me like an adopted son and pretended, with the air of a man who has made a foolish error, that he had long thought of me as a boon companion.

THE VARIOUS COUNSELS PUT FORWARD TO
THE EMPEROR WITH REGARD TO THE
REBELLION

Well, I bore him no malice and my advice to him was to take the following three measures at once. I knew that there was a difference of opinion between himself and the patriarch, and I knew that the latter was angry with Michael. So my first counsel was this, that he should put an end, once and for all, to his quarrel with the patriarch and come to some common agreement with him, because his position in the present circumstances was particularly strong. Unless the emperor made quite sure of his adherence first, he was likely to join the rebel party in their attack. My second proposal was that an embassy should be dispatched to the enemy leader, with instructions to disband his forces: a reward should be promised him – a reasonable sum of money – and the prospect of further inducements later on. The embassy should moreover seek to undermine discipline in the enemy's camp and try to disorganize his army. To these I added a third suggestion, the most convincing of all and more cogent than the others, that he should mass the armies of the west, centralize whatever forces remained to him in one group, invoke the alliances concluded with the neighbouring barbarians, strengthen the mercenary army then in Byzantium, put them under the command of a brave general, build up an adequate corps of men for him, and everywhere resist the hordes set in motion against us. These proposals were actually accepted by the emperor.

THE DISPATCH OF THE ARMY AGAINST
ISAAC COMNENUS

Later, however, he rejected the first plan – and the disregarding of that alone was enough to cause his downfall – but he did apply himself to the second and third. Nevertheless, nothing was accomplished in respect of the second. As for the armies in the West, they were prepared in the most warlike fashion and reinforced by other allied forces.[1] So, after being divided up into companies and grouped by regiments, they faced the eastern armies not only well equipped but with confidence. The two sides were entrenched at no great distance from each other and the no-man's land between was quite small, but that space remained empty, for neither party sallied out to do battle. Clearly the emperor's men were more numerous, but the enemy had the advantage in discipline and strength, and – more important and still more astonishing – their army was coherent, with an unwavering belief in its leader, whereas in our camp there were gaps and empty places, when every day bodies of men deserted to the rebels. Moreover, our commander [2] – I need not mention his name – was divided in his loyalties; in fact, as I see it, he was biased against us.

We were therefore at a disadvantage in two respects, and, even before it was decided to make war, the attitude of our generals proved our undoing. The rank and file, on the other hand, together with what had been left of our own national army, were still unaware of their leader's vacillation. They faced the enemy, 'men of war and breathing courage',[3] as the poet says, ready with the finest weapons and all the best armour, both for offence and defence. So, with the war-cry on their lips, they gave rein to their chargers and bore down on the foe with irresistible force, and our right flank, having turned their left, pursued them afar.

When the rebel right flank saw what had happened, they made no attempt to hold their ground or face the emperor's

---

1. Commanded by Theodorus, a eunuch, and Aaron Ducas, brother-in-law of Comnenus. They crossed to Nicomedia and broke down the bridge over the River Sangares.
2. The eunuch Theodorus.   3. Homer, *Iliad*, iii, 8 ff.

troops roaring to the attack, but retired and dispersed at once. The truth is, they were afraid the victors might divert their attack, and, by relieving pressure on the routed left wing, bring the full force of their charge on to their own flank. So both right and left joined in the flight and victory clearly rested with the emperor. Firmly rooted in the centre, master of victors and vanquished alike, was the rebel leader. Some of our men saw him (they were Scyths from the Taurus region, and not more than four at that) and attacked him with spears, driving in on both flanks, but the iron shafts proved ineffective, for they missed him. Meanwhile he budged in neither direction, for as they pushed him with equal force this way and that, he remained poised and balanced in the middle. To Isaac this seemed a favourable omen, when attacks from right and left both failed to dislodge him, and he promptly bade his followers set about their adversaries with more vigour. He urged them to take heart, rout their enemies, and pursue them far and wide.

The news of this reverse,[1] inflicted on us in the manner I have described, was even more terrifying and serious than anything we had heard before. It astounded us, and the emperor was thrown into utter confusion. He was now convinced that his cause was hopeless, for it was impossible to summon to his aid the western army after its defeat, at least for the moment, and he could not get ready other men by a fresh levy. The general in charge of his forces, moreover, the eunuch Theodorus, who had previously been appointed to the office of *proedrus* by the Empress Theodora, and who had afterwards taken over the eastern armies, resolutely opposed a military expedition, not so much because he lacked the necessary confidence to engage the enemy, but because he had already concluded a treacherous and secret agreement with Comnenus.

1. The Battle of Hades, not far from Nicaea, on 20 August 1057. Cedrenus describes the engagement in some detail (801-2, p. 628 ff.).

THE SENDING OF THE EMBASSY TO
COMNENUS

The emperor, therefore, after waiting a few days, asked me to come to terms with Comnenus. I was to lead an embassy on his behalf, with secret proposals to the enemy. By my eloquence and powers of argument I was to soften him down and induce a change of attitude towards the emperor. My first reaction to this idea, which came upon me like a bolt from the blue, was to refuse the honour. 'I would not voluntarily undertake such a commission,' I said, 'fraught as it is with considerable danger, the outcome of which, so far from being a matter of doubt, is quite obvious to everyone. It is clear that a man who has just won a victory and is elated by his success will not agree to surrender his superior position, or so abase himself as to accept inferior office.'

The emperor had a prompt reply to this. Shaking his head and accusing me of forgetting all the ties of mutual attachment and friendship, he went on: 'So the purpose of your unceasing studies was to cultivate a persuasive eloquence, but when your friends suffer misfortune, or rather your *masters* – God forgive me for using the word! – you care not a jot how you may give them assistance. When I became emperor, my relations with you underwent no change: I speak with you as I have always done; I greet you and embrace you in my usual way, and every day – it is right that it should be so – "I taste the honey of your lips". But I thought to be repaid in equal measure. But you – you do not even give me as much consideration as a gentleman accords an enemy when he is down and out. Never mind, I will go along the path that destiny has prepared for me, and, as for you, be sure that some day someone will bring on you censure and reproach for having betrayed your master and friend.'

At the sound of these words I was almost struck dumb with amazement. It was impossible to maintain my original objection, so I suddenly changed my attitude. 'But, Sire,' I said, 'I am not refusing to carry out your instructions because I am *afraid* of this duty. My idea is rather to observe proper precautions in the matter. I am merely postponing action because I suspect that most of the others will be jealous.' – 'And what, may I ask,' said he, 'is it that makes you so careful? Why have you no confidence in this embassy?' – 'The man you are asking me to visit', I replied, 'has already won a victory. He is full of confidence in his own future. I hardly fancy, then, that he will show any kindly feeling towards me, nor will he be diverted from his plans by any arguments I can put before him. Possibly he will address me in a haughty fashion, bring dishonour on my embassy, and send me away without accomplishing anything. The others will then slander me, saying that I have betrayed my trust. They will argue thus: when he succeeded beyond his expectations, I only made him more arrogant than ever; in any future negotiations, therefore, he would ignore all the emperor's orders. Any embassy sent to him afterwards would be disregarded. Why? Because Comnenus is under the impression that he himself is soon to become supreme ruler of the Empire. Nevertheless,' I went on, 'if it is your wish that I should obey this order, please give me a colleague, one of the senior members of the Senate. Our proposals will thus be put forward by two of us, jointly, and his replies will be addressed to both of us. The negotiations will then be conducted without secrecy.'

Michael was pleased with this idea. 'Choose any member of the Senate you like,' he said. I chose the most distinguished and sensible man, one who, I was quite sure, would have the courage to accompany me on the embassy.[1] No sooner had this gentleman heard my proposal than he agreed to act in this capacity and share my duties. Then, after consultation and an exchange of thoughts, we coopted a third person to join in the deputation, a man who held high rank among the

1. Theodorus Alopus, a senator.

Romans, a leading member of the Senate, distinguished no less for his oratory than because of his powerful intellect.[1] In former times he had been guide and counsellor to the Emperor Monomachus, and later he brought glory to the office of Patriarch. Having devoted his own life to the service of God, he afterwards consecrated Isaac, too, as a priest.[2]

When he also expressed his readiness to join us – his patriotism was never in doubt – he became the most delightful member of our mission. We then received letters for Isaac from the emperor, or rather we ourselves concocted these messages and composed them in a form as expedient as might be. Our object was to effect a compromise: Isaac was to wear the crown and the insignia of the Caesar, and yet, at the same time, remain subject to the emperor. So we confidently set out on our journey to meet him, and, after covering the first stage out from the city, we acquainted him of our arrival and assured him, most emphatically, that we would under no circumstances enter into any negotiations, unless he first undertook by the most solemn oaths not to detain us once our task was done, nor to do us any other injury, but to treat us with the honour due to our position and guarantee our safe return.

All these assurances being given and other, additional, promises being made, we immediately set sail in our triremes and landed near the spot where he was encamped.[3] We were greeted at once, even before the conference with Isaac began, and they received us most cordially. One after another the leaders of his army came up and addressed us in the pleasantest manner. Kissing our heads and hands, they protested with tears that, though they wore on their brows the garlands of victory, they were weary of shedding the blood of their

1. Constantine Lichudes.
2. He succeeded Cerularius and presided at Isaac's tonsuration in 1059.
3. At Nicomedia, 24 August.

fellow-countrymen and of bringing destruction upon their
kinsfolk. Then, putting us in their midst, they escorted us to
the tent of their general (for he too was encamped there, like
themselves, in the open air). After dismounting themselves,
they made us do likewise and bade us wait outside. Permission
was then given us to enter the tent alone, for the sun had
already gone down and Isaac was unwilling to allow a big
assembly in the imperial tent.

He greeted us as we came in, seated on a high throne, with
a small bodyguard in attendance. He was dressed not so much
like an emperor as a general. He rose slightly as we entered
and told us to sit. No questions were asked about the purpose
of our visit, but after a few brief remarks in explanation of his
own campaign, and after sharing a drink with us, he allowed
us to retire to our own tents, which had been pitched very
near his. We went out in amazement. The man had made no
long speeches at this first meeting; his only inquiries had concerned our voyage. Had we had a smooth crossing? Nothing
more. So, after dispersing to our respective tents and sleeping
for a while, we met again at dawn and decided how we were
to conduct negotiations at the next interview. We were convinced that it was wrong to delegate the duty to one member alone: better that all should frame our questions and all
together receive his answers.

While we were engaged in these discussions, day broke and
the sun crept up over the horizon and was up in the sky,
shining brightly. But it was not long before the leading counsellors arrived and summoned us to his presence. They practically became our escort and led us away to their general. We
found him in a bigger tent this time, big enough for an army
and its mercenary forces as well. Outside it and all around
there stood a great multitude of men, not at ease or mingled
together, but drawn up in ranks, in a series of concentric
circles, with a short interval between each group. Some were
armed with swords, others with the heavy iron *rhomphaia*,

others with lances. Not a sound was heard from any of them.
Every man stood stiffly to attention in an attitude of fear,
their eyes steadily fixed on the soldier who was in charge at
the door of the tent. He was actually the captain of the
emperor's personal bodyguard, a brave-hearted man, quick-
witted and energetic, good at speaking, better at holding his
tongue, and at his best when in deliberation – the Duke John,
who had from a long line of ancestors inherited a spirit at
once courageous and steadfast.[1]

When we had drawn near, this man told us to stand by the
entrance while he himself went inside the tent. After a short
pause he came out again, and, without a single word to us,
threw open the tent door, suddenly. The sight that met our
eyes within was astonishing. It was so unexpected, and truly
it was an imperial spectacle, capable of overawing anyone.
First, our ears were deafened by the roars of the army, but
their voices were not all raised at once: the front rank acclaimed him first, then the second took up the cry, then the
next rank, and so on. Each rank uttered its own cry with a
different intonation from the rest. Then, after the last circle
had shouted, there was one great united roar which hit us
almost like a clap of thunder.

When they eventually became quiet, they gave us leisure to
observe what was inside the tent (for we had not immediately
entered when the door was thrown open, but stood at some
distance waiting for the signal to go in). I will describe that
scene. The emperor himself was seated on a couch decorated
with two head-rests. The couch was raised on a high plat-
form and overlaid with gold. Under his feet was a stool. A
magnificent robe gave him an air of great distinction. Very
proudly he held up his head and puffed out his chest (an
effort that caused his cheeks to take on a deep red tinge), while
his eyes, with their far-away gaze, showed plainly that he was
thinking profoundly and wholly given up to his own medi-

1. Brother of Isaac.

.tations. Then the fixed gaze relaxed, and it was as if he had
come from troubled deeps to the calm of some haven. All
round him were circles on circles of warriors. The nearest
circle, and the smallest one, was composed of the most important persons, the leading representatives of the nobility,
men who rivalled the stately grandeur of the Ancient Heroes.
And there they stood, their own exalted rank an inspiration
to their juniors. Around them were their lieutenants and the
front-rank fighters, grouped in a second circle. With these
stood some soldiers of inferior battalions and certain high-
ranking company commanders, on the emperor's left. Surrounding these again we saw the light-armed troops without
armour, and behind them all the allied forces which had joined
him from different barbarian nations. There were Italians, and
Scyths from the Taurus, men of fearful appearance, dressed in
fearful garb, both alike glaring fiercely about them. They were
not alike in other respects, for while the one tribe painted
themselves and plucked out their eyebrows, the other preserved their natural colour; the one made their attacks as the
spirit moved them, were impetuous and led by impulse, the
other with a mad fury; the former in their first onslaught were
irresistible, but they quickly lost their ardour; the latter, on
the other hand, were less impatient, but fought with unspar-
ing devotion and a complete disregard for wounds. Those
then were the warriors who rounded off that circle of shields,
armed with long spears and single-edged battle-axes. The
axes they carried on their shoulders, and with the spiked ends
of the spears jutting out before and behind them the intervals
between the ranks were, so to speak, roofed in.

So much for the warriors. As for us, we were given a sign
to come in by the emperor, with a motion of the hand and a
slight nod of the head, just enough to tell us that we were to
move over to his left side. When we had passed through the
space between the first and second circle and were quite
near him, he again asked us the same questions as before, and,

being satisfied with our replies, he continued in a louder voice, 'Well, now, let one of you turn about and stand in the midst of these men here' (pointing to those who stood about him on either side) 'and put in my hand the letter from him who has sent you. You can also tell me the message that you have brought to us here.'

At this each of us declined the honour of making reply, and each asked the others to do so instead of himself. We held a conference among ourselves and my two companions pressed the duty on me. I was best equipped, they said, for speaking freely because, unlike themselves, I was a philosopher. They would come to my aid if, by any chance, my arguments were refuted. So I at once calmed the beating of my heart and stepped into the middle, collected my wits, and gave him the letter. Then, taking the signal to speak, I began my discourse. If the noise which was going on there had not scared me while I was speaking, and if it had not so frequently interrupted me that I forgot my long harangue, perhaps I would have recalled the actual words I had prepared beforehand. They would have occurred to me in their proper setting and sequence wherever I was developing my argument in periods, or stressing my ideas with a series of clauses rising to some climax. Nobody there noticed that there was subtlety in my plain speaking, but the fact was that, by a careful imitation of Lysias[1] in his use of common everyday speech, I took simple expressions known to the ordinary man, and decked them out with delicate philosophical touches. Anyway, I will recall now the main points of my discourse, as far as my memory serves me.

The introduction was most emphatic. I spoke clearly enough, but it was artfully done, for to begin with I avoided all reference to their guilt, and started with the Caesar and the acclamation he shared with the emperor. I enumerated other favours, and honours greater still, which had been con-

1. The Athenian orator (*c.* 459–*c.* 380 B.C.).

ferred on them by their true sovereign. Those who stood nearest us received this preamble with satisfaction and held their
peace, but the crowd in our rear shouted as one man that they
refused to acknowledge any other role for their leader but
that of emperor. Maybe the majority did not approve of this,
but they slavishly said so and accommodated themselves to
circumstances. At all events they put to shame the orderly
element in my audience and forced them to shout defiance
too. Probably because he wished to avoid the appearance of
disagreeing with the mob, the emperor supported their objection, using precisely the same words.

I was in no way disturbed by this. Indeed, I was now in a
solid position based on very substantial arguments – and I am
not the sort of man who shrinks away when I am once engaged in a fight. So I interrupted my speech and stood in
silence, waiting for the crowd to grow quiet. And, after they
had bawled their heads off, they did steady down, and I, continuing in the same strain, began gently to reveal my more
damaging points, although still not blaming the rebels. I
reminded them how one climbs a ladder, pointed out the
mistake of over-reaching with the foot, and praised the
reasonable progress to the imperial throne. The proper order,
I said, was this: first, experience, and afterwards, philosophical
speculations; the man of affairs first, and afterwards the
theorist. Most of those who had ruled as emperors, and the
best of them, had been promoted to imperial power from the
rank of Caesar.

At this remark, some individuals objected that I was quot-
ing one particular kind of promotion. Isaac, they said, had
been invested with power already. 'But', I flashed back,'he
has not become emperor yet! What is more, if your objec-
tions are not to be perfectly ridiculous, your position' (I was
afraid to use the word 'rebellion' expressly) 'has not even a
respectable name at all.' Then I went on as follows: 'Give up
the title of Emperor and your accession to the throne will

have the sanction of legality.' When I mentioned the adoption proposed by the emperor, they broke in. 'Do you mean to tell us', they asked, 'that an emperor's son will be deprived of his power, the sovereign power?' – 'Yes,' I answered, 'the greatest emperors have treated even their *real* sons like that.' And I straightway reminded them of the divine Constantine[1] and certain other rulers who had honoured their sons with the title of Caesar first and afterwards promoted them to the exalted position of emperor. Then, drawing together the threads of my argument, more in the manner of a syllogism, I made this comparison: 'That is how they treated their own sons, men of their own flesh and blood. Isaac here is only a son by adoption . . .' and, having thrown in the word 'adoption', I left the rest of the sentence in suspense.

However, they knew what I meant, and they proceeded to enumerate a host of reasons for their 'common movement' – a euphemism they produced for 'rebellion'. Instead of refuting their arguments out of hand, I replied as if I were taking their part. I exaggerated their misfortunes. 'Yes, I know these things and often my heart has bled because of them. Your anger,' I said, 'your anger is justified, and so is the despair you feel at your sufferings.' And having pacified them with these words, I shook them with a sudden assault from the flank. 'Those are terrible things, terrible indeed, but they do not justify revolution: nothing whatever is a legitimate excuse for that. Now suppose that you were emperor' (here I carried on the argument with a direct reference to their leader) 'and suppose you were to become very ill-tempered, and the leader of the Senate, shall we say, or the commander-in-chief of the army entered into a conspiracy and got accomplices to aid him in his evil designs, engineering a plot to dethrone yourself and at the same time excusing himself with a recital

1. Constantine the Great appointed his sons Caesars before his death: Crispus and Constantine II in 317, Constantius II in 323, and in 333 Constans. The last three afterwards became emperors.

of all his sufferings and a description of the indignity with
which he had been treated – would the pretexts he put forward justify the plot in your eyes?' When Isaac said 'No!' I
went on, 'But in your case you have not even suffered indignity, except inasmuch as you have failed to get what you
had previously set your heart on. As for the terrible sufferings
you speak of, those have been caused by other men, not by
the present emperor.' As he did not reply to this (for he was
not so much concerned with arguing persuasively himself as
with listening to the simple truth from me) I pressed him still
further: 'Well then, change your mind. Be persuaded by your
better judgement. Honour your father in his old age, and
you will inherit the throne by legal means.'

My words, assisted by numerous other arguments, had
already convinced him, when a cry rose up behind me, a cry
which from that moment has never ceased to ring in my ears.
It was a confused cry, for everyone there attributed to me a
different quality. Some spoke of my invincible rhetoric,
others of the power of my words, others again of the force of
my arguments. I myself made no reply to any of them, but
the emperor, holding up his hand for silence, addressed them.
'This man has said nothing at all which gives the appearance
of chicanery or wilful deception of his audience. He has followed the course of events, and his explanations have been
proffered in simple language. There is no reason therefore
why you should upset our conversation or throw our meeting
into disorder.' Those were his very words, but some of his
entourage, wishing to intimidate me, begged the emperor 'to
save the orator, who is sure to be destroyed out of hand, for
most of the soldiers have already drawn their swords against
him, and they will cut him in pieces the moment he leaves the
tent!' I smiled at these words. 'If I, who have brought to you
an Empire and all the power which you have achieved, am in
recompense for these good tidings to be torn in pieces by
your own hands, surely you are merely confirming the fact of

your rebellion. You become your own accusers. No, your purpose in these threats is either to gag me or force a recantation, but I will neither change my opinions nor alter my words.'

When I made this declaration the emperor rose from his throne and dismissed the assembly, after honouring me with several complimentary remarks. The soldiers were ordered to go on ahead and Isaac took us aside by ourselves. 'Do you really believe', he said, 'that this imperial robe has been put on me with my approval? Do you think that if it were possible for me to run away I would refuse to escape? Of course not. They persuaded me to take this course in the first place, and now I am in their power, hemmed in on all sides. However, if you will take a solemn oath to convey certain private information to the emperor on my behalf, I will tell you, now, my own secret intentions.' We swore to preserve the secrecy of this confidential information, and he went on: 'For the present I do not covet supreme power. I am satisfied with the position of Caesar. Let the emperor therefore send me fresh dispatches, to the effect that when he dies he will bequeath the Empire to nobody but myself; that he will not deprive any of my colleagues of the honours I have bestowed upon them; and that he will share with me some, at any rate, of his imperial power, so that I may be able, if I wish, to dispense the less important civilian posts to some of my followers, and in other cases even control military promotions. I am not making these requests for my own sake, but for my men. And if he confirms them, I will come to him without delay and pay him the honour due to an emperor and a father. Naturally, these terms are not to the liking of my army.[1] So I will give you a two-fold message. One letter I will submit courteously to their inspection and let them read it; the other (the secret one) will be memorized by yourselves. And one other favour

1. Catacalon, who was chiefly responsible for the victory of 20 August, is said to have opposed any compromise with the emperor.

for my men: make sure that little fellow[1] is deprived of his position in the government. In the past it was obvious that he was bitterly opposed to our ambitions, and we still suspect him. Today then, you will dine with me. Tomorrow you will set out and carry my secret injunctions to your master.'

So we sat at his table and marvelled still more at his perfect manners, for he condescended to us in a most friendly way. There was nothing of the proud tyrant about him. Early next morning we presented ourselves to him again, and, after receiving the second message secretly, we went down to the sea, escorted by the same guard as before. We found the water calm, slipped our mooring-cables, and sailed for Byzantium. Day had broken when we reached the palace harbour. We gave the emperor a description of the whole affair and explained the secret proposals after handing him the two letters. He read them through several times and then urged us to recapitulate what Isaac had suggested. 'Well,' he said, 'they must all be carried out. Let him have whatever he wants. He can even wear a crown – that will give him more prestige than ever. He wears a garland now, not a crown, but there – he can have it, however unusual it may be for a Caesar. He must exercise power together with myself, he must share in the appointment to offices. A special imperial tent will have to be set aside for his use and a noble bodyguard must be allowed for his protection. And as for those who have served with him on this rebellious campaign, each of them can retain with impunity whatever privileges Isaac has granted him, money, or property, or high office. What I have promised shall be ratified in writing, and by word of mouth. It shall be carried out. I will have documents drawn up and sealed. I will moreover swear on oath never to break these promises in any particular. As he has entrusted you with secret proposals to me, so I also make my counter-suggestions to him. You shall convey these proposals, even more confidential than his

1. Leo Paraspondylus.

own. Do you therefore swear solemnly to Isaac that a few days hence I will make him my partner, after I have made the necessary excuses for his promotion. If for the moment I postpone this action, he must forgive me. The fact is, I am afraid of the people and the Senate, and I am not at all sure that they will approve my plan. To avoid stirring up trouble against myself, therefore, I beg him to excuse me at present – at the proper moment it shall be done. As for the other promises in my letter to him, mark them well; but please keep secret the one I have just mentioned. Go back to him as quickly as possible. No more delay.'

So, after one day's interval, we sailed back together to the Caesar and handed over to him the emperor's message.[1] Isaac was not dressed in the same clothes in which we had seen him before, when he was seated on his throne, but in some modest and inferior garb. When he had received our letter he gave orders for it to be read aloud, so that all might hear it. It was apparent that what he had done met with general approval, because he had acted in the interests of his fellow-conspirators rather than for himself. Both he and they, therefore, were unanimously resolved that their revolutionary activities must be abandoned. Later we had a private interview and passed on to him our secret information. The effect of this was instantaneous. He was like a man inspired. Immediate orders were given to the army: the men were to dismiss to their homes for the present, but to return to the colours when his affairs were firmly established. Isaac was even more disposed now to trust us, for he knew that the man who had formerly been entrusted with the administration of the Empire had since been forced to resign his office. He spoke, too,

1. Comnenus had moved to Rheae. No doubt these negotiations were deliberately prolonged, and Psellus with his fellow-ambassadors was plotting to get rid of Michael. According to Cedrenus (803, p. 633) Catacalon was to oppose the terms in order to delay the final decision until all was ready at Byzantium.

of the straightforward, honest character of the emperor. As he wished no time to be lost in concluding the negotiations, he bade us return next day and tell Michael that he (Isaac) would come to the capital and that all his former suspicions were now dissipated. Preparations were thereupon made for his departure on the third day. He was to leave camp with a small bodyguard and come down to the seaboard opposite the imperial palace. He had extraordinary faith in the emperor, so much indeed that he did not even insist on a magnificent reception in Byzantium. He merely required us to go out to meet him and we were to escort him personally to the palace. In this, our second embassy, success again attended our efforts, and we were filled with unspeakable joy to think that by our oratory and wisdom we had made some contribution to our country's welfare. So we made ready to depart on the morrow.

It was not yet evening, however, before some messengers arrived from the camp and gathered round the emperor's (Isaac's) tent, with what was no doubt good news for the Caesar. Michael, they said, had been forced to abdicate. A plot had been set on foot against him by senators who had obliged him to put aside his imperial robes and fly for refuge to the Church of St Sophia.[1] This tale had no great effect on Isaac, nor were we very much perturbed by it then. We imagined the whole story to be a fiction, and turned to our own affairs.

But the first bearers of good tidings had not dispersed before others came up, and then again others, one after another, all confirming the truth of the rumour. Naturally we were extremely worried at this, and having met together, we conferred on the possible causes of this belief. The occupant of

1. Cedrenus (804–5, pp. 635–6) says the patriarch *pretended* reluctance to proclaim Isaac; he was advising Michael to abdicate and warning Comnenus to hurry to the palace. In fact, Michael did not fly to St Sophia.

the first tent, anyway, assured us that the rumour was true, for one of his own servants, he said, had just arrived from the city, a most reliable and serious fellow, and he had given a vivid account of the whole affair. Apparently, certain seditious and troublesome persons – and here he mentioned individuals who, as we ourselves know quite well, had insinuated themselves into favour with the Senate – these persons, he said, had first thrown the city into a turmoil and thoroughly upset the government, threatened peaceful citizens with burning and other misfortunes, stolen into the sacred precincts of St Sophia and dared to violate its sanctuary, and then, after enlisting the sympathies of the patriarch, without any opposition from him, had made him the leader of their faction.[1] After which, with wild shouts of exultation, they called down curses on the emperor, uttered all kinds of slander to discredit him, and hailed Isaac as alone worthy of ruling the Empire. That, said he, was all his informant knew, but if anything further had happened since, no doubt we should soon hear of it.

At this news we determined to make our way to the Caesar's tent, to see if there was any further news to be learnt from him. So we gathered there, and found him dictating his letter to Michael. What he had to tell us was the same as before: the stories were, to him, just incredible. But while he was in the open with us – the sun had not yet set – there came another messenger, panting for breath while he was still some distance off, and when he had almost reached us he fell down (on purpose, I fancy), and his words came in gasps. Then, pretending to collect his wits, he told us the emperor had abdicated, the city was making preparations to receive his successor, already an imperial galley had been equipped for

1. Michael Anastasius, Theodorus Chryselius, Christophorus Pyrrhus were the persons concerned. The patriarch sent his nephews, Nicephorus and Constantine, to negotiate with them, but the crowd threatened to strangle these emissaries unless Cerularius himself condescended to meet the conspirators.

Isaac, and his escort were standing by with their torches. He assured us that he himself had witnessed these things. He had seen Michael, who only that morning had been our sovereign, become an ordinary citizen and soon afterwards he had been dressed in the coarse cowl of a monk, with no outward sign of imperial rank. The fellow's account was still unfinished when another messenger came up, and after him a third, all with the same story. Finally, there reached us one of the more intelligent and educated class, and he too gave us a dramatic account of the whole scene. The emperor believed him – the only courier he did believe. We were thereupon ordered to remain quiet by our tents. The reign of Isaac had begun.

How my fellow-ambassadors passed that night[1] I cannot say, but to me life seemed hopeless and I thought it was a matter of minutes before I should be sacrificed like a beast. You see, I knew that everyone was violently angry with me: there could be no escape. I would perish miserably, and all manner of throat-slitting and maiming would be my lot. Above all I was afraid of the new emperor. Perhaps he would recall the things I had said to him, and how I had persuaded him to remain an ordinary citizen; probably he would subject me to all kinds of vengeance and torture. So, while everyone else had dropped off to sleep, I waited in solitude for my executioners. At the slightest sound of a voice or any noise round my tent, I was at once petrified with fear, thinking death was at hand. When the greater part of the night had passed in this way – I had no idea the time had elapsed – and when the dawn was about to break, I recovered somewhat, for it seemed a lesser evil to die in the light of day. Bending forward a little to peep out of my tent, I saw watch-fires burning and round the emperor's quarters lighted lamps. There was hurry and bustle everywhere, for the whole army had been ordered to make ready and pack for the journey to the capital. The sun had not yet risen, when suddenly Isaac rode out on horseback

1. The night of 31 August 1057. Isaac was now at Chrysopolis.

and we too left camp, not in his immediate entourage, but in
the rear.

For my part, I expected, after a reasonable distance had
been traversed, that he would send for me: I should be commanded to explain why I had given my former advice. When
he did summon me, my hopes and fears were exhausted. To
my surprise, however, he spoke in a perfectly straightforward
manner; there were no rhetorical propositions, no balanced
arguments, no refutations, no artful insinuations or systematic
discussion, no attempt to influence my judgement or to lead
me astray. Instead, he proceeded to tell me his secret plans and
confided in me about the cares he had for the Empire. He
asked me what in my opinion was the best way to govern,
what course of action he should follow in order to rival the
greatest sovereigns. I recovered my spirit at these words.
My courage revived, and, as I expatiated at great length on
this subject, my reputation with him was much enhanced. In
fact the emperor had nothing but admiration for my discourse, so that he persisted in asking me questions and carefully pondered my answers, not satisfied with any superficial
reply. After our talk, he summoned my fellow-ambassadors
to his presence also, and he expounded to them his immediate
policy, treating them as partners in the scheme. Such was the
position in our relations when the sun rose and the whole
scene was flooded with its light.

All the populace of the city poured out to honour him.[1]
Some brought lighted torches, as though he were God Himself, while others sprinkled sweet perfumes over him. Everyone, in his own peculiar way, tried to please him. Without
exception the people regarded the occasion as a festal day.
There was dancing and rejoicing everywhere. You would
think Isaac's entry into the capital was some revelation of the
Deity Himself. But how could I, in a few brief words, describe to you the magnificence of that wonderful sight? I have

1. On 1 September.

taken my part in many imperial processions, and I have assisted at ceremonies of a more religious character, but in all my life I have never seen such splendour. It was not merely the people of the city, nor the Senate, nor the host of farmers and merchants, that made up that happy throng: there were students of the theological colleges there, and dwellers on the mountain-tops, and hermits who had left their communal homes in the carved rock-tombs; the stylites, too, who lived in mid-air, joined the crowds. All of them, whether they had slipped out from their rocks, or come down from their aerial perches, or exchanged the mountain heights for the level plains, all made the emperor's procession into the city a most memorable sight.

Isaac himself was neither deceived by this hollow triumph nor unduly elated. His first reaction was to suspect the extraordinary changes in his fortunes. It was typical of the man's shrewd perception. He was still meditating on the subject when he turned and spoke to me, rather unexpectedly. 'Philosopher,' he said, 'this amazing piece of good luck seems to me a fickle business. In my heart I am not at all sure it will have a happy ending.' – 'The thought of a philosopher,' I answered, 'but fortunate beginnings are not *invariably* followed by disaster. If Fate has set a limit, it is not for us to probe. In fact, my acquaintance with learned books and propitiatory prayers tells me that if a man betters his condition, he is merely following his destiny. When I say that, I am, of course, expressing the doctrine of the Hellenes,[1] for according to our Christian Faith, nothing is predetermined, nothing foreordained in our lives. Nevertheless, there is a logical connexion between effects and their immediate causes. Once you change that philosophic outlook, however, or become elated with pride because of these glories, Divine Justice will assuredly oppose your plans, and very quickly at that. So long as your heart is not filled with pride, you can take courage, for

1. Psellus uses this generic term for pagans.

God is not jealous where He gives us blessings. On the contrary, He has many times set men on the path of glory by one swift move. But, setting aside all such considerations, my own case offers a fine opportunity for you to exercise justice. Make a good start and bear no malice for the reckless speeches I made as an envoy. I was obeying an emperor's command and I served him well. So it was not through any ill-will towards you, but in loyalty to Michael that I argued as I did.'

At these words his eyes filled with tears. 'Do not speak so,' he said, 'for I appreciated your tongue then, when you spoke in insolence, more than now, when it flatters and praises. However, I will make a beginning, as you suggest, with your own case. In fact I regard you as first among my friends, and I will mark the occasion with a special honour, the title of President of the Senate.' While we were talking the sun had already reached its zenith, and we saw the gulf on which we were to sail. The imperial galley came into sight. Isaac, pelted with flowers and deafened with cries of 'Good luck!', immediately went on board and made his triumphal progress across the sea from the Propontis to the Imperial Palace. Even in the midst of these preparations he remained seated by us. So, with all due legal sanction, Isaac Comnenus acceded to the throne.[1]

The Emperor Michael the Aged had spent one whole year in power. He died soon after his abdication, a private citizen.

THE REIGN OF ISAAC COMNENUS[2]

Having inherited the throne, Comnenus, always the man of action, lost no time in making himself complete master of the

1. He was crowned by the patriarch in St Sophia.
2. Isaac was about fifty years old. Essentially a soldier-emperor, he had little respect for courtiers. His reply to someone who reproached him for rebelling against Michael was typical: 'I couldn't bear to serve my fellow-slave any more!' (Scylitzes, 813, p. 650).

Empire. From the very start he personally supervised the affairs of State. In the evening on which he entered the palace, and before he had time to shake off the dust of battle or to change his clothes and order baths for the morrow, he was issuing instructions to the army and the people of the city. There was no pause for rest. He reminded me of a man who has barely escaped a mighty storm at sea, and after swimming for his life, has been lucky enough to reach harbour but has not yet spat the salt brine out of his mouth or recovered his breath. The rest of that day, and all that night, he spent on matters of State.

His army had flocked into the city, at least those who had risked their lives with him and dared to face danger in his ranks, and Isaac was afraid they might run amok in the streets, or, trusting in his indulgence, cause trouble for the civil population. His first care, therefore, was to pay them the usual tributes and send them off to their own countries. They were to rest at home for a while and report to the colours later, in order to serve under the emperor in war against the barbarians. It was supposed that the operation of disbandment would take place in a matter of months, but one had scarcely time to guess his plans before he dispersed these forces and withdrew them from the capital. He reminded them individually of their deeds in the war, decorating some for bravery in the field, others for distinguished leadership; for others he had some word of commendation. All alike were mentioned in some way and received their appropriate reward from the new emperor. For my own part, I was glad to see them go. The affair reminded me of clouds in the sky suddenly penetrated by the sun, its bright rays scattering the shadows.

So the city was freed of the troublesome presence of the soldiers and the inhabitants marvelled at the way in which Isaac had handled them. A great future was predicted for his reign. This was natural enough, for his actions had already confounded their expectations and the future promised to surpass their wildest dreams. In fact, they anticipated a time of wonderful prosperity. With regard to the emperor's character, people who met him only at certain times, when he was seated on the throne, in the process of dealing with State affairs, or giving audience to some embassy, or uttering the most dreadful threats against the barbarians, had the impression that he was abrupt and hard. To such folk it was inconceivable that there could be a softer side to the man's behaviour. But if one saw him in his home-life, or choosing his officials, one realized the extraordinary duality of Isaac's nature. It was like hearing the string of some musical instrument pitched to one certain note, but producing two sounds, one soft, the other harsh. I myself have seen him in both moods, in moments of tension and moments of relaxation, and in my opinion his character was indeed two-fold. When he was relaxing, it was incredible to me that he would ever concentrate again; when he was fiercely concentrated on some purpose, that he would ever relax again or forget his serious deliberations and come down to earth. He was so gracious and pleasant in the one case, and in the other – why, even his face changed, his eyes flashed, and his brow, to put it metaphorically, hung threatening over the clear light of his soul like some dark cloud.[1]

When the throne was ready for him and the senators were standing in groups on either side of it, Isaac would at once relapse into silence, a perfect imitation of Xenocrates'[2] picture, his mind open, as it were, to receive ideas. This silence of his struck no little fear into the hearts of the Senate. Some

1. Cf. Scylitzes (813, p. 650): 'Isaac was a man of fixed habits, fair-minded, sharp-witted, strong, intelligent, a great leader in war, a terror to his foes, kindly to his friends.'

2. Xenocrates of Chalcedon, a follower of Plato, was head of the Academy from 339 to 314 B.C., a philosopher of great earnestness. Psellus may however be referring to the sculptor of the school of Lysippus, who lived in the third century B.C., and wrote on art (Pliny, *Historia Naturalis*, xxxv, 10, 36; Diogenes Laertius, iv, 15).

stood rooted to the spot, as if they had been hit by lightning, in the same position as when the thunderbolt fell, dry and bloodless, like men without souls. Others reacted differently: one standing stiffly to attention, another folding his arms more tightly than usual across his chest, a third staring at the ground. Another (and this was true of all, for they were all filled with terror) repressed a desire to move by sheer will-power, shifting his posture as quietly and unobtrusively as he could. Every time the emperor refused his consent to proposals set before him, their breath would come fast, and you recognized the change in them by the beating of their hearts.

More than any other man he was laconic in the extreme, not expressing all his ideas in so many words, yet leaving no doubt as to his meaning. Those who describe Lysias (the orator Lysias, the son of Cephalus) attribute to him, among other virtues to which they bear witness, the ability to bridle his eloquence at the appropriate moment. They tell us, more-over that, despite his command of language, he was satisfied with saying only what was essential, so that his audience might infer from them those things that were left unsaid. In the same way Isaac also had a tongue which by gentle showers, so to speak, and not by heavy rain, fattened the nature ready to receive them, and, as the moisture quietly sank deep into the soil, he aroused his listeners to the knowledge of what had been passed over in silence; the truth was that he wished to avoid refutation, and being now emperor and lord of all, he had no desire to foster any inopportune rivalry with himself in the sphere of eloquence.

For that reason he left the study of rhetoric to us lesser folk, and to ordinary citizens. In his case, a nod, a movement of the hand, an inclination of the head to one side or the other, were all that he considered necessary to indicate his wishes. He was not particularly conversant with the laws, so he improvised a legal procedure of his own. For instance, where a verdict had to be pronounced, he would not take the initiative himself, but refer the matter to his judges, and, when they decided the case, he used to support the majority, and only then would he take the lead and record his vote, all the time pretending that his own judgment had not been influenced by the others. To avoid any mistake in legal phraseology, he left that to his juniors, but invariably he added something which he said should have been included in the documents, or else erased something on the ground that it was superfluous.

When dealing with ambassadors he pursued no set policy, except that he always held converse with them dressed in the most magnificent apparel. On those occasions he poured out a flood of words, more abundant than the rising Nile in Egypt or Euphrates plashing against the shores of Assyria. He made peace with those who desired it, but with the threat of war if they transgressed so much as one term of his treaty. Such was the contract he made with Parthia and Egypt. In the case of other nations, however, he was not so agreeable. Some, having ceded many towns and surrendered their armed forces, were even prepared to leave their native soil and emigrate at once, but Isaac refused his consent and they were ordered to remain quietly where they were. He did this, not because he grudged the Roman Empire the acquisition of new territory, but because he knew that an imperialist policy of that sort could not be effected without much expenditure of money and men, as well as sufficient reserve. Where these were lacking, expansion became merely a diminution of strength. On most of the barbarian generals he cast aspersions – I have myself heard these things being said – charging them with want of manliness and reprimanding them for the careless manner in which they carried out their duties as officers. Their morale had fallen very low, but he revived it, with the intention of using them as a bulwark against the aggression of stronger nations.

What I have written is sufficient eulogy for Isaac. If in addition there is some lesson to be drawn for the future, that task is one the historian will find to his liking. I will try to do so. In matters other than the civil administration he advanced the welfare of his Empire by *gradual* progress, and had he followed the same policy in the non-military sphere also, by purging the State of its rotten elements, first reducing the gross evil and then applying his remedy, two things would have happened: he himself would have earned undying honour; and the body politic would not have been brought to utter ruin. But Isaac wanted to revolutionize everything. He was eager to lose no time in cutting out the dead wood which had long been accumulating in the Roman Empire. We can liken it to a monstrous body, a body with a multitude of heads, an ugly bull-neck, hands so many that they were beyond counting, and just as many feet; its entrails were festering and diseased, in some parts swollen, in others wasting away, here afflicted with dropsy, there diminishing with consumption. Now Isaac tried to remedy this by wholesale surgery. He attempted to get rid of the bulges and restore the body to a normal shape, to take away this and build up that, to heal the intestines and breathe into this monster some life-giving breath; but the task was beyond him, and in consequence he lacked faith in his own success. However, to avoid any confusion in our history, let us first explain how our body politic got into this gross condition, then how Isaac attempted to cut out its rottenness, and, thirdly, how these efforts of his were not universally successful.[1] When I have done all this, I will add an account of the end of his reign and finish my history.

After the death of Basil the Great (Basil the son of

1. Isaac's coinage gives the clue to his reign. Instead of the *labarum* (the imperial standard), a drawn sword appears in his hand. The days of eunuch-rule were over: henceforth the Empire was to be governed by a soldier. Hence he had little sympathy for the court party. All kinds of economy were practised. The monasteries suffered first and many noble families were forced to give up property and wealth; certain allowances given to men in office were cancelled; taxation became heavier and was merciless; donations made by other rulers were withheld.

Romanus,[1] whose family inherited the Empire to the third
generation), his brother, Romanus's younger son, succeeded
to the throne. He inherited great wealth, for Basil had been
emperor for many years, longer than any other sovereign, and
had made himself master of many nations whose riches he
transferred to the imperial treasury. In Basil's reign, therefore,
the revenues greatly exceeded expenditure, and when he died
immense sums were at the disposal of his brother Constantine.
The latter was already an old man. Many years had passed
before he finally realized his ambition, yet, once that ambition
was attained, he not only made no attempt to win military renown and add to the dominions he possessed, but did not even
care to preserve the bounds of his power inviolate. On the contrary, he plunged into a life of pleasure, determined to squander and spend everything, and if death had not quickly carried
him off, Constantine alone would have sufficed for the destruction of the Empire.

He was the first emperor to corrupt and swell out the body
politic, partly by fattening some of his subjects with great
wealth, partly by raising them to positions of honour and
giving them opportunities to live in depravity and vice. At his
death, his kinsman Romanus became emperor, with the intention of being a real autocrat. The family of the Porphyrogeniti[2] was now extinct, and Romanus's ambition was to lay
firm foundations of a rival dynasty. In order, therefore, that
the civil population, as well as the military class, might be
ready and willing to accept the hereditary succession in his
own family, he proceeded to anticipate their approval with
the distribution of largess on a generous scale, thus adding to
a body which was already gross, and aggravating the disease,
and filling the corrupted part with superfluous fat. His ambitions ended, however, in utter failure, not only in his ideas

1. Romanus II.
2. The title ('born in the purple') gave special distinction to the
ruling dynasty.

about his family, but also in his hopes of bequeathing to his descendants a well-organized state.

At his death Michael ascended the throne. He stopped most of the evil practices, but he was not strong enough to deny some small additions of fat to this body, so accustomed to its nourishment of bad juices and unwholesome, fat-making foods. Even Michael contributed something to its grossness, however niggardly. Doubtless he would have perished on the spot if he had not followed, in some small measure, the policy of his predecessors. On the other hand, had Michael continued a few years longer in power, his subjects would one day have learnt to live wisely. In any case, a bursting-point was inevitable one day, for they were gorged to the limit of well-being.

This emperor also having quickly met his end – I will pass over his nephew who, after a wretched reign, came to an even more wretched death – Constantine Euergetes, the nickname by which he is known to most folk (I refer to Monomachus), succeeded to the imperial throne. He took over the State as though it were a merchantman loaded to the safety-line, so that it barely topped the wash of the waves, and, having crammed it up to the very decks, he sank it. To put it more plainly, and at the same time revert to my former comparison, he first added a host of new limbs and new parts to a body already long-corrupted, injected into its entrails liquids even more unwholesome, and then, having done this, took it out of its natural state and deprived it of peaceful and civilized existence. He practically drove it mad and brought it to the verge of savagery, by making many-headed, hundred-handed monsters of the majority of his subjects. After him, Theodora became empress, with more legal claim to power. Although she apparently refrained from reducing this strange animal to a state of complete insanity, yet she too imperceptibly added some hands and a few feet to it.

Theodora's drama played out to its finish, the reins were put into the hands of the old man Michael. Unable to bear the

movement of the imperial chariot, with his horses running
away with him from the start, he made the show more confused than ever, and, being scared out of his wits at the uproar,
he retired from the race and took his place by the non-runners.
Of course he ought to have held on; he should have kept a
pretty tight hold on the rein. In practice, however, he was
like a man who is dismissed the service – in his case, the
throne – and returns to his former manner of life.

Here then we have the first crisis. The greater part of the
nation had been changed from men into beasts. They had
been fattened up to such an extent that it was necessary to administer purgative drugs, and that in considerable doses. A
second course of treatment was demanded – I mean, of course,
surgical operations, cauterization, cathartics. The opportunity
for healing recurred, and Isaac Comnenus, wearing his crown,
climbed into the Roman chariot. In order that we may consider him, too, in the light of allegory, let us liken his position
partly to that of a charioteer, partly to that of a doctor.

Isaac was a devotee of the philosophic life: he abhorred
anything that was physically diseased or corrupt. But his hopes
were disappointed, for he found nothing but disease and festering sores, the imperial horses running at full speed from the
starting-post, quite impossible to master, heedless of the reins.
In the one case he ought to have waited for the appropriate
moment before he applied surgical remedies and cautery; it
was wrong to operate on the internal organs with the sur-
geon's heated iron without reasonable premeditation. In the
case of the horses, the right course was to discipline them
gently with the reins, and break them in, caress them lightly
in a professional way, and make a fuss of them, then climb
aboard his chariot and give them the rein, after the style of
Philip's son when he taught Bucephalus to answer the bit.[1]

1. Alexander the Great, who mastered his favourite horse by turning
him towards the sun. In its memory (it died in battle) he founded the
city of Bucephala.

But Isaac wanted to see the chariot borne along on a straight course at once, before this initial training. He wanted to see the sick body restored to health immediately. What with his burning and cutting here, and his mighty pulling and tugging with the reins on his runaway horses there, he somehow or other failed to notice that he himself had caught the disease before he got control over these troubles and restored them to a good condition. Do not imagine that I am finding fault with the man for trying. I do accuse him, however, for choosing the wrong time for his vain efforts. As for the third stage of the disease, that must wait. Let us dwell on the second a little longer.

As I have often remarked, the emperors before Isaac exhausted the imperial treasures on personal whims. The public revenues were expended not on the organization of the army, but on favours to civilians and on magnificent shows. Finally, to ensure that after their death the funerals should be more impressive and the interment more extravagant, they made ready monuments of Phrygian or Italian marble, or of Proconnesian slab. Houses were then built round them and churches lent them sanctity. Groves were planted, while parks and meadows encircled the whole area. Then, as they had to enrich their places of meditation (the name they invented for these buildings) with money and possessions, they not only emptied the palace treasury, but even cut into the money contributed by the people to the public revenues. Nor were they satisfied with the presentation of a mere sufficiency to their places of meditation – we had better call them that. The imperial wealth was divided into three parts: one to pay for their pleasures, another to glorify their new-fangled buildings, and a third to enable those who were naturally lazy and made no contribution to the balancing of the nation's budget to live in luxury and bring dishonour on the practice and name of virtue, while the military were being stinted and treated harshly. The present emperor, of course, had been commander-in-chief of the army. He was already aware, for many reasons, of the cause of the Roman Empire's deplorable state. He knew why it was that our neighbours prospered while all our affairs had declined, and why not one Roman had been able to stop the attacks and robberies carried out by the barbarians. When he had the additional prestige conferred by the title of 'Emperor', Isaac at once rooted up the cause of our troubles. So far his actions were worthy of his exalted position, but I am by no means disposed to commend his efforts to do everything at once. However, let me describe what he did.

In the first place, once he had taken the government on his own shoulders – from the moment of his coronation indeed – and once he had, by his coronation, legalized his position as emperor, his policy was radically opposed to that of the aged Michael. Donations which Michael had given, Isaac took away; wherever Michael had done something of note, Isaac destroyed it. Then, becoming gradually more bold, he went too far in his reforms, and here too he wiped out and rescinded much of his predecessor's work. Quite a number of his measures he completely annulled. The consequence was that the people came to hate him, and no small section of the army agreed with them – all those soldiers, in fact, who found themselves deprived of their wealth by the new ruler. Having gone so far, instead of relaxing his programme somewhat, he went further, like the grammarian who in analysis starts with the complex and then proceeds to the simple. He classed under one heading the acts of previous emperors, thus attacking all and bringing all into discredit at once. In pursuit of such a policy it was inevitable that he should add to his other victims the priests of the Church. Indeed, he cut off the greater part of the monies set aside for their sacred buildings, and, having transferred these sums to the public funds, he estimated the bare necessities for the clergy, thereby making the name 'place of meditation' really appropriate. He did this with the insouciance of a man picking up a grain of sand from the sea-

shore. He just set his hand to the task, and it was all done without the slightest commotion. Indeed, I never saw any man on
earth so deliberate in his reasoning, or so quiet in the execution of vast ideas.

This conduct at the time seriously alarmed most of his subjects, but after a while the majority became more resigned to
it. Obviously, if men wished to vilify the emperor's actions,
it was sufficient for him to point out that they were in the
public interest. And the policy would have been hailed with
applause, if only the emperor, like a man who has swum to
shore out of the sea, had given himself some time to recover
his breath. Isaac, however, did not know what it was to lie
at anchor for a while, or rest in harbour. On the contrary, he
braved the sea a second time, a different sea this time, and a
third, and after that a greater and most fearful one, as if he
were not merely engaged in stirring up the waves of politics,
but in cleaning up the dung of Augeas's stables.[1]

As I have emphasized before, if this emperor had chosen
the proper time for his reforms; if he had condemned one
practice, shall we say, and allowed another to stand for the
time being, destroying it at some later date; if, after the am-
putation, he had rested before attempting another operation;
if he had advanced thus, step by step, in his extermination of
evil, quietly and without attracting attention, like the Creator
in Plato, this man who like him had inherited a world – in his
case the world of politics – in a state of flux, without harmony,
without order, then he too, I affirm, would have brought it
back from chaos to calm, and he too would have introduced
real harmony into the affairs of State. God is described by
Moses, the leader of his people, as creating the universe in six
days, but if Isaac did not complete his whole task in a *single*
day, he reckoned the failure intolerable, such was the excessive zeal with which he tried to accomplish his purpose.
Nothing on earth restrained him, no proffering of wiser

1. The sixth labour of Hercules.

counsels, no fear for the future, no hatred of the mob, none of the other factors which in normal men curb vanity or check mighty ambition. Had some rein kept him under control, he would have overrun the whole inhabited world, country by country. He would have won glory on every battlefield, and none of the emperors before him would have been his rival. But lack of restraint, refusal to accept reason as his guide, these were the ruin of his noble character.

I have described, more or less, the alarm and confusion he caused in the political world. In the world of foreign affairs, his ambition was to effect a union of the eastern and western barbarians. They themselves were heartily afraid of him. For the first time they changed their usual tactics, and having observed the quality of the man they had to deal with, instead of pursuing an aggressive strategy they sought safety in obscurity. The Sultan of Parthia, for example, the arch-revolutionary of former times, now adopted an almost retrogressive policy. In no place would he stay for any length of time, had no fixed abode, and – a thing which is really astonishing – went into complete retirement, cutting himself off from intercourse with anyone. The ruler of Egypt too, even to this day, is terrified of the man and still courts his favour with flattery. He even goes so far as to lament Isaac's downfall. The truth is, the emperor's appearance and the emperor's words were as potent as his hands were strong, hands with which he had torn down many a city and destroyed walls defended by thousands of warriors.[1]

He preferred to be ignorant of nothing, even down to the smallest detail, but, since he knew this to be impossible, he would try to obtain his information by indirect means. He used to send for an expert and, without questioning him on the subject about which he was ignorant, by clever manoeuvring round it, he would make the other reveal what he himself

1. Judging by Isaac's conduct of the Patzinak campaign of 1059, one could hardly call him an outstanding strategist.

did not know, in such a way that the expert was apparently
explaining something that was common knowledge to both
of them alike. He often tried to catch me in that way too, but
when on one occasion I ventured to tell him it was a secret,
he was taken aback and blushed as if he had been caught doing
something wrong. Being a man of great pride, he had a hor-
ror of being rebuked, whether openly or subtly.

An example of this is to be found in his treatment of the
Patriarch Michael.[1] The latter had spoken frankly to him on a
certain subject, using language that was somewhat bold. At
the time the emperor passed it over and checked his anger, but
he cherished resentment deep in his heart. It broke out unexpectedly, and, in the belief that he was following a precedent,
he expelled Michael from the city. He was condemned to exile
in a circumscribed area, and it was there that he died. However, I will not explain how this came about now, for it is a
long story. If anyone cares to examine the quarrel between
these two, he will blame the one for the start of it, the other
for its ending, when the emperor cast the patriarch off as if he
were a load on his shoulders. One point here that I almost
forgot: a messenger returning from a distant mission brought
to him the news of the patriarch's death, with the air of a
a man who was freeing him from all trouble in the future,
but Isaac, when he heard of it, his heart immediately touched,
bewailed loudly – an unusual thing for him – and mourned

1. Cerularius. Isaac owed his throne to the patriarch's intervention in
1057. In return the emperor renounced certain jurisdiction over Church
affairs. Emboldened by this, Cerularius tried to extend his power: he
wore (or perhaps destined for his relative Constantine Ducas) the purple
buskins that were considered the prerogative of the emperor. In November 1058 Isaac arrested him and exiled him to Proconnesus. As the
patriarch refused to abdicate, Psellus, at the emperor's request, drew up
the *Accusation*, an interesting and informative document which charges
him with heresy and treason and gives corroborative details. However,
Cerularius died before coming to trial and was succeeded by Lichudes
in 1059 (Scylitzes, 809, p. 644).

him sincerely. He was sorry for the way he had treated the patriarch and often tried to propitiate his soul. As if to justify himself, or rather to appease the dead man, he at once granted to Michael's family the privilege of speaking freely in his presence, and they were allowed to join his nearest retinue. As Michael's successor in the sacred office, he presented to God and honoured with high rank one whom his previous life had shown to be blameless, one whose eloquence had left him without a rival, even among the most eminent scholars.

THE CHOICE OF THE PATRIARCH CONSTANTINE

This gentleman was none other than the famous Constantine, who in the past had on more than one occasion restored peace to a storm-tossed Empire and had been much sought after by many of the emperors. The crowning-point of his career came with his elevation to the Patriarchate.[1] All other candidates for the office yielded to his claims.[2] All were agreed that he had pre-eminent qualities which fitted him for the duty above the rest, and to the glorification of this dignity he dedicated all his efforts, a man who lived the life of a priest, yet possessed qualities of statesmanship and great public spirit. In the case of other men, virtue is supposed to be some such thing as not yielding to circumstances, not tempering one's freedom of speech, not attempting by one's own mildness of character to turn men of sterner material into slaves. So it has come about that mankind has dared every sea, gone in the face of all winds, and some, caught by the waves, have sunk, while others have been rebuffed with much violence. With Constantine, however, the varied pattern of his life enabled him to deal successfully with every precise philosophic problem,

1. February 1059.
2. Yet Lichudes was not allowed to become patriarch without submitting to some inquiry before the Synod (Scylitzes, 809, C–D, p. 645).

and at the same time with all questions of practical government. Moreover, he handled affairs, not like an orator, but as
a philosopher would deal with them: there were no wasted
words, no histrionics. He played either role, churchman or
politician, without deviating one iota from his natural habits.
As a politician, he impressed his interrogators by his priestly
dignity, yet when you approached him in his capacity of
patriarch, even if you stood in considerable awe of him and
trembled a bit, he still appeared human, with the graceful
manners of a diplomat, a man of sturdy character and smiling
gravity. His whole life inspired confidence: on the one side,
his military and political career; on the other, his great dignity,
his courtesy. It was natural, even before this appointment,
that I should often predict for him promotion to the Church's
highest offices. His manner of life taught me what to expect
in the future, and now, after he has actually become High
Priest, I still see in him a gentleman of the noblest character.

By appointing such a man as Michael's successor, therefore,
the emperor paid a compliment to the late patriarch. I will
now deal with the barbarians. In the east Isaac put an end to
their incursions; in that part of the world the task proved to
be well within his power. Now he proceeded to march in full
force against the western enemies. In the old days they had
been called Mysians,[1] but later their name was changed to its
present form: they live in all countries divided from the
Roman Empire by the River Ister (Danube). Suddenly they
left these districts and emigrated to our side of the river. This
movement was caused by the activities of the Getae, their
neighbours, who by their plundering and ravaging compelled

1. The Patzinaks crossed the Ister in 1059. The Hungarians also
threatened the Romans, but peace was arranged with them. The Patzinak campaign was nearly successful, but an unusually early fall of snow
and heavy rain caused Isaac to withdraw under great difficulties (September). Rumours that the Turks were about to invade the eastern provinces made him return quickly to the capital.

them to abandon their homes and seek new ones. So, at a time
when the Ister was frozen over, they crossed as though on
dry land and emigrated from the Trans-danubian territories
to our province. The whole nation was transported, bag and
baggage, over our borders, incapable of living at peace themselves, and bound to spread consternation among their former
neighbours.

More than other nations they are difficult to fight and hard
to subdue. They are neither vigorous of body, nor brave in
spirit, they wear no breast-plates, put on no greaves, and no
helmets protect their heads. They carry no shields of any kind
whatsoever, neither the long sort like those traditionally
borne by the Argives, nor the round shield, nor do they gird
on swords. The only weapon they carry in their hands is the
spear, their sole defensive armour. They are not divided up
by battalions, and when they go to war they have no strategic
plan to guide them. The terms 'vanguard', 'left wing', 'right
flank' mean nothing to them. They build no palisades for
their own protection, and they are unacquainted with the
idea of defensive ditches on the perimeter of their camps. In
one mass, close-packed and pell-mell, fortified by sheer desperation, they emit loud war-cries, and so fall on their adversaries. If they succeed in pushing them back, they dash
against them in solid blocks, like towers, pursuing and slaying
without mercy. On the other hand, if the opposing force
withstands their assault and if their ranks preserve an unbroken
line in face of the barbarian onslaught, the latter forthwith turn
about and seek safety in flight. But there is no order in their
retreat. They scatter in all directions, in small groups. One
hurls himself into a river, and either swims to land or is
engulfed in its eddies and sinks; another goes off into a thick
wood and so becomes invisible to his pursuers; a third escapes
in some other way. They all disperse at the same moment, but
later, in some strange fashion, they meet again, one coming
down from a mountain, another from some ravine, another

from a river, all from different hiding-places. When they are
thirsty, if they find water, either from springs or in the
streams, they at once throw themselves down into it and gulp
it up; if there is no water, each man dismounts from his horse,
opens its veins with a knife and drinks the blood. So they
quench their thirst by substituting blood for water. After that
they cut up the fattest of the horses, set fire to whatever wood
they find ready to hand, and, having slightly warmed the
chopped limbs there on the spot, they gorge themselves on
the meat, blood and all. The refreshment over, they hurry
back to their primitive huts and lurk, like snakes, in the deep
gullies and precipitous cliffs which serve as their walls.

Taken in the mass this is a nation to be feared, and a treacherous one. Treaties of friendship exercise no restraining influence over these barbarians, and even oaths sworn over their
sacrifices are not respected, for they reverence no deity at all,
not to speak of God. To them all things are the result of
chance, and death they believe to be the end of everything.
For these reasons they make peace with great alacrity and
then, when they find it necessary to resort to war, they at once
violate the terms of their treaty. If you conquer them in war,
they invoke a second treaty of friendship; if it is they who win
the combat, they massacre some of their captives and hold a
great auction of the rest. For the rich prisoners they fix the
price high, and if no ransom is forthcoming, they kill them.

Determined to drive this people from Roman territory,
Isaac set out against them with a strong force. He was particularly confident before an enemy that was so scattered and
had such a different conception of war. He led his army in an
attack on the strongest enemy concentration. It was difficult
to fight them and no less difficult to take them captive. As he
drew near, they were filled with terror, not only on his own
account, but also because of his army. In fact, they had not
the courage to defy a man whom they looked on as 'wielder
of the thunderbolt', and when they saw the unbroken line of

Roman shields, they abandoned the idea of fighting in mass and attacked in isolated groups, howling their war-cries. But they found the Romans too compact for them, and having discovered that they could neither catch them by ambush nor face them in open battle, they made a proclamation that they would fight on the third day from then. Thereupon, on the self-same day on which they made this declaration, they left their tents, forsaking all those incapable of flight, that is, aged people and the very young, and then dispersed in the inaccessible regions of that country. According to the agreement the emperor marched out to meet them on the third day, with his troops lined up for battle, but not a barbarian was to be seen. As he thought it unwise to pursue them, partly because he was nervous of secret ambushes, and partly because they had three days' start on their flight, he destroyed their tents, and, taking away what booty he found there, returned laden with the trophies of war. The return journey, however, proved unfortunate, for a sudden storm fell upon his army with great violence and he lost many of his soldiers.[1] Still, he did return to the capital, his head crowned with the garlands of victory.

From that time there appeared in the man new qualities, foreign to his normal behaviour. I am speaking from personal observation, as I was pretty familiar with his character. He became more haughty, to such an extent that he held everyone else in contempt. In fact, he treated his own relatives just like the others, and his brother (John), whenever he approached the outer entrances to the palace, at once dismounted from his horse, in accordance with the emperor's express command, and there was nothing whatever to distinguish him from the rest when he had audience with Isaac. Indeed, he was the finest gentleman I ever met; he accepted the change of attitude without rancour and, far from showing irritation at this new state of affairs, he obeyed the emperor's commands and treated him with due respect. He was

1. 24 September.

generally unobtrusive, an example to other men to alter their demeanour in like manner.

With this change in the emperor's character the second period of his reign came to an end. Now begins the third. Isaac was passionately devoted to hunting: no one was ever more fascinated by the difficulties of this sport. It must be admitted, moreover, that he was skilled in the art, for he rode lightly, and his shouts and halloos lent wings to the dogs, besides frightening the coursing hare. On several occasions he even caught the quarry in full flight with his hand. He was, too, an expert shot with a spear. But crane-hunting attracted him more, and when the birds were flying high in the air he still refused to give up the hunt. He would shoot them down from the sky, and truly his pleasure at this was not unmixed with wonder. The wonder was that a bird so exceptionally big, with feet and legs like lances, hiding itself behind the clouds, should in the twinkling of an eye be caught by an object so much smaller than itself. The pleasure he derived was from the bird's fall, for the crane, as it fell, danced the dance of death, turning over and over, now on its back, now on its belly.

The emperor took delight in both kinds of chase. However, to avoid reducing the number of animals kept in special reserves by hunting them down, he used to go out when the fancy took him to find beasts in their natural habitat, hunting them both on horseback and with the falcon, at his leisure. He would stay at an imperial lodge outside the city, a place surrounded by sea and equipped well enough to please ordinary huntsmen of either kind, but not to the satisfaction of Isaac. He would rise early in the morning and continue hunting till late evening. With this constant throwing of spears at bears and hogs, and with the repeated strain on his right arm, he caught a chill in his side. At the time the trouble was not especially obvious, but on the following day he had fever, with fits of shivering.[1]

1. November 1059. Scylitzes' account is different (811A, p. 647).

THE EMPEROR'S ILLNESS

I, knowing nothing of this, went out to see him and pay my respects as usual. He greeted me lying on a bed. A small body-guard stood near and there was also present his chief physician. After greeting me he remarked, with a cheerful look, 'You come at an opportune moment', and promptly gave me his hand to feel his pulse, for he knew that besides my other activities I had also practised medicine. I recognized the illness from which he was suffering, but made no immediate comment. Instead, I turned to the aforementioned doctor. 'In your opinion,' I said, 'what sort of fever is this?' In a some-what loud voice, so that the emperor might hear, he replied, 'Ephemeral. But if it does not pass off today, there is no cause for alarm. The fever sometimes takes that form as well—the name "ephemeral" is deceptive.' 'Well,' said I, 'I do not exactly agree with your diagnosis. The artery pulsation tells me it will be a three days' fever. However, let us hope your Dodonian cauldron is right and my Delphic tripod wrong.[1] Probably it will be wrong, for my own studies have not been advanced enough for me to play the oracle.'

Well, the third day arrived and the critical stage of the illness had already run on past the normal period. It proved that one of us was a skilled physician, and it also proved that my calculations were not quite accurate. Afterwards some not very solid food was prepared for the emperor, but before he had time to taste it a sudden violent fever assailed him. They do say that Cato,[2] when he was in a fever or suffering from some other illness, used to remain completely motionless and still, resting until the attack passed and the state of his health took a change for the better. Isaac, however, unlike Cato, kept altering the position of his body and twisting about. His

1. Dodona and Delphi were noted oracles in the ancient world.
2. M. Porcius Cato (234–149 B.C.) was regarded as the typical Roman, the perfect example of a *vir moribus antiquis*.

breathing was quicker, and laboured, and Nature gave him no respite whatever. When at last he did get some rest, he thought of returning to the palace.

At once he embarked on the imperial trireme and put in at Blachernae. Back in the palace he felt easier and revelled in the change. He talked in a rather provincial dialect, cracking jokes more than was his wont, and kept us till evening with stories of the old times, recalling all the witty sayings of Romanus's son, the Emperor Basil the Great.

At sunset he dismissed us and prepared for sleep. For my part, I left the palace full of confidence and buoyed up with fond hopes of the emperor's recovery. I returned rather early the next morning. Just before I reached the doors someone gave me the most alarming news: the emperor was suffering from a stabbing pain in his side, his respiration was difficult, and the breathing was not very strong. I was astonished at this information. Quietly entering the bedroom where he lay, I stood there in silence, filled with instant dismay. He looked at me as if he were asking whether there was no hope, whether he was on the point of dying, and at once stretched out his hand to me from under the coverlet. Before I put my fingers on his wrist, the chief physician – there is no need to mention his name – interrupted, 'Don't test the artery. I have already taken his pulse. It's irregular. I could detect only half the pulsations. Each alternate beat is very weak, like the teeth of an iron saw.'

I myself paid little attention to the fellow, but at every break in the pulsation I carefully watched the movement of the artery. I did not recognize the 'saw' pulse, but it was beating rather faintly, not so much reminiscent of the movements of a palsied foot, but rather of one held by chains and trying hard to move. The illness afflicting the emperor had now reached its crisis. Most of the others there did not know this; all of them, or nearly all, were in fact doubtful whether he would survive.

From that moment confusion reigned in the palace. The empress [1] – a most remarkable woman, descended from a very noble family, foremost in works of piety – and her daughter by Isaac,[2] herself a beautiful girl, not only at the time when her hair was cut early in life but even after tonsuration, her simple robes showing off to advantage the warmth of her complexion and the gold-red of her hair – these two women, and the emperor's brother,[3] and his nephew,[4] formed a circle round his bed, giving him their last messages and shedding tears of farewell. They exhorted him to go at once to the Great Palace, so that there he might make any decisions that were necessary. They were anxious, too, lest the family should fall on evil times at his death: they might lose the fortunate status they then held as the emperor's kinsfolk. So Isaac made ready to leave. During these preparations there came to him, none too soon, the High Priest of St Sophia, offering spiritual advice and all kinds of consolation.

As I said, the emperor agreed with his family that it was desirable for him to move, and here he showed he had lost none of his pristine courage. He left the bedroom leaning on no one's arm. It was typical of the man's independent spirit. Like some towering cypress being violently shaken by gusts of wind, he certainly tottered as he walked forward, but he did walk, although his hands trembled; and he did it unaided. In this condition he mounted his horse, but how he fared on the ride I do not know, for I hurried on by the other road to get there before him. I was successful, but when he arrived I saw that he was extremely agitated and in a state of utter

1. Catherine (or Aecaterina), daughter of John Vladislav, a Bulgarian prince.

2. Maria. After Isaac's death she and her mother retired to a convent. The empress changed her name to Helena.

3. John.

4. Probably Manuel, afterwards a noted general. But John had four other sons. The person concerned could have been Theodorus Docceianus, his sister's son.

collapse. All the family sat round him lamenting. They would have willingly died with him, had they been able. Leader of the chorus of dirges was the empress; answering her mother's lamentations and weeping in a manner even more lugubrious, was the daughter.

While they were engaged thus, the emperor, remembering that he was about to pass to a higher life, expressed a desire to enter the Church. It was his own wish – we had not influenced him at all, but the empress, who did not know that, blamed all of us for the decision rather than him. Then, seeing me there as well as the others, she exclaimed, 'Pray Heaven we benefit from your advice as much as you hope, philosopher! But what a fine way to show your gratitude – planning to convert your emperor to the life of a monk!'

I gave her my word of honour, before she could say another word, that I had never entertained such a thought. More than that, I asked the sick man who had advised him to take this course. 'Not you,' he replied, 'but this lady' (the very words he used), 'this lady, true to her womanly instincts, first tries to prevent us from following wiser counsel, and then blames everyone else for a suggestion that I make myself.' – 'Indeed I do,' said she, 'and take on my own shoulders all the sins you ever committed, and if you do get well again – at least I have what I seek and long for; if not, then I myself will defend you before your Judge and God. I will answer for the wrongs you have done. Please God you may be found guiltless, but in any case I would gladly be devoured – yes, even by worms – for your sake. The deepest darkness can cover me, the outer fire can burn every bit of me – I would welcome it. And you – have you no pity now for us in our desolation? What sort of feeling have you, to take away yourself from the palace, and leave me behind, condemned to a widowhood full of sorrow, and your daughter, a wretched orphan? Nor will that be the end of our sufferings. More dreadful things will follow. Hands, maybe not even friendly hands, will carry us off to far-away places of exile. They may decide on some worse fate. It may be some pitiless fellow will shed the blood of your dear ones. No doubt you will live on after you enter the Church, or perhaps you will die nobly, but what will be left for us? – A life worse than death!'

Yet she failed to convince him with these arguments, and when she had given up all hope of winning him over to her own point of view, she went on, 'At least, then, nominate as emperor the man who serves you with greatest loyalty and devotion. As long as you live, he will treat you with due honour, and he will be just like a son to me.' At these words the emperor gained fresh strength. The Duke Constantine[1] was immediately sent for and joined us. Constantine was a man of great renown whose ancestors had been most distinguished: his descent in fact was traced from the celebrated Ducas (I refer to Andronicus[2] and Constantine[3]) who are the object of much attention in the writings of historians, both for the keenness of their intellect and for their brave deeds. The duke was no less proud of his more immediate ancestors.

His lineage, therefore, was enough to cover the man with glory, but no one in attempting a biography of Constantine himself would be wrong if he referred to him as an Achilles. Just as that hero's family had a mighty origin – his grandfather was Aeacus, who the myths say was begotten of Zeus, and his father was Peleus, whom the Greek stories exalt and represent as a husband of Thetis, herself a goddess of the sea – and yet Achilles' own deeds surpassed the glories of his fathers, and, far from Achilles being honoured because of those who begat him, it is they who win renown from the fact that he was their progeny; so it was also in the case of Duke Constantine, who must be the next emperor in my history. Brilliant as the

1. Constantine Ducas, President of the Senate. It is said that he offered the throne first to his brother, who refused it.

2. He was implicated in a plot against Leo VI the Wise in 906.

3. One of the rivals for the throne after the death of Alexander (913).

early records of his family were, still more brilliant are the
deeds that had their origin in his own nature and moral purpose.

But the story of his reign must wait a little. While he was
still living as an ordinary citizen, he rivalled even the greatest
emperors, as far as aptitude for government was concerned,
or pride of lineage. Above all other things, he strove to live
prudently, to avoid giving offence to his neighbours or treating anyone with a patronizing and lordly condescension. He
was most careful to prove his loyalty to the reigning emperors, while his own brilliance, like the sun behind clouds,
was kept in obscurity to avoid attracting attention to himself.

I say these things, not on the evidence of other men, but
relying on my own senses and my own opinions, after personal observation of a careful and quite exceptional nature.
Others may boast of his many splendid successes, but, so far
as I myself am concerned, one thing counterbalances all the
rest: the fact that this man, who was so admirable, not only
in appearance, but in reality, should place more confidence in
my judgement than in the scheming of my rivals. Whether
he had noticed somewhat more evidence of wisdom in my
opinions than in those of the others, or whether it was because
my character pleased him, I know not, but he was so much
attached to me and loved me so much more than the rest, that
he listened intently to every word that I uttered, depended on
me absolutely for spiritual advice, and entrusted to my personal care his most precious possessions.

Despite his qualities, Constantine had a hearty contempt for
offices of great dignity and preferred to live in retirement. He
used to dress in a rather careless fashion, going about like a
country yokel. Lovely women, of course, enhance their
beauty by the wearing of simple clothes; the veil with which
they conceal it only serves to make more evident their radiant
glory, and a garment carelessly worn is just as effective, when
they wear it, as the most carefully-prepared make-up. So it

was with Constantine. The clothes he threw round him,
far from hiding his secret beauties, only rendered them more
conspicuous. It was inevitable that all tongues should be loud
in his praise. Men naturally referred to him as destined for the
imperial throne. Some prophesied his future with all the
solemnity of an oracle; others were more guarded in their
language, careful to refrain from causing him any embarrassment. All the same, it was not the openly hostile, but his own
admirers, who made him most nervous, and he put up all
manner of barriers to keep them at a distance. Unfortunately,
from his point of view, they proved to be the most pugna-
cious dare-devils, and made light of the obstacles he put in
their path.

His extraordinary caution and sound judgement were
proved when the army elected its leader and Comnenus was
preferred to all others, for Comnenus, the man who had
actually been designated as the next emperor, was ready to
hand over the command of the army to Constantine, after
the soldiers' decision was made known; but he renounced all
claim to it in writing and voluntarily gave up his ambitions
in that direction, considering the circumstances in which the
offer was made. Certain it is that those who attended that
conference would never have reached a unanimous decision
on the subject had he not intervened in the debate himself. By
sheer force of character he united the various factions. The
army, now acting in concert, had, so to speak, two strings to
its bow, a stronger and a weaker, or perhaps I should say a
weaker and a stronger, for although Isaac had been elected
emperor and Constantine had been promised the lesser
honour of Caesar, the latter's more noble ancestry and his
extremely lovable nature made him a favourite among the
people. To show even more clearly what an admirable person he was, when the rebellion ended in Isaac's accession to the
throne and he was firmly established in power, Constantine
gave up to him the Caesarship as well, though he could have

disputed with him the highest position of all. The man's character was, in fact, without parallel. I would like to add an observation of my own here. There can be no doubt that his failure to obtain election at the time of the conference, and his present promotion, were both the result of Divine intervention, for instead of being elevated to the supreme position in the Empire by means of a revolution, a circuitous route, he was chosen directly from the inner circle of the court.

CONCERNING THE DUKE'S PRESENTATION TO COMNENUS, HIS NOMINATION AS EMPEROR, AND THE OPINIONS OF ISAAC'S RELATIVES ABOUT HIM

It was not surprising, therefore, that when he was summoned on this occasion by Isaac, apparently breathing his last, he came blushing and showing signs of his accustomed modesty, his hands hidden beneath his robe (a habit of his). The emperor, speaking with great deliberation, addressed him. 'Of those who stand around me here,' he said, pointing to his family, 'one is my brother, another my nephew, and, dearest of all, here is my wife, the empress, and here my daughter, my only child, in fact. But my choice falls on you rather than on them. Your qualities have a greater claim on me than the ties of kinship. It is to you that I bequeath the Empire, and more than that my beloved family. Nor are they unwilling that this should be so: indeed, they have strongly advised me to take this course. This is no new idea, conceived on the spur of the moment, nor is it my unfortunate illness that has driven me to adopt it. Even at the time when I was elected emperor, I knew that you were the better man, more fitted for the office, and since then I have come to the conclusion, after a detailed examination of your claims in comparison with other candidates, that you are without any doubt whatsoever the man most suited to follow me as emperor. As for myself, you see that I am finished: my life is nearing its close. From now on you will assume power, and the government will be in safe hands, for in the past God has judged you worthy. Now the Empire is your inheritance. My wife and my dear daughter I place in your care as a sacred trust. As for my brother and nephew, I beg you earnestly to look after and cherish them.'

At these words there was applause, not unmingled with tears, and the emperor's entourage acclaimed Constantine. He, having now been chosen to succeed Isaac, stood respectfully and modestly at the latter's side, with the air of a man being initiated into some holy mystery or introduced to some strange rite. Such was the ceremony that commenced his reign. The events that subsequently occurred did not run so smoothly as the account of them would lead one to suppose. Certainly he had some immediate successes, but there were difficulties, even reverses.

If he was assisted in any way by myself, it is surely not for me to say so. I would not dream of claiming such an honour. Doubtless the emperor himself would know that wherever opposition arose I resisted it, and when his affairs prospered, I was at hand to help on the good work. Such was the extent of my enthusiasm and my devotion to his cause, that when he was in desperate straits I seized the helm myself, and, by drifting with the tide here and pulling hard on the tiller there, I brought him into the imperial harbour in safety.

It is now my purpose to examine, and describe in detail, the events of his reign, his general policy, the part he played in the government. I will discuss the principles on which he based his rule and the modifications he introduced into them, the ideals for which he strove as emperor, the measures he carried through successfully, the innovations for which he was personally responsible, his prejudices for and against certain lines of conduct, his handling of civil administration, his attitude to the army, and so on.

CONSTANTINE X

1059–67

CONSTANTINE DUCAS RULED THE ROMAN EMPIRE FOR SEVEN YEARS[1]

I WILL abbreviate my account of this emperor as far as is convenient, devoting the usual space that I allot to these descriptions. Afterwards I will go into greater detail and write of his family, the appearance of his house, his personal habits, his likes and dislikes, both before he came to the throne and after. There is no other emperor whom I am qualified to describe with such intimate knowledge, for here was a man who as an ordinary citizen earned my praise, as a crowned emperor my admiration, one from whom I was never estranged in the slightest degree. I had a special place of honour at his side whenever he took his seat on the imperial throne, was constantly engaged in conversation with him, shared the same table, received at his hands favours that baffle description.

As soon as he acceded to power, this man, an emperor in very truth appointed by God, made it his first concern to ensure in his Empire fair dealing and good order, to put an end to fraudulence and introduce a moderate and just system of government. Being endowed with a natural aptitude for all kinds of duties, he was fully capable of dealing with his responsibilities as a sovereign.[2] For instance, when acting as

1. Seven years and six months (from November 1059 to May 1067).
2. The truth is that Constantine X was a mediocre person. He neglected the army, allowed the barbarians to attack the Empire almost with impunity, devoted his time to civil administration (particularly to legal problems) and openly admitted that he preferred to be known as a great orator rather than as a great emperor (Scylitzes, 813–4, pp. 651–3).

judge in lawsuits, he showed himself by no means ignorant of the principles of civil law. He was, in fact, extraordinarily clever in getting straight to the point. Without making a special study of philosophy and rhetoric, he proved to be in no way inferior to the philosophers and orators when he engaged in controversy, or made a speech, or dashed off a letter. In military affairs, too, the superiority of his methods was no less pronounced.[1]

Finding the Empire reduced to serious straits – all its revenues had been squandered – he inaugurated a moderate financial policy. There was no foolish spending, no reaping (if I may quote) where he had not sowed, no gathering of what he had not scattered. On the contrary, he was careful to determine in advance what capital he was prepared to expend, thereby saving himself from trouble in the future. As a result he left the imperial treasury not full, certainly not overflowing, but half-replenished. Of all the emperors he was the most pious; nobody, in fact, rivalled him in that virtue. In war he achieved several successes, without undue effort, and wore the garlands of victory.[2]

He administered the Empire for slightly over seven years, and when he died, a victim of disease, he left abundant material for would-be eulogists. He controlled his temper, did nothing by instinct, always followed the dictates of reason.

1. He had earned some reputation as a general, but during his reign he was lacking in initiative and dilatory in the extreme.

2. In the east the Turks plundered and ravaged Armenia and Iberia; and the provinces on the Euphrates suffered at their hands. Ani was lost. Meanwhile in the west some 600,000 Uzes crossed the Danube, defeated the Roman and Bulgarian forces who opposed them, captured the Roman generals Basil Apocapes and Nicephorus Botaneiates, broke into Thrace and Greece, and threatened Macedonia. After much delay Constantine marched out against them with 150,000 men, but before he could join battle he heard that the enemy, attacked by Patzinaks, Bulgarians, famine, and disease, had retreated over the Danube. Scylitzes (816C, p. 656) ascribes this reverse to Divine intervention (1065).

No one was ever put to death by him, even where the most dreadful crimes had been committed.[1] No one suffered mutilation at his command. He rarely uttered threats and even these were forgotten soon, for he was invariably more inclined to shed tears than to resort to cruelty.

Having thus given a brief outline of the man, I will now proceed to a fuller description and fill in the details, as I promised I would in the case of this admirable and remarkable ruler.

His family, as far back as his great-grandfathers, had been both distinguished and affluent, the kind of persons historians record in their works. Certain it is that to this very day the names of the celebrated Andronicus, of Constantine, of Pantherius,[2] are on everybody's lips – all relatives of his, some on the paternal, others on the mother's, side. His immediate ancestors were no less prominent. And just as Achilles, descended from the famous Aeacus and Peleus, won more renown than they, so this emperor also, having before him such examples in his own family, not only followed their pattern, but far surpassed his forefathers, being himself conspicuous for all the virtues. From earliest childhood he had seemed a likely candidate for imperial honours, and when he did ascend the throne he conducted himself so well in his duties that he won universal approbation. Constantine was careful to avoid the wild gossip and petty talk of the Forum, and most of his time was spent in the country, where he busied himself on the father's estate. After his marriage he led a life of studied moderation. His wife was herself a member of a famous family (she was the daughter of the great Constantine Dalassenus, a man well known throughout the civilized world for his strength) and she was a lady of much beauty. When death

1. The City Prefect and some nobles were implicated in a plot to kill the emperor on St George's Day (1060), but they were only punished by the confiscation of all their property (Scylitzes 813D, p. 652).
2. Grandfather (?) of the legendary Digenes Akritas.

carried her off, lest he should again be exposed to obloquy or give ill-natured folk any opportunity for slander, he married a second time. This lady was also of noble birth, a woman of great spirit, and exceptional beauty.[1] By her he had both sons and daughters, not only before his accession to the throne but afterwards.[2] The eldest of these children was Michael, who succeeded him as emperor and shared that position with his brothers, surpassing all other rulers before him. When I have told the story of the father's reign, I will pass straight on to a description of him.

At this stage of the history I would like to introduce myself into the narrative, deriving from the virtues of Constantine some reflected glory. At that time I was a prominent orator. In fact, my renown was due rather to eloquence than to any family connexions. The emperor himself was passionately fond of rhetoric, an enthusiast if ever there was one, and my friendship with him and the intimacy we enjoyed owed its origin to this fact. A mutual admiration sprang up after our first conversation and trial of skill, and we became so attached to one another that we frequently visited each other's homes, revelling in this delightful comradeship. Another factor, too, contributed to the high regard in which we held one another. Owing to my oratorical skill I was introduced at court and became secretary to the reigning emperor, none other than Constantine, head of the Monomachi, a position which was in very truth his by right.[3] I was then twenty-five years old. Of course I had to adopt a more distinguished mode of living and a finer house had to be found to live in. Even in this matter the emperor provided for me. He allowed me to take over my friend's[4] house, giving him a mansion in exchange, and thereby uniting us more firmly still in the bonds of friend-

1. Eudocia Macrembolitissa, a relative of Michael Cerularius.

2. Michael and Andronicus before his accession, and Constantine after. There were two daughters, Theodora and Zoe.

3. Constantine IX.   4. Constantine X.

ship. I trusted him (my friend) implicitly on all occasions and
painted a glowing picture of his virtues to the emperor. I was
even able to gain for him certain advantages. Then, of course,
this emperor died and his place on the throne was taken by
Michael the Aged (I will not recall again the many events that
occurred between the two reigns). There was a crisis in the
State, when the military felt it incumbent on *them* to enter
the struggle for power, prepared to risk their lives in order
that they might rule the Empire. Chief responsibility for this
crisis rested on the Senate, because of its choice of magistrates
in the government and because it failed to see the dangers involved. No doubt, too, the emperor gave them a pretext for
disloyalty and added fuel to the flames. Well, the soldiers
decided to rebel on their own initiative, holding a council of
war in Byzantium and immediately afterwards setting out
for their chosen rendezvous. I have told the whole story in
detail in the section devoted to Comnenus.

The people were unanimous in their support of Constantine and wished him to become emperor. They urged him to
seize power himself, but he refused, nobly withdrawing his
own claims and making way for Isaac Comnenus. So God, long
before his accession guided his actions, wishing him to come
to the throne by legitimate means. I prefer not to repeat the
history of the subsequent happenings, but briefly Comnenus
did become master of the Empire, and forgot most of the
promises he had made to Constantine. The latter contented
himself once more with a minor role. He prudently avoided
giving any offence to the ruling monarch. However, when
Comnenus fell ill and nearly died, he remembered the agreements previously made with his lieutenant. He sought my
advice on the situation (none of the emperors in my lifetime
had a higher opinion of me, or admired me more than he did).
The result of this conversation was that he set aside the claims
of his own family and turned wholeheartedly to Constantine.

I will dwell for a few moments on this affair and the reasons for it. It was midday, and the emperor was suffering from a recurrence of his illness, a more than usually violent attack. Believing that he was about to die almost at once, he sent for Ducas, gave him a verbal assurance that he was the new emperor, and openly entrusted to his care those whom he held most dear, his wife and daughter, his brother and the rest of his family. The insignia of the sovereign had not yet been handed over to Constantine, but the promise was explicit.

Later, the emperor recovered somewhat, and as it appeared that he was now restored to his normal health, he regretted what was done, while Constantine, after being promoted to the throne, now found himself in a dangerous and embarrassing position. Not only was he afraid that his hopes were confounded, but he was fearful of the misfortune and the suspicion that might follow his collapse. So, abandoning all others, he took counsel with me, in the name of our old friendship. Whatever I proposed to do, whatever initiative I took, he was ready, he said, to follow without hesitation. Divine, spotless soul (I am moved to write as though you indeed heard me), I did not fail you. My friendship was true. You know yourself how from the very start I stood by you, how I encouraged and upheld you, how I cheered you in moments of despair, how I promised if need arose to share your perils, how I won over to your side the Patriarch, satisfied all the demands of friendship, allowed no opportunity to slip.

To complete the story, the emperor was seized with a worse attack and everyone despaired of his life, but nobody at all, except myself, dared to array Constantine in the imperial insignia. I spoke out freely and seated him on the imperial throne, putting on his feet the sandals of purple – the sandals hitherto denied him – and the Senate gave its unanimous approval. The other ceremonies followed, the meeting of the magistrates, their presentation to the sovereign, the homage due to an emperor, the prostration, and all the formalities usually observed when a new ruler is proclaimed.

When he saw me leading the act of homage, he at once rose from his throne and openly embraced me, his eyes filled with tears. He was quite overcome, and the favours he then promised in his great thankfulness were more than he could ever have fulfilled – though he did carry into effect most of them.

These events took place in the evening, and not long after, Isaac, now utterly despairing both of his throne and his life, allowed himself to undergo the ceremony of tonsuration and assumed the robe of a monk. About midnight the illness became less severe and he revived a little. Then, realizing his predicament and giving up all hope for the future, when he saw that Constantine was now in power, he admitted that the affair had his full approval and without more ado left the palace. A journey by sea brought him to his retreat in the monastery at Studium.

I have already described how he went off there, to die a lingering death, in the history of the last reign. Constantine was now complete master of the Empire and firmly established on the throne. In the privacy of the throne-room, with the separating curtain still drawn, and with only myself standing beside him at his right hand, his first act was to render thanksgiving to God, his hands raised above his head, his eyes filled with tears. After this preliminary act of dedication, he drew aside the curtain and called in the Senate, all the soldiers who happened to be there at the time, the keepers of the public records, and the magistrates who presided in the courts of justice. When all were assembled, he made an extempore speech on the subject of justice and mercy and righteous dealing. The address was suited to his audience, as he appealed now to their sense of justice, now to their humanity and the responsibilities of Empire. At the end he invited me to say a few words appropriate to the occasion, and then dismissed the assembly.

He proceeded at once to put into practice the advice he had given, guided by the two principles just emphasized, namely,

337

'Do good' and 'Dispense justice'. Not a single man out of
that assembly was sent away without some reward. The
government officials, their deputies, the minor dignitaries,
even the manual workers, all received something. In the case
of the last-named, he actually raised their social status. Until
his time there had been a sharp distinction between the class
of ordinary citizens and the Senate, but Constantine did away
with it. Henceforth no discrimination was made between
worker and Senator, and they were merged in one body.

Seeing that the majority of his subjects were disturbed at
the injustice of their lot, some persons exercising more power
than they should have done, while the rest were oppressed by
them, he decided to act as a judge himself, 'seeing things', as
the Prophet-King has it, 'with an unbiased eye'. Wrongdoers
he treated with severity, but to the injured parties he showed
himself most gracious and kind. So long as a trial was in progress there was no prejudice for or against either litigant,
plaintiff or defendant, and both were cross-examined with
equal respect. This impartiality led to the disclosure of secrets:
not only was the character of individual witnesses exposed to
scrutiny, but more often than not fresh delinquencies were
brought to light. New customs made their first appearance at
court, their initiation being proclaimed with the utmost
solemnity. Unjust contracts were annulled. Every order issued
by the emperor, every written instruction, had the same, or
even greater, force than the law. As for the country-folk, who
in former times did not even know who the ruling emperor
was, they were unwavering in their loyalty to Constantine,
while the kindly affection he had for them was evident in the
way he spoke to them, and still more from the way he treated
them.

These were not his only measures, for the public revenues
also demanded attention. I am not composing a panegyric,
but a true history, so I must admit here that there were occasions on which his policy fell short of perfection, when he

relied on his own judgement and refused outside advice. For example, international differences, according to his ideas, had to be settled, not by recourse to arms, but by the sending of gifts and by other tokens of friendship – for two reasons: in the first place, he would avoid having to spend the greater part of the imperial revenues on the army, and secondly his own manner of life would not be disturbed.

Actually he was greatly mistaken in this, for, when the military organization broke down, the power of our enemies increased and they became more active in opposition. Of course emperors should be above such foolishness – refusal to accept advice, I mean, and lack of foresight – but selfishness on the one hand, and on the other the flattering speeches of ordinary folk, who persuaded some of them that they could do everything unaided, these for the most part were the things that caused their downfall and led them astray, off the path of duty. If a man speaks his mind in defence of what is good, they suspect him, whereas a warm welcome awaits the parasite: *he* is allowed to share their secrets. Herein lies the cause of the Roman Empire's decline. It was this that brought discredit on our affairs. Yet more than once I tried to save this emperor, if no other, from such a mistake. On this point, however, he was emphatic and quite inflexible. Let us leave it at that, and examine his reputation for humanity, as well as for wisdom. We have already dealt with his claim to be just. But here I recall a point that had escaped my memory, and I will mention it now.

At the time when he was crowned, he made a vow to God that he would never inflict corporal punishment. It was a promise that he kept, and more than kept, for not only did he abstain from physical violence, but usually from violent language, except when he purposely assumed a terrible expression and uttered threats of vengeance that he never intended to carry out. As a judge, he went straight to the point, dealing with cases on their merit and giving each party a reasonable chance to state their claims, careful to maintain justice where injustice had been done.

The reader may like to know something of his home-life. With the children he was delightful, joining gladly in their games, laughing at their baby-talk, often romping with them. From infancy he saw to it that they had a good education, both in mind and body. Three sons had been born before he acceded to the throne, and two daughters. The second boy lived only a short time after his father became emperor and then died, a most beautiful child. Of the daughters the younger had already been betrothed.[1] She was a lady of great charm and virtue. The other, who bore the significant name of Arete (Virtue), dedicated her life to the service of God.[2] She is still with us. May she live to a ripe old age!

The sun had not yet completed its yearly cycle after Constantine's promotion when another child was born, and was at once dignified with the imperial title. The other two brothers, having been born before his accession (the remarkable Michael and the younger son, Andronicus), counted as ordinary citizens. However, it was not long before his father adorned the eldest and most handsome son, this same Michael, the truly devout Michael, with the imperial diadem; but, just before he took his seat on the throne, Constantine put him to a severe test, to find out if the young man was really suited to be emperor. The question he asked him concerned political theory. As Michael solved the problem and gave the correct answer, the emperor regarded it as an omen that he was destined to win great renown in his future reign, and the ceremony of enthronement was at once performed.

Later on certain individuals set on foot a plot against the emperor's life.[3] Their object was to depose him and set up

1. Zoe married Adrian Comnenus, brother of the future Alexius I.
2. She was also known as Theodora Anna.
3. They planned to sink the imperial galley and drown Constantine on his way back to the palace from Mangana.

someone else as head of state. The conspirators included among their number men of obscure birth, persons who were quite unknown, but there were also implicated some of the nobles and distinguished men. The plot was preconcerted in such a way that some of the rebels made their attempt from the sea, while others were carrying on their disreputable business on land, but, at the very moment when things reached a crisis, the affair was brought to light through Divine intervention and their evil plans were discovered. Constantine might well have had them beheaded. They might have lost their hands or been mutilated in some other way. Instead, some of them were forcibly shaved and the rest condemned to exile. The emperor, as if to celebrate his narrow escape from danger, invited me to his private apartment and ordered me to dine at his table. But he had not finished the meal before he burst into tears. 'Philosopher,' he said, 'what a pity our exiles cannot share in such pleasures! I cannot possibly enjoy myself like this when others are in distress!'

When an alliance had been concluded between the western Mysians and the Triballi, and these two nations formed a united front, the Roman Empire found itself in a very serious position. At the first opportunity Constantine hurried off to fight them, but, later, thanks to me – I snatched him from danger almost by main force – he returned to the palace. However, he did mobilize a small army and sent it off to oppose them. At this point God worked a wonder no less strange than the miracles performed by Moses, for the barbarians immediately took to their heels, terror-struck, scattering in all directions, and most of them were cut down by our men's swords as they followed them in hot pursuit. It was as if the enemy had seen a host of angelic beings. Their dead were left to the birds of prey, while the runaways dispersed all over the countryside. If I had proposed to write a panegyric, therefore, instead of a comprehensive history, in this marvel I would have found enough material for praise beyond all bounds. As it is, I must divert my enthusiasm to other matters.

It would be possible for me to name emperors who rivalled, even equalled, Constantine in other things, but not where belief in God was concerned, or the mystery of the ineffable dispensation of God the Word. This latter, to Constantine, was more than anything else beyond conception: no words could possibly explain it, however simple, however clever. Every time I tried to expound to him the Mystery enacted on our behalf, his heart would fill with joy, his whole body tremble in exultation, and the tears would stream from his eyes. He had made a study of Holy Writ in all its fullness, and his knowledge was not confined merely to the text, but extended to the deep spiritual ideas that underlie it. Whatever leisure from public duties he enjoyed was spent in the reading of the Sacred Books.

He took peculiar pleasure in my company. No one else had the same restful influence on him, and if therefore I failed to present myself several times a day, he would complain about it and fret. He respected me more than anyone else and 'drank his fill of waters at my fount': to him they were as nectar. I told him once that a certain citizen was dead. To my astonishment he displayed extraordinary pleasure and, when I asked him why, he replied: 'Because, if you must know, I have heard many complaints about the fellow before and now . . .', but here I broke in (actually I was afraid he might give way to violence and burst into a rage against the man): 'Well, since he is dead, let the accusations against the man die too. It would be well for his detractors to forget them, for all hatred perishes when a man meets his end.'

Constantine promoted his brother John to the dignity of Caesar. He showed great affection for him, especially after his elevation, and shared with him the administration of the Empire. This was not surprising, for the brother was endowed with wisdom. He was, moreover, a man of high ideals and great practical ability. It was natural, then, that when the emperor (some time before his death) fell victim to a serious illness, he should place under John's tutelage his own children. John was to be a father to them, together with the man whom Constantine had appointed Patriarch.[1] The latter gentleman was a person of great virtue and thoroughly suited to be Head of the Church.

However, the emperor recovered from that illness, though it was not long before there were signs of physical decay and he gradually declined. On this occasion he entrusted all his duties to his wife, Eudocia. In his opinion, she was the wisest woman of her time and he thought that no one was better qualified to educate his sons and daughters. Later on in the history I will give a more detailed account of Eudocia. Constantine himself did not long survive the administrative changes I have mentioned, and after committing the children to her care, he died.[2] He had lived slightly over sixty years.

I doubt whether any emperor lived a life more glorious, or died more contented. Apart from the one conspiracy against his life and the disaster from which he was saved, the rest of his reign was spent in tranquillity and pleasure. What is more, he left behind sons to succeed him on the throne, sons who were the living image of their father, resembling him both in character and in physique.

Having given an adequate account of his deeds, let us now

1. John Xiphilinus of Trebizond was elected patriarch in 1064, after the death of Lichudes, against his will (Scylitzes, 817C, p. 658) for he was anxious not to leave his monastery. He was Abbot there (Psellus, *Funeral Oration on John Xiphilinus*, ed. C. N. Sathas, *Bibl. Graec. Med. Aev.*, iv, p. 448).

2. His illness began in October 1066 and lasted until the following May. On his deathbed he compelled his wife to swear that she would never marry again, and the Caesar John and other intimates were required to promise that they would recognize no other emperor but Constantine's sons.

record a few of his sayings.[1] When speaking of those who had plotted against him, he used to remark that, far from depriving them of honour or money, he would treat them as slaves, not as free men. 'But it is not I who have taken away their freedom: it is the law that has exiled them from their country.' He was a keen student of literature and a favourite saying was this: 'Would that I were better known as a scholar than as emperor!' He was a valiant fighter himself, and, when someone professed that he would gladly shield the emperor with his own body in battle, Constantine answered: 'Good! And please don't forget to deal me a blow yourself, when I have fallen!' To a person who was making a careful study of the laws, so that he might do some wrong with impunity, he remarked, 'These laws are the ruination of us!' With that I end my account of this emperor.

1. It is noteworthy that the whole of this section dealing with his sayings is found verbatim in Scylitzes, 818C, p. 660. Medieval writers regarded the work of their predecessors or even contemporaries as common property. (Cf. Anna Comnena, *Alexiad.* v, 9, where she uses a passage taken from Psellus, *Chronographia*, Romanus III, 2–3.)

EUDOCIA

EUDOCIA BECOMES RULER OF THE EMPIRE, WITH HER SONS MICHAEL AND CONSTANTINE

WHEN the Empress Eudocia, in accordance with the wishes of her husband, succeeded him as supreme ruler, she did not hand over the government to others. Far from choosing to spend most of her life in idleness at home, while the magistrates had charge of public affairs, she assumed control of the whole administration in person. At first she behaved modestly enough: neither in the imperial processions nor in her own clothing was there any mark of extravagance. She made herself conversant with all her duties, and wherever it was practicable she took part in all the processes of government, the choice of magistrates, civil affairs, revenues, and taxes. Her pronouncements had the note of authority which one associates with an emperor. Nor was this surprising, for she was in fact an exceedingly clever woman. On either side of her were the two sons, both of whom stood almost rooted to the spot, quite overcome with awe and reverence for their mother.

That Constantine should respect her, being a child and still incapable of understanding political matters, will hardly be unexpected, and I cannot bring myself to praise him for a modesty that was natural, but Michael's case was different. He was already long past his boyhood and able to think for himself. His intellectual powers were fully developed, had been frequently put to the test, and it is no easy matter, therefore, to find a parallel to his obedient attitude, or to the way he left the whole administration to his mother. I find it altogether impossible to praise the young man enough for this. On several occasions I have seen him myself, when he could have spoken in his mother's presence, keep silent, as if speech were beyond him, and, though he had the ability to undertake any task you like to name, he took no part in matters concerned with the Empire.

Yet it would not be true to say that his mother despised him, at the beginning of her reign. As a matter of fact, she personally trained him for his future career, and later on allowed him to appoint magistrates and encouraged him to act as a judge. She often demonstrated her affection for him with kisses. There were times when she commended him, expressed her pride in what he had done, and always she was building up his character, quietly preparing him for the various duties that an emperor has to perform. She frequently handed him over to me and suggested that I should instruct him in the functions of his office and give him advice. He used to sit on the imperial throne beside his brother Constantine, and being endowed with an exceptionally generous nature, he had no intention of keeping all power to himself. In fact, he often let his brother share in his duties as emperor. Such was the state of affairs at that time, and these arrangements would have been preserved without alteration to the end, if they had not suffered interruption from a cruel blow of fortune.

At this stage in my narrative I would like to say just this about the Empress Eudocia: I do not know whether any other woman ever set such an example of wisdom or lived a life comparable to hers, up to this point; I will not go so far as to say that she became *less* wise after this event, only that she lost some of her old precision: her ideas changed as she grew older. I would offer this defence on her behalf, that, even if there was some alteration in her, she did not become a slave to pleasure nor give way to voluptuous emotions. The truth is, she was very worried over her sons, and feared they might be deprived of the crown, if there were no one to protect and guide them. Actually, life at the palace held no attraction so far as she herself was concerned. The following incident will prove this quite convincingly. The present author was a brother (I am using the word in a spiritual sense) of her father, and she had a great respect for me. In fact, she looked upon me as something divine. I happened on one occasion to be with her in a sacred church, and, when I saw the earnestness of her faith in God and how devoted she was to her Lord, I was deeply moved and prayed with all my heart that she might enjoy power as long as she lived. But, she, turning round, rebuked me for it. The prayer, she said, was really a curse. 'I hope it will not be my fate to enjoy power so long that I die an empress.' These words filled me with such terror that ever afterwards I regarded her as more than human.

However, man is a very inconstant being, especially when external circumstances give him an excuse for changing. This particular empress was a woman of steadfast character and noble spirit, but her tower of wise counsels was violently shaken by the rivers that dashed against it, and she was persuaded to marry a second time. A number of people knew what was going on, and they even suggested that Destiny had a hand in the matter. Yet she never so much as hinted at her intentions to me. No doubt she held her tongue for shame. She wished to avoid naming the husband-to-be and at the same time put an end to the conflicting rumours about his identity. On the other hand, she wanted me to know of her plan. Consequently I was visited by one of her evil counsellors. He urged me to speak freely to her on the subject, and to suggest that she should put a nobleman on the throne.[1] My

1. Eudocia was particularly concerned at the attitude of the patriarch: he insisted that she should remain faithful to the oath given to her dying husband. To get his consent to the marriage, she conspired with one of the court eunuchs, a man of bad character. He suggested to the patriarch that his brother Bardas should marry the empress. Xiphilinus, flattered

answer was concise: I would neither offer this advice, nor seek to persuade her by arguments, nor would I use my eloquence if a good opportunity presented itself.

In the meantime there had been whispered rumours, and the court got to know of the affair. The future emperor had already been chosen by her, and, according to the arrangements they had made, this was the very day on which the prospective bridegroom was expected to arrive in the city. On the morrow the ceremony of coronation was to be performed. That evening the empress sent for me. When we were alone, she spoke to me with tears in her eyes. 'You must be aware', she said, 'of our loss in prestige and of the declining fortunes of our Empire, with wars constantly springing up and barbarian hordes ravaging the whole of the east.[1] How can our country possibly escape disaster?' I knew nothing of the things that had been going on, nor that the future emperor was already standing at the palace doors, so I replied that it was no easy matter to decide. 'It requires careful consideration,' I said. 'Better propose today and listen tomorrow, as the proverb says.' With a little laugh she went on, 'But deliberation is superfluous now. The matter has been considered already and the decision is made. Romanus, the son of Diogenes,[2] has been invited to rule as emperor, in preference to all others.'

These words filled me with instant consternation. I could not conceive what would become of me. 'Well then,' I said, 'tomorrow I too will give my advice on the matter.' – 'Not tomorrow,' she replied, 'but now. Give me your support.'

---

by this proposal, consulted the Senate, but could not press Bardas's claim (he was quite unsuitable); however, he agreed that Diogenes Romanus should be the lucky man (Scylitzes, 821–2, p. 664 ff.).

1. The Turks were successful in Cilicia (helped by a Roman deserter, Amertices, who had attempted to assassinate Constantine X) and in Syria, where Nicephorus Botaneiates fought them with an ill-equipped force and eventually gave up his command. The Patzinaks in Europe were troublesome but were repelled by Romanus.

2. Romanus was born in Cappadocia.

I returned to the attack, with just one question: 'But your son, the emperor, who will presumably one day govern the Empire alone – does he know what has happened too?' – 'He is not entirely in the dark, although he does not yet know all the details,' she said. 'However, I am glad you mention my son. Let us go up to him together, and explain how things stand. He is sleeping above in one of the imperial apartments.'

So we went up to him. How she felt about it I do not know, but I was most agitated. A sudden fit of trembling shook me through and through. She sat down on her son's bed, called him 'her emperor', 'her best of sons'. 'Rise up', she said, 'and receive your step-father. Although he takes the place of your father, he will be a subject, not a ruler. I, your mother, have bound him in writing to observe this arrangement.' Well, the young man got up from his bed at once, and although he looked at me suspiciously I have no idea what he was thinking. Together with his mother he left the room in which he had been sleeping, and immediately came face to face with the new emperor. Without the slightest trace of emotion, his visage quite expressionless, he embraced Romanus, becoming at once his colleague on the throne and his friend.

Thereupon the Caesar was also summoned. Never were his diplomatic qualities seen to better advantage. First he made some tactful inquiries about his nephew the emperor, then added a few words of commendation in praise of Romanus. This was followed by congratulations for all the imperial party. One could almost hear him singing the wedding song and see him taking his fill from the nuptial drinking-bowl. And that is how the government of the Empire passed into the hands of the next sovereign, Romanus.[1]

1. The marriage took place on 1 January 1068 and the new reign begins from that date.

ROMANUS IV

1068–71

THE REIGN OF ROMANUS DIOGENES

THIS emperor, Romanus, son of Diogenes, came of an ancient and distinguished family. Only in one respect was it dishonoured – by his father. The latter had been arrested on a charge of attempted revolution during the reign of Romanus Argyrus and had committed suicide by hurling himself over a precipice. There were occasions when he did act in a straightforward fashion, but for the most part he was a hypocrite and a braggart. Even Romanus himself did not escape the imputation of treachery at the time, but any designs he may have cherished during the rest of his life passed unnoticed, until Eudocia became empress (I have described this lady in the preceding chapters). It was not until her reign that he revealed his secret intentions. He was at once apprehended, and his audacity would have met with its just deserts, had not the empress exercised her clemency on his behalf and saved him from condemnation – an error of judgement on her part. She ought to have put him to death. Instead she preserved his life, and, having done so, she thought that her own supremacy would be assured if she made him emperor. He would, she believed, never again oppose her wishes. It was a reasonable conjecture, but her plans went astray. After pretending for a few days to be her loyal subject, he suddenly reverted to his normal habits. The more she tried to dominate him, to treat him, who was really her master, like a lion in a cage, the more he fretted at her restraining influence and glared at the hand that kept him in check. To begin with, he growled inwardly, but as time passed his disgust became obvious to everyone.

I must admit that his attitude to myself was one of great

deference. The fact is, when he was still a private citizen, he
had courted my favour with the most abject servility, and I
had in some measure helped him in his career. Far from forgetting these services when he ascended the throne, he showed
such affection and regard for me that he would rise up when
I came into his presence and treated me as his greatest friend.
However, that is by the way and outside the general scope
of my narrative. The main point is that he wished to reign
unchallenged by anyone else and to govern the Empire entirely on his own. Unfortunately he had made no notable
contribution to public affairs in his previous career. Nevertheless he waited patiently for the opportunity, and the declaration of war against the Persians owed its origin no less
to his personal ambitions than to a desire to safeguard the
whole commonwealth.[1]

It was my habit to give the emperors useful advice, so I
tried to restrain him, pointing out that it was first necessary
to discuss the question of military forces, to draw up lists of
names, to call on help from abroad, and then, when all preparations had been completed, to declare war. But the bab-
blers who make a habit of contradicting all I say (with a few
exceptions) have brought ruin on our affairs. They did it then,
and they are doing it now. So the worse opinion prevailed,
and he, donning his warlike armour in the palace, taking a
shield in his left hand and a spear in his right, 'well compacted
with bands, twenty-two cubits in length,'[2] thought that with
the one he could bar the enemy's inroads, while he plunged
the other in his adversary's flanks. Others uttered their war-
cry, clapped their hands at this, but my face was clouded with
gloom, for I guessed what the result of it all would probably
be.

1. The elevation of Romanus was clearly a victory for the military
party. In Psellus's account one can detect some bias – Psellus being prominent among the courtiers.
2. Cf. Homer, *Iliad*, xv, 678.

At all events, he left the city with all his army[1] and advanced against the barbarians, not knowing where he was marching nor what he was going to do. He wandered over the countryside, planning to go one way, marching by another, traversing Syria, as well as Persia – and all the success he met with was to lead his army into the interior, establish his men on some high hills, bring them down again, cut them off in narrow passes, and suffer heavy casualties through his manoeuvring. However, he returned, still to all appearances victorious. Neither from the Medes nor from the Persians did he bring us any spoils of war. One thing alone satisfied him: that he had marched against his foes.

Therein lay his first excuse for vainglory. From now on he affected contempt for the empress, completely despised the officers of state, refused advice, and – incurable malady of emperors – relied on no counsel, no guidance but his own, under all circumstances without exception. As for myself, I swear by God, the God whom philosophy reveres, that I tried to turn him from his ambitions. I knew his treacherous designs. I feared for the empress and the commonwealth, lest all should be lost in revolt and disorder. I reminded him of his solemn undertakings. Wherever possible, I even tried to frighten him with the prospect of ultimate failure: his schemes might turn to his own destruction. And when, as often happened, the Empress Eudocia was stirred to indignation at his insults, and when she was grieved, I

1. Romanus had a conglomerate force of Macedonians, Bulgarians, Cappadocians, Uzes, Franks, and some poor levies from Phrygia. The army was ill-paid and ill-equipped – a state of affairs entirely due to his predecessor. Psellus is not quite fair to him, for his strategy was not so aimless as he infers. The enemy had the initiative and could strike at many points, while the emperor had generals he could scarcely trust. Certainly he himself was brave enough and often saved the day. He was defeated by the Turks on 20 November 1068.

took both sides and tried by my words to reconcile their differences.[1]

Not long afterwards, at the very beginning of spring,[2] in fact, there was trouble from the enemy, and the emperor's previous campaign was shown to have been a hollow triumph. So once more there were preparations for war and (to pass over the intervening occurrences) I myself took a small part in the expedition. The fact is, he put such overwhelming compulsion on me to join him on the campaign that I could not possibly refuse. I would rather not say anything at the moment of the reason why he was so insistent that I should accompany him, because I am abridging most of this story, but I will speak of it when I write the history of these events. I am still under an obligation in the matter, although nobody can accuse me of any disloyalty to him, nor blame me because all his plans went astray.

He agreed that in all matters connected with literature he was my inferior (I am referring here to the sciences), but where military strategy was concerned it was his ambition to surpass me. The knowledge that I was thoroughly conversant with the science of military tactics, that I had made a complete study of everything pertaining to military formations, the building of war-machines, the capture of cities, and all the other things that a general has to consider, this moved him not only to admiration, but also to envy. So far as he could, he argued against me, and tried to outdo me in these debates. Many of those who shared that campaign with us will know that this description is not exaggerated.

This second war of his was no more successful than the first. It was, in fact, altogether indecisive and the enemy held their own everywhere. If our men fell in their tens of thousands, while a mere handful of our adversaries were taken prisoner,

1. Nicephorus Palaeologus and John Ducas were leaders of the peace party, with Psellus.
2. Spring 1069.

at least we were not beaten – and we succeeded in making a lot of noise at the barbarians! The result of it all was that Romanus became more proud and more insolent than ever, because, forsooth, he had twice commanded an army. He lost respect for everything and – worse still – the evil counsellors to whom he listened led him completely astray.

As for the empress, he treated her like a captive taken in war. For next to nothing he would have agreed even to drive her out of the palace. The Caesar he suspected, and on several occasions hastened to arrest and put him to death, but changed his mind afterwards and gave up the idea. For the present, at all events, he was content to bind him and his sons to swear on oath that they would be loyal. Having no reasonable pretext for carrying out the plans which he secretly cherished against the Caesar, he set out on his third and last expedition against the barbarians, who were now distinctly hostile.[1] Actually, they were engaged in plundering raids on Roman territory, and as soon as spring came they overran it in considerable force. So Romanus once again left the capital to fight them, accompanied by a larger contingent of allies and native troops than before.

With his usual contempt of all advice, whether on matters civil or military, he at once set out with his army and hurried to Caesarea. Having reached that objective, he was loath to advance any further and tried to find excuses for returning to Byzantium, not only for his own sake but for the army's. When he found the disgrace involved in such a retreat intolerable, he should have come to terms with the enemy and put a

1. Psellus does not mention that the campaign of 1070 was carried on by Manuel Comnenus. He was defeated and captured, but persuaded his conqueror to desert to the Byzantines and unexpectedly returned to the capital. Romanus's third war, against Alp Arslan, the Seljuq leader, took place in 1071. The Sultan offered peace, but the emperor refused his terms and a pitched battle was fought at Manzikert (26 August 1071). Romanus was defeated, but showed great gallantry (Scylitzes, 841, p. 699).

stop to their annual incursions. Instead, whether in desperation, or because he was more confident than he should have been, he marched to the attack, without taking adequate measures to protect his rear. The enemy, seeing him advance, decided to lure him on still farther and ensnare him by cunning. They therefore rode on ahead of him and then retired again, as though the retreat was planned. By carrying out this manoeuvre several times, they succeeded in cutting off some of our generals, who were taken captive.

Now I was aware (though he was not) that the Sultan himself, the King of the Persians and Kurds, was present in person with his army, and most of their victories were due to his leadership. Romanus refused to believe anyone who detected the Sultan's influence in these successes. The truth is, he did not want peace. He thought he would capture the barbarian camp without a battle. Unfortunately for him, through his ignorance of military science, he had scattered his forces; some were concentrated round himself, others had been sent off to take up some other position. So, instead of opposing his adversaries with the full force of his army, less than half were actually involved.[1]

Although I cannot applaud his subsequent behaviour, it is impossible for me to censure him. The fact is, he bore the whole brunt of the danger himself. His action can be interpreted in two ways. My own view represents the mean between these two extremes. On the one hand, if you regard him as a hero, courting danger and fighting courageously, it is reasonable to praise him; on the other, when one reflects that a general, if he conforms to the accepted rules of strategy, must remain aloof from the battle-line, supervising the movements of his army and issuing the necessary orders to the men under his command, then Romanus's conduct on this occasion would appear foolish in the extreme, for he exposed himself to danger without a thought of the consequences. I myself

1. The Battle of Manzikert.

am more inclined to praise than to blame him for what he did.[1]

However that may be, he put on the full armour of an ordinary soldier and drew sword against his enemies. According to several of my informants he actually killed many of them and put others to flight. Later, when his attackers recognized who he was, they surrounded him on all sides. He was wounded and fell from his horse. They seized him, of course, and the Emperor of the Romans was led away, a prisoner, to the enemy camp, and his army was scattered. Those who escaped were but a tiny fraction of the whole. Of the majority some were taken captive, the rest massacred.

I do not intend at this moment to write of the time spent by the emperor in captivity, or of the attitude adopted towards him by his conqueror. That must wait till later. A few days after the battle, one of those who escaped, arriving before his comrades, brought the terrible news to the city. He was followed by a second messenger, and by others. The picture they painted was by no means distinct, for each explained the disaster in his own fashion, some saying that Romanus was dead, others that he was only a prisoner; some again declared that they had seen him wounded and hurled to the ground, while others had seen him being led away in chains to the barbarian camp. In view of this information, a conference was held in the capital, and the empress considered our future policy. The unanimous decision of the meeting was that, for the time being, they should ignore the emperor, whether he was a prisoner, or dead, and that Eudocia and her sons should carry on the government of the Empire.

At this conference some councillors wished Michael, and his young brother, to control the administration entirely:

1. Psellus conveniently ignores the fact that if Andronicus, son of John Ducas, had not run away and deliberately spread the rumour that the battle was lost, Romanus might never have been compelled to take such a risk (Scylitzes, 840D, p. 698).

their mother was to take no active part whatever. Others again favoured the complete restoration of Eudocia's rule, to the exclusion of her sons. For my own part, neither solution of the problem seemed satisfactory. My personal opinion – I will speak frankly – was that both should act in concert: the son should pay her respect, because she was his mother, and she should govern the whole Empire as sovereign on equal terms with her son. This was in fact the proposal which the Emperor Michael himself favoured and he supported me. There were persons who wished to get supreme power for themselves and to govern the State for their own profit, and these were just the people who urged her to rule alone. At the same time they were busily engaged in trying to force a quarrel between Michael and his mother.

It is difficult for me, at this stage, to express adequately the admiration I feel for this young man. He discussed the constitutional question with me privately, and he was prepared, if his mother so desired, to abdicate. He was most anxious to avoid any mark of disrespect for her: at all costs she must be treated with all due consideration. Again and again I managed to effect a settlement between them, but Michael was so obsessed with the idea that he must never oppose his mother that even the thought of meeting her face to face would cause him to blush. He insisted on humiliating himself altogether. Such was the position, with the whole matter undecided, when the Caesar arrived in the city, at Eudocia's invitation, and lent his support to my scheme. He was strongly in favour of joint-rule by the family.

This trouble had not completely died down before another howling tempest broke over our heads, and on the self-same day. The commander-in-chief of the enemy forces, when he perceived that the Roman Emperor had fallen into his hands, instead of exulting in his triumph, was quite overcome by his own extraordinary success. He celebrated his victory with a moderation that was beyond all expectation. Offering his condolences to the captive, he shared his own table with him, treated him as an honoured guest, gave him a bodyguard, loosed from their chains those prisoners he cared to name and set them free. Finally, he restored liberty to Romanus himself also, and, after making a treaty of friendship and after receiving from him assurances on oath that he would loyally abide by the agreements they had made, sent him back to Roman territory, with as numerous an escort and bodyguard as anyone could wish for.[1] Actually, this proved to be the beginning of trouble, the main cause of a multitude of disasters. The emperor, having obtained more concessions than he had thought possible, was under the impression that he could now recover his throne without any difficulty, and, to signalize the good fortune that had followed on his defeat, he wrote a letter in his own hand to the empress, telling her of his adventures.

Immediately there was wild confusion in the palace, with comings and goings everywhere. Some professed astonishment at the news, others would not believe it. Eudocia found herself in an embarrassing position. She was unable to decide what to do next. When I myself arrived in the midst of the turmoil, there was a general demand that I should advise on the best policy. My beloved emperor (Michael) was particularly insistent and joined the others in urging me to speak. I declared, therefore, that it was no longer necessary to receive Romanus in the Empire: he should be outlawed, and instructions should be forwarded to every place in the Roman dominions that his reign was over. The moderate element were convinced that this policy was in our best interests, but the opposition favoured a different plan.

1. A full account is preserved in Scylitzes (842, p. 700). The Sultan asked Romanus what *he* would have done if the Romans had won. The emperor, without any dissimulation, replied, 'I would have flogged you to death!' 'But I', said Arslan, 'will not imitate you. I have been told that your Christ teaches gentleness and forgiveness of wrong. He resists the proud and gives grace to the humble.'

That was the state of affairs when Michael, fearing for his own safety and distrusting the cruel nature of Diogenes, decided on his own course of action. The plan he adopted undoubtedly saved him, and it was admittedly a wise move. He cut himself off from his mother and henceforth became his own master. Then, on the advice of his cousins, the Caesar's sons,[1] he won over to his allegiance the palace guards.[2] (These men are, without exception, armed with shields and the *rhomphaia*, a one-edged sword of heavy iron which they carry suspended from the right shoulder.) Well, the guards banged on their shields all together, bawled their heads off as they shouted their war-cry, clashed sword on sword, with answering yells, and went off to the emperor, thinking he was in danger. Then, forming a circle about him, so that no one could approach, they carried him off to the upper parts of the palace.

So much for them. Meanwhile those who were with the empress – and I was one of that number – not knowing what was happening, were almost petrified with fear. We thought that terrible things were about to befall us. The empress did indeed lose her nerve, and pulling her veil over her head she ran off to a secret crypt below ground. While she was hiding in the depths of this cavern, I stayed by the opening that led to it. I had no idea what to do, nor where to turn for safety. However, once his own security was guaranteed, Michael remembered me. I was the first person he thought of, and messengers were sent to all parts of the palace, to find out where I was. Having discovered me, they lifted me up in their arms and carried me in cheerful triumph to their sovereign, as if I were some lucky find, or some precious gift. And he, as soon as he set eyes on me, was like a man who heaves a sigh of relief when a storm has passed. At once he handed over to me the responsibility of taking all decisions that might be necessary.

1. Andronicus and Constantine Ducas.
2. The famous Varangian Guards.

So I busied myself with affairs of State. There were plans to be made, precautions to be taken, if the administration of the city was to ride this storm. Meanwhile the others were dealing with the question of the dowager empress. To cut a long story short, it was decreed that she must leave the city and live in a convent that she herself had founded by the sea in honour of Mary, the Mother of God. No time was lost in carrying out this decision, although her son refused to ratify it: he could not agree to his mother's exile. I know that for a fact, and I am prepared to maintain it before all the world, with God as my witness. The truth is, circumstances were too strong for him and overruled his wishes.

In matters of this kind, history is apt to repeat itself. You find the same sort of things happening, the same sort of things being said. In this case, men differed widely in their opinions about the empress, and a constant stream of propaganda was directed against her. The result was a second decree, to the effect that she must now take the veil of a nun. Without more ado this order was also carried out, and the empress's career was brought to an abrupt conclusion.[1]

Diogenes, meantime, instead of rejoicing in his deliverance, was filled with chagrin at the prospect of losing his throne. Actually, a large body of soldiers had already flocked to his standard, and as he moved from place to place, with the comforting knowledge that there was no one to oppose him, he appropriated to his own use the money from the public funds. Finally he arrived with his army at the famous city of Amasea, the place that everyone is talking about.

Michael's immediate answer to this was to appoint the Caesar's younger son commander-in-chief of the Roman Army. The new general was a man of great energy, blessed with a quick wit and a remarkable flair for discerning the

1. According to Scylitzes (843, p. 702) Eudocia was exiled by Caesar John and his sons, and above all by Psellus, who 'glories in his deed in one of his books'.

right course of action, and for explaining it in language that all could understand. Having approached the city – Diogenes had already established himself in Amasea – he first concentrated his army. This done, he began a series of skirmishes, using all manner of wily tricks in order to capture his opponent, or else drive him out of the city. As his position grew steadily worse, Diogenes made a daring sally and drew up the whole of his forces in battle-array against the attacker. In the ensuing struggle both sides suffered considerable losses. Our general charged the enemy like a horseman on wings, and falling on the hostile ranks, a veritable tower of strength, forced them back and smashed their line in many places. Some of those who resisted fell fighting on the battlefield, others were captured, while a small number escaped by flight. Among these last was Diogenes, riding as fast as his horse could carry him. For the first time we had reason to feel confident in the future.

As a matter of fact, this defeat marked the beginning of Diogenes' downfall. With a handful of his followers, he took refuge in a minor fortress,[1] and he would very soon have fallen into our hands but for the intervention of someone else.[2] An Armenian by birth, a crafty individual opposed to us on principle, this man had been promoted to high rank by Diogenes, while he was still reigning emperor, and now, seeing in the latter's present misfortune an opportunity to repay the favours he had received from him in the past, he came to meet him with a strong band of soldiers. He encouraged Romanus to take heart, made him wonderful promises, and, instead of allowing him to fight our troops, carried him off to Cilicia. The remote valleys of that country, he argued, would give him a respite from our attacks. Next he equipped an

1. Tyropaeum. The defeat of Chapter 24 was really suffered by Theodorus Alyates, one of the emperor's lieutenants who was captured and blinded.
2. Chatatoures, the Duke of Antioch.

army for him, gave him money, clothed him in the robes of an emperor, and then, having armed him for battle, the clever rogue waited for a favourable chance to renew the struggle against us.

Once again, therefore, we held a council and debated our future policy. One party was in favour of making peace: it was better, they contended, to allow him some share in the government, and to do nothing more in the matter. Others were determined to prosecute the war and make sure that he had no second chance to embark on his reckless schemes. Well, we decided to try the course of peace first. A friendly and sympathetic letter was dispatched to him from the emperor. Diogenes, however, regarded Michael's kindly attitude as an outrageous insult. He maintained that he himself was entirely free from blame, and he proceeded to make specific demands. He refused to abdicate or in any way moderate his claims to the throne. In fact, to judge from his reply, he was more presumptuous than his plotting had led us to believe.

So the emperor was reluctantly compelled to abandon his plans for peace. Andronicus, the elder of the Caesar's sons, was given command of the imperial armies. This Andronicus was an amazingly tall man, generous, kindly, and extremely fair. He was now entrusted with the conduct of all the forces of the Eastern Command, and was sent out to do battle with the enemy. His first object was to instil into his army a corporate spirit: the loyalties of his men must be centred in one common purpose. With this in view he treated all ranks with meticulous fairness. He tried to understand his soldiers as individuals, and to prove that he was their friend. His second aim was to escape Diogenes' notice when he drew near the passes into Cilicia, to make his way quietly through the tortuous mountain defiles, and, after traversing all the difficult parts, to present himself unexpectedly before the enemy. Our men set about this task, and in accordance with the plan they marched through the pass on a narrow precipitous path. Meanwhile the emperor was terribly worried in case his rival should be caught by our soldiers, and either fall fighting, or having been taken alive be mutilated in some part of his body.

Many a time I have seen him weep over this, risking his own life if only his adversary might be spared any suffering. The man was his friend, he said, and there were covenants between them, which he was afraid might be broken. So certain priests, men of peace, were entrusted with a message of friendship to Diogenes.[1] They had a letter from Michael in which he made all kinds of promises, but at the same time counselled him, stubborn though he was, to submit.

Before this message arrived, however, Diogenes was already engaged in war. He himself remained inside the fortress previously seized by him with a handful of men, but practically all his army was under the command of the Armenian Chatatoures, whom I mentioned in a preceding chapter, and had been sent out to do battle, apparently with every chance of success. The Armenian, advancing with infantry and cavalry, had seized the points of vantage before our men arrived, and his forces were drawn up in battle order. For the most part they were fine physical specimens, and most eager for combat.

Facing Chatatoures, with his army also arranged for battle, was Andronicus. Before the soldiers formed up in close order and the two armies came to grips, Crispinus the Frank[2] (I am writing these words on the very day he died) was

1. The Bishops of Chalcedon, Heraclea, and Colonus.

2. Crispinus had joined Romanus on his first campaign, but, because he was not treated with the respect he thought his due, he revolted (Easter 1069) and apparently became a freebooter, plundering the tax-collectors and defeating those sent against him. After routing the emperor's brother-in-law, Samuel Alousianus the Bulgarian, in Armenia, he asked for pardon and was temporarily restored. Not long after he was again exiled and sent to Abydos.

standing with Andronicus and they were encouraging one another. This Crispinus had at first appeared as an enemy to the Romans, but later he changed his attitude, and his new loyalty was no less evident than his former hostility. Seeing Diogenes' men now prepared for battle, Crispinus exhorted Andronicus to trust him, saying that he was going to charge the enemy cavalry. With that, he and his men rode at full gallop against their centre. He cut right through the ranks and, when he saw resistance was feeble, the rebels only withstanding his attack for a few moments and then running away, he pursued the fugitives with a handful of his knights. Thus he inflicted heavy losses and took still more prisoners.

Diogenes' army was broken and routed. Andronicus meanwhile returned in triumph with Crispinus to the tent which had been prepared for him. Later, one of the knights came up, bringing to the general an enemy captive. It was the Armenian Chatatoures. In the flight, he said, he had fallen from his horse at a ditch and had crept under a bush. One of the pursuers had spotted him and would have made short work of him, but, when he saw the Armenian's tears, he merely stripped him of his clothes and went away, leaving him naked under the bush. Then a second warrior, seeing him in this sorry plight, rushed up to kill him, but Chatatoures told him that if he would spare him and take him away to a certain general (whom he mentioned by name) he would be most handsomely rewarded. Recognizing who the man was, Andronicus felt doubly victorious. However, clothes and equipment were provided for him, and, though he was kept a prisoner, no constraint was put upon him, as befitted a brave leader.

Diogenes, of course, could feel no confidence in the small remnants of his army, but he still hoped that assistance would speedily come from his Persian allies. Indeed, he encouraged his men with this assurance and held out prospects of relief in the near future. Yet the very troops on whose loyalty he was relying, the men to whom he entrusted the keys of his garrison, were the first to betray him. They made an agreement with our general, and, being promised on oath that they themselves would suffer no harm, they threw the gates wide open and admitted our soldiers. Then they led them to the house where Diogenes was living. There he stood, a strange, melancholy spectacle, all his hopes gone, his hands fettered as though he were a slave, surrendering himself unconditionally to his captors. At once he was forced to don the black robe of a monk, and, taking off his head-dress, he allowed his hair to be cut short, not caring who did it. So the ceremony of initiation was hurriedly performed, not by the persons who should have carried it out, but by individuals who chanced to be there. Having made him a monk, they then led him out of his fortress and, with the greatest joy imaginable, took him off to Andronicus. Instead of receiving him in a high-handed, arrogant fashion, he really sympathized with the prisoner. He shook hands and invited him to his own tent. Finally, he asked him to be his guest at table, where a magnificent banquet was prepared.

So far the story has proceeded without a hitch: I have taken you along 'the royal, smooth highway', as the Holy Scripture has it. To pass on to what happened thereafter is a most disagreeable task. I am reluctant to describe a deed that should never have taken place; and yet, if I may alter my words slightly, it was a deed that should have taken place by all means. On the one hand, the scruples of religion, as well as a natural unwillingness to inflict pain, would forbid such a deed: on the contrary side, the state of affairs at the time, and the possibility of sudden changes in the fortunes of both parties, proclaimed that it *must* be done. The thing came about as follows. The more enthusiastic element in the emperor's council were afraid that Diogenes might succeed in his plots and once more embarrass the emperor. So, concealing their intentions from Michael, they wrote a letter to a certain person who was conveniently able to carry them out, with orders to blind him.[1]

The emperor was quite ignorant of what was being done – and God knows I am not saying that to flatter Michael. This is a perfectly true account. When therefore he found out, too late, what had occurred, he wept more bitterly even than Diogenes did before undergoing his torture. The news had the most distressing effect on him. Indeed, Michael did not leap for joy, nor show any other sign of pleasure, even when he first heard that his enemy had been taken prisoner. There is no doubt but that he would have long continued to mourn him openly, had he not feared public resentment. As for Diogenes, he was brought in his blindness to the monastery which he himself had founded, on the island of Prote, and there he died, not long afterwards. His reign had lasted less than four years.[2] Michael was now undisputed ruler of the Empire.

1. Scylitzes (845B, p. 705) asserts that it was John Ducas who gave this order, without the knowledge of Michael.

2. From the time of his accession to his capture at Adana he reigned three years and eight months (i.e. to September 1071). Further details are to be found in Scylitzes, who cannot conceal his dislike of Psellus and the Ducas family. He writes (821, p. 664) that Romanus was a man of fine appearance, with broad shoulders and a deep chest. He pays tribute to the emperor's personal bravery and to his fortitude at the final calamity of blinding.

MICHAEL VII

1071–8

Now that I am about to write an account of the Emperor Michael Ducas, or at least to give a rough outline of his reign, as far as the limited space of this history allows me, I must first beg my readers not to look upon my version of the man's character and deeds as exaggerated. On the contrary, I shall hardly do justice to either. As I write these words, I find myself overcome by the same emotions as I often feel when I am in his presence: the same wonder thrills me. Indeed, it is impossible for me not to admire him. And I would ask my readers not to distrust my account, nor to regard with suspicion the words that I shall presently write here, because they are penned during this emperor's lifetime. The very reason why I undertook to write this history was, in fact, none other than this, that men might know there exists a human nature of such divinity, one that far surpasses all others that we have ever known before.[1]

It is difficult to decide which of his qualities I am to delineate first, but I consider the following characteristic most worthy of note: despite the fact that none of his subjects, however humble, however distinguished in any way, however illustrious, remained for long personally unknown to the emperor, not one was ever abused by him, or insulted in public, or refused admittance to his presence because of some

1. The truth is that Michael Parapinaces was a despicable person and some of the blame for his inefficiency must fall on Psellus. The young emperor was being trained in logic and philosophy, but the situation of the Empire called for a soldier. On all sides the enemy were meeting with success, the Serbs, the Normans, the Muslims, the nomad tribes from over the Danube; and the Roman armies were discontented and disorganized.

delinquency. Further than that, even when Michael had been deliberately affronted, he preferred to disregard bad manners rather than to rebuke them openly. The supreme example of this trait occurred when he caught certain individuals – and they were, incredible though it may seem, members of his own bodyguard, entrusted with his own safety – actually hastening to do him some injury. Yet their impudence earned them neither reproof nor threats of terrible vengeance. There were several cases, too, of attempted robbery from the imperial treasury, where the burglars were caught red-handed. They also were released, and, far from treating them with any severity, Michael did not even impugn their motives. He was a man of extraordinary intelligence, and through careful observation he acquired a knowledge of affairs. He had, for instance, a thorough grasp of the whole system of taxation, of revenues and public expenditure, of the incomes paid from the exchequer and the percentage of income paid back to the treasury in the form of taxes. He knew all about the mint, the exact weight of a *stater*, how a touchstone functioned, what proportion of precious metal was included in every gold coin. In short, his information on the whole business of finance was extremely accurate, with the result that the experts on any particular subject found themselves at a disadvantage when he talked with them. Men who devoted their lives to a study of these things were unable to rival him in their own sphere.

Even when he was a youth, with the down of his first beard still fresh on his cheeks, he was in no way the inferior of his elders in wisdom. He was addicted to no pleasures, was no slave to gluttony, did not encourage sumptuous banqueting. From the delights of love he abstained so rigorously that of most of them he had no knowledge at all and was quite ignorant of sexual practices condemned by law. So excessive was his modesty, in fact, that an indecent jest, or even a mere mention of the word 'love', would immediately bring a deep blush to his cheeks.

The reader will probably like to know what were the emperor's favourite occupations, on what he prided himself most. Nothing pleased him more than reading books on all kinds of learned subjects, studying literary essays, pithy sayings, proverbs; he delighted in elegant compositions, subtle combinations of words, changes of style, coining of new words, poetic diction; but, above all else, he cultivated a love of philosophy, of books that enrich the spiritual life, of allegory and its interpretation. None of his predecessors on the throne, I should imagine, was more thoughtful, none quicker in getting to the central point of any given problem. But I will be more explicit. It is agreed that certain standards of behaviour, certain manners of speaking are appropriate to an emperor, others to a philosopher, others to an orator, others to a musician. Similarly, each class specializes in its own subject: astrologers spend their time in studying the heavens; geometricians in demonstrating with geometrical figures; the syllogism is reserved for philosophers, the secrets of nature for the scientists – everyone has his own particular *métier*, his own particular subject. With Michael, however, it was different, for he specialized in them all. He took his place with the philosophers, conversed with the orators on emphasis or zeugma, talked with the opticians about the refraction or diffraction of rays; and often, when we spoke of allegory, he surpassed his present historian, whom in preference to all others he chose as his tutor, and whose name he mentioned with extraordinary honour. Although he does not apply himself to iambics, he dashes them off extempore, and, if the rhythm is generally defective, at least the sentiments are sound. In brief, Michael is a prodigy of our generation, and a most beloved character.[1]

1. Scylitzes (856D, p. 725) is scathing in his condemnation of the emperor's pursuits: 'While he spent his time in the useless pursuit of eloquence and wasted his energy on the composition of iambic and anapaestic verse (and they were poor efforts indeed) he brought his

In appearance he somewhat resembles an old man, with
something about him of the thinker or pedagogue. His eyes
are intent, his brow neither haughty nor beetling, like that of
a man who suspects his fellows. His expression is frank,
marked with a suitable gravity. There is nothing hurried
about his gait, nothing of disorder; on the other hand, he is
neither slow-moving nor indolent. A musician, who from
the nature of his vocation must understand the regulated
succession of notes, would praise his movements. His voice,
too, is both harmonious and rhythmical, without a suggestion
of harshness or impetuosity, clear and distinct.

There are many things that can be said or done to take the
heart out of a man, or to provoke him to some course of
action; but Michael keeps his head. He is neither dispirited by
the one, nor exasperated by the other. He has a most pleasant
laugh, weeps in the most piteous manner imaginable, very
rarely becomes angry, and generally is in better humour than
ever afterwards. Not having made a special study of legal
matters, he takes a broad view of their interpretation, and
passes judgment rather in accordance with the spirit than with
the letter of the law. He is very prone to blush, but there is
never in his conduct the slightest hint of any impropriety.
Although he is a clever ball-player, his enthusiasm is reserved
for one ball only – the heavenly sphere, for he is well aware
that the course of life, and all its changes, depend on the throw
of a dice-cube, and that it is a cube – the geometric cube
– that Plato attributes to the earth.[1] In the chase he takes
pleasure, but only provided that he sees the quarry escape

Empire to ruin, led astray by his mentor, the philosopher Psellus.'
Again (846, p. 706): 'While he (Nicephoritza, the emperor's favourite)
concentrated all power in his hands, Michael found time for nothing
but trifles and childish games. The leading philosopher, Psellus, had
made him quite unfitted for the position he occupied.'

    1. Obscure, but maybe a reference to Plato's perfect number (*Re-
public*, viii).

unharmed, and, if the huntsmen get near it, he is worried and refuses to watch.

The magnificent apparel of an emperor holds no particular charm for him; he prefers to crown his head, not so much with material diadems, as with unseen virtues. And not every word that is whispered in his ears affects him deeply; harmful remarks, stories that usually inflict pain, he ignores altogether; others, which ordinarily produce most pleasure in the hearer, he erases completely from his mind. For inspiration he looks to his father, and, although in most things he surpasses him, he professes that he is in every way his inferior. Here I must mention something that I feel is beyond praise, the most remarkable fact about Michael's reign. At a time when our affairs, no less in the east than in the west, were at their lowest ebb – a condition brought about in the first place by the sovereigns who preceded him – any other man, however resolute, would have allowed himself to drift with the tide of misfortune, would have given up the struggle. With what result? The cable that held the ship of State would have cracked under the strain, and we should have seen the roof of the edifice come crashing down, the foundations torn up. But the tide of misfortune was checked by Michael's steadfast spirit, by his unshakeable resolve, and if, so far, we have not beached our vessel in harbour, at least we are riding the storm in deep waters and we have not been driven back into the open sea.

His attitude to the others I have described.[1] Now I will examine his relations with myself. There was, in fact, no comparison at all between the way he treated them and his behaviour towards me, his biographer. Not one of his brothers enjoyed the confidence that he placed in me, nor did the great nobles, nor the churchmen. Favours were heaped upon me, gifts, in ever-increasing profusion, were sent to

1. Michael's worst mistake was to appoint the eunuch Nicephoritza *logothete* – an unscrupulous rascal of the worst type.

me, and boons followed one another in rapid succession, augmenting the wealth that I already possessed. Others, of course, have done much the same thing, but there are certain characteristics that mark him out as different from all the rest: the depth of his feeling for me, not only on mental, but spiritual, grounds; his unhesitating frankness and the obvious pleasure he takes in my company; his belief in my supremacy as a man of learning, both here, among men with whom he is personally acquainted, and among others, of whom he has heard only by repute. I pray that the darts of jealousy and malice may never disturb that friendship.

In my efforts to compress this account, I have inadvertently passed over many things: for example, Michael's love for his wife,[1] by whom he has a baby son;[2] and his affection for his two brothers, who, though admirable in themselves, are not his equal. It would be superfluous to praise the empress because of her family, although its wealth and antiquity cannot fail to confer lustre on the highest offices; her own pre-eminence, not only in virtue, but also in beauty, is commendation enough. If, as the tragic poet[3] says 'silence is a woman's glory' then she above all other women is worthy of honour, for she speaks to no one but her husband, and her natural loveliness is far more effective than any artificial adornment dictated by convention.

The reader will probably wish to know what is the emperor's attitude to his brothers. Far from keeping them in subjection, perpetually tugging at the reins, so to speak, he gives each of them a chance to exercise imperial power, with complete freedom of action. Nor must I forget his uncle, the Caesar, on whose opinions he places considerable reliance.

1. Maria, an Alan princess afterwards married to the Emperor Nicephorus Botaneiates. Often mentioned in the *Alexiad* of Anna Comnena.
2. Constantine, betrothed to Helena the daughter of Robert Guiscard, but later to Anna Comnena.
3. Sophocles, *Ajax*, 293.

His wise counsel and all-round ability are, in fact, greatly admired by the nephew. Michael devotes his attention to civil administration, but everything pertaining to military affairs is left to the Caesar.

There is one thing that I must add here. The emperor knew that I was preparing to publish his biography and instructed me not to write until he had first given me a brief outline of his own character. Later, his secretary read to me what he had written. I myself, before I heard this effusion, was expecting something too intimate, something rather on the grand scale. What he did in fact produce was quite the reverse. Such was the humility, such the diffidence with which he described himself, and so critical the way in which he examined his innermost being, that even a heart of stone could not forbear to wonder at the depths of his self-abasement. God-like emperor, no other virtue, no other good quality could demonstrate more clearly your real character.

CONSTANTINE, THE SON OF THE EMPEROR MICHAEL DUCAS

I saw Constantine, the son of the Emperor Michael Ducas, when he was a tiny baby. He was being fed in the arms of his nurse and was wearing an imperial headband. To him I can attribute neither sayings nor deeds, for he has not yet done anything, nor spoken a word, but I can comment on his appearance and on the character that it expresses, as far as it is possible to judge anyone's nature from his looks, for never have I seen such beauty on earth. His face is rounded into a perfect circle, the eyes grey, very big and most serene, with the eyebrows forming an absolutely straight line, slightly separated at the base of the nose and gently curving towards the temples. The tip of the nose is straight, but there is a tiny rise on the bridge and towards the base it is somewhat aquiline. His head is covered with hair golden as the sun, and his lips are dainty, his eyes gentle, gentler than the angels. In them you may see a nature neither proud nor humble, but charming, divinely inspired.

There is a story that Heracles saw Ajax, the son of Telamon, while still a nursling, and wrapt him in his lion-skin. Likewise I have many a time held in my arms this little prince and prayed that he may benefit from my words. In time to come I will take him in my arms again, very often, and I hope that when he grows to manhood and inherits the Empire from his father, I too may benefit from him. Nestor of Pylos, after the capture of Troy, told Neoptolemus, Achilles' son, how a man might cultivate shrewdness; I would give only this advice to the little one – for maybe, when he becomes a youth, he will read my history – this advice, to follow the example of his father and to ask himself how nearly he approaches that model. Yes, little one, may you indeed be like your sire: you would 'grow up no mean man'.[1] If I live on beyond the normal span, I will compose another history, for you, when you have given me deeds to write of; if not, then what I have written here will satisfy you and provide for other historians a starting-point, when they record your reign.

ANDRONICUS, BROTHER OF THE EMPEROR MICHAEL DUCAS

This charming prince is just past his boyhood. Although an eager student of oratory, he is not disposed to neglect the more profound subjects – at any rate, he embarrasses me when he discourses on the antipodes and denies their existence, contending that, if they *did* exist, they would have to walk upside down! His hands are somewhat large, but he is clever with them and has a delicate touch. He takes to athletic training easily, is lighthearted, unaffected and altogether frank,

1. Sophocles, *Ajax*, 551.

refined in his tastes, a useful horseman, passionately fond of the chase, not content with keeping abreast of the hare, but anxious to fly along with the crane. He is only a moderate speaker, but concludes gracefully whenever he lapses into nonsense.

CONSTANTINE, HIS BROTHER[1]

Not very quick-witted, but, being wrapt up in himself, he has all the appearance of a thinker. He is generally observant, however, and when words are called for, he is a pretty clever speaker. He is not one to give way to his adversaries quickly, but answers argument with argument, and tries to win his point. Yet he finishes with a smile and derives a quiet satisfaction from his efforts. He has an old head on young shoulders, great tenacity of purpose and steadiness. He is moderately generous, not too liberal, nor yet tight-fisted, a clever horseman, a great huntsman, the darling both of his mother and of his brothers.

JOHN DUCAS, THE CAESAR[2]

How can I do justice to the noble qualities, the virtues, of this gentleman? Such versatility, such outstanding gifts, baffle description. Two characteristics, rarely found in conjunction, are extremely marked in him – a lively intelligence (I never saw or heard of anyone so quick-witted) and kindness of heart.

1. After Michael's abdication, Constantine (or Constantius) was confined in a monastery by the new emperor. He apparently died in battle at Durazzo (1082).

2. John's subsequent history was eventful enough. He had no reason to be grateful to Michael, for the emperor acted with his usual duplicity and in the end John became a monk. However, the marriage of his grand-daughter Irene and Alexius Comnenus united the two most powerful families at Constantinople, and he continued to play an important part in the State.

He reminds me of a river of oil flowing noiselessly on its way, so mild he is. And as for military strategy, he has acquired a knowledge of the science of the ancients comparable to that of the famous Caesars themselves. He has studied the brave deeds and victories of the Hadrians, the Trajans, and others of the same company. This knowledge, moreover, has not developed spontaneously, nor by chance, but from the reading of books on tactics and strategy and siege-craft, from the works of Aelian[1] and Apollodorus[2] and their disciples. It might be inferred that one so versed in military science would be deficient in the arts of civil administration, of jurisprudence, of finance, but such a belief would be quite erroneous. The truth is, to whatever noble study he devotes his energies, John excels in it, sharp as the proverbial razor. Perhaps, someone may suggest, he is bad-tempered. Not a bit of it, although he does show a certain amount of spirit. Perhaps vindictive? No man was ever less revengeful: his forgiving nature is even more marked than his self-control. Maybe he is too ready with his tongue, too outspoken, too presumptuous in the presence of his brother, and, to a less degree, when talking to his nephew? Wrong again. In fact, John sets us all an example of diplomacy, always careful to avoid extremes, tempering his serious pursuits with levity. Only in this matter of pastimes does he show lack of restraint and lose a sense of proportion.

He indulges in all kinds of hunting, observing carefully the flight of birds and the tracks followed by wild beasts. He urges on the dogs and chases the dappled hind. He is mad about bears, too – I have often reproached him for that, but all to no purpose for the pastime never fails to give him amusement. His life is spent in two pursuits – books and hunting; in other words, his leisure hours are devoted to the latter,

1. Author of a book on strategy (*c.* A.D. 100).
2. Apollodorus of Damascus wrote on *Engines of War* in the first century A.D.

and when he works, the whole world is his study, everything in its place. Nor is he less conversant with the functions of war than with the occupations of peace. He can discourse on companies, battle-formations, army groups, how to set out a phalanx, how to defend in depth, how to form a hollow square. He understands what is meant by hollow wedge or forming close column. He knows all about wall-fighting, cavalry skirmishing, the arrangement of infantry appropriate to different circumstances or different terrains. But why go into further details? Whatever aspect one considers, the man is without a rival.

THE EMPEROR'S LETTER TO PHOCAS[1]

In this letter the emperor began with a reference to the harshness of Phocas's exile,[2] and to the time he had wasted. He recalled the desolation of his friends, the financial difficulties, the filthy tunics and tattered garments. After this preface, he wrote of Phocas's restoration, a change of fortune for which he (Michael) had been personally responsible, and of the great honour accorded him at his reception in the palace (here he reminded him of favours 'worthy of a satrap' and of indescribable scenes of welcome). He pointed out how quick he had been to confer on Phocas all the greatest and most coveted honours of the Roman State; how from the first he had exalted him to positions of power, both in the civil and in the military sphere; how he had promoted him above all others and assured him of an income which, everyone would agree, was commensurate with the high office he enjoyed. To quote his own words, 'Who has received at my hands a

1. Nicephorus Botaneiates, who claimed to be descended from the ancient Roman Fabii. After defeating his rival Bryennius, he forced Michael VII to abdicate and retire to a monastery. He reigned for three years before being compelled to do the same.

2. Perhaps a reference to his dismissal by Romanus IV in 1071.

greater reward than yourself? Who was adjudged to be the
emperor's friend, his ears and eyes, but you? Who but you
obtained from me his every desire? With whom did I share
the most important functions of government? There were
secrets, kept hidden from my brother and my mother, which
I disclosed to you alone. And who now has the power to give
away or withhold the highest offices in the realm? Those
offices, remember, have brought you great renown and much
aggrandizement. I will not speak of the favours I have conferred, for your sake, on your father and brother and kinsmen;
I will not mention all those whom I have promoted from
obscurity and indigence to high rank, merely to please you;
nor will I speak of the many who have acquired not inconsiderable riches, and now, instead of existing in the penurious
manner of their forbears, hold commands in the army and fill
responsible posts in the civil administration. Their injustices,
whether committed in secret or in the broad light of day,
were purposely ignored by me, for I knew these malefactors
were legion and held my peace at their wrongdoing, being
prepared to tolerate anything for your sake. My one comfort
in the hour of trouble was, I believed, yourself – after God,
of course. I chose you to stand by me throughout the time of
my tribulations, and elected you to supervise my affairs constantly, because I thought that in you, alone of all men, I had
won an ally and a partner, and because I was confident that
the perplexities which assailed us would be settled by your
aid. But my plans – how vain they appear now, how ground-
less my hopes! Through your senseless pride, the treasure
that I sought has turned out to be nothing but rubble. Hope
will not always spring eternal: a host of evils takes the heart
out of a man. But there – we have brought this trouble on
ourselves, deluded into thinking that fire can be extinguished
with oil.

'In place of the comfort that I looked for, you bring on me
disaster: instead of an ally, I find in you an open enemy, in-

stead of a fellow-worker, a destructive agent. So, at least, it
appears, if the rumours that are spread abroad about you are
true. Men say that you are arming yourself for the fray, intent
on vengeance, as if you had suffered at my hands the vilest of
injuries, the supreme disservice. They tell me that you are
earnestly striving to thrust me forth from my home, the
palace of an emperor, and preparing to win it for yourself and
make it your own. I beg of you, *magistros*, with all my heart
and soul, never, never to contemplate such a course. A plague
on the rumour-mongers and the inventors of idle tales, the
wicked who sow tares among the wheat, who magnify into
prodigies what does not even exist, inspired only by their
jealousy! Their monstrous absurdities are beneath contempt,
lies fabricated, I am sure, with one special intent – to break
up our unity of purpose and to smash the harmony that binds
us together. These evil men are nothing to us. If the adversary
speaks again, let him not rejoice at our discomfiture. And as
for yourself, I pray that you may for ever cast from your
mind the thought of a deed so abominable in the eyes of God,
so utterly depraved. I plead with you not to show yourself
so unfeeling, so unjust as to attack those who have treated
you with kindness and are blameless. Do not allow yourself
to become an object of loathing to men, a model of wickedness.'

The emperor went on to remind Phocas that he had called
on God as his witness, with oaths most terrible. He pointed
out that Divine Providence each day scans the whole inhabited world, but with unsleeping eye it also watches over
the affairs of individual men, and metes out to the just recompense for their deeds, and to each of them renders measure for
measure. Those who walk in the path of unrighteousness are
caught in the net of Providence, and through the working of
Providence even the dictates of Fortune are reversed. 'If you
stand in awe of the Judgement of God, if you expect Him to
pass sentence on your deeds, then tremble for the success of

this enterprise. Let wisdom guide your steps, let prudence direct your plans. Discretion before disloyalty! He who follows bad counsel plots, from the very beginning, his own destruction!'

[At this point the *Chronographia* ends abruptly. Psellus never completed it.[1]]

1. What happened to Psellus after the abdication of Michael in January 1078 is not known.

BIBLIOGRAPHY

Readers who wish to learn more about the late Byzantine Empire (i.e. the period from the ninth to the fifteenth century) will find the following books helpful. An asterisk denotes that a full bibliography is included.

The fourth volume of the *Cambridge Medieval History* has been thoroughly revised under the general editorship of Professor Joan Hussey. The formal dates for this volume are 717–1453, but in certain cases the events of previous centuries are discussed. Part I has already been published; Part II should appear in 1966.

BAYNES, N. H. and MOSS, H. ST. L. B., *Byzantium, Oxford University Press, London, 1948.

BAYNES, N. H., *The Hellenistic Civilization and East Rome*, Oxford University Press, London, 1946; and *The Thought World of East Rome*, Oxford University Press, London, 1947: these are both good introductory essays.

BECKWITH, JOHN, *The Art of Constantinople*, Phaidon, London, 1961. 'Byzantine Empire' in *Chambers's Encyclopedia*, new edition, George Newnes, London, 1950, is valuable.

HEARSEY, JOHN, *City of Constantine*, John Murray, London, 1963.

HUSSEY, PROFESSOR J. M., *Church and Learning in the Byzantine Empire, 867–1185*, Oxford University Press, London, 1937.

HUSSEY, PROFESSOR J. M., *The Byzantine World*, Hutchinson's University Library, London, 1957.

LIDDELL, ROBERT, *Byzantium and Istanbul*, Jonathan Cape, London, 1958.

MATHEW, GERVASE, *Byzantine Aesthetics*, John Murray, London, 1963.

OSTROGORSKY, GEORGE, *History of the Byzantine State*, translated from the German by Professor J. M. Hussey, Blackwell, Oxford, 1956.

RICE, D. TALBOT, *Art of the Byzantine Era*, Thames & Hudson, London, 1963.

RICE, D. TALBOT, *Byzantine Art*, Penguin Books, Harmondsworth, 1961.

Bibliography

RICE, D. TALBOT and HIRMER, M. *The Art of Byzantium*, Thames & Hudson, London, 1959.

RICE, D. TALBOT, *The Byzantines*, Thames & Hudson (Ancient Peoples and Places series), London, 1962.

RUNCIMAN, S., *Byzantine Civilization*, Edward Arnold, London, 1933.

STEWART, CECIL, *Byzantine Legacy*, Allen & Unwin, London, 1949.

VASILIEV, A. A., *History of the Byzantine Empire*, Blackwell, Oxford, 1952.

For the place of Psellus in eleventh century life in the light of recent research, see Professor J. M. Hussey in *Transactions of the Royal Historical Society*, 4th series, Volume 32, 1950.

The above list is, of course, by no means exhaustive; much good work has been done by the French, for example, and by German scholars.

APPENDIX I

THE MACEDONIAN HOUSE

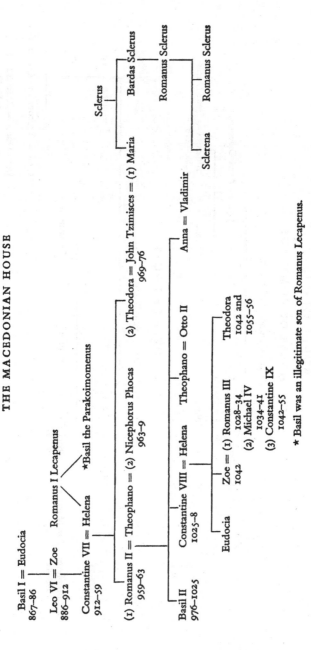

Basil I = Budocia
867–86

Leo VI = Zoe
886–912

Romanus I Lecapenus

*Basil the Parakoimomenus

Constantine VII = Helena
912–59

(1) Romanus II = Theophano = (2) Nicephorus Phocas
959–63   963–9

(2) Theodora = John Tzimisces = (1) Maria
                969–76

Basil II
976–1025

Constantine VIII = Helena
1025–8

Theophano = Otto II

Anna = Vladimir

Sclerus

Bardas Sclerus

Romanus Sclerus

Sclerena

Romanus Sclerus

Eudocia

Zoe = (1) Romanus III
1042   1028–34
      (2) Michael IV
           1034–41
      (3) Constantine IX
           1042–55

Theodora
1042 and
1055–56

* Basil was an illegitimate son of Romanus Lecapenus.

APPENDIX II

THE HOUSE OF COMNENUS

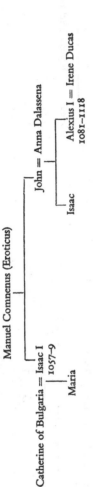

Manuel Comnenus (Eroticus)

Catherine of Bulgaria = Isaac I
1057–9

Maria

John = Anna Dalassena

Isaac

Alexius I = Irene Ducas
1081–1118

THE HOUSE OF DUCAS

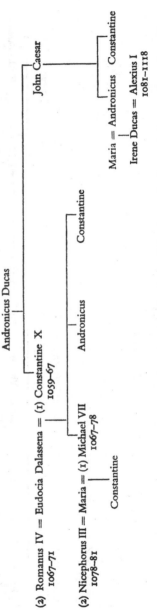

Andronicus Ducas

(2) Romanus IV = Eudocia Dalassena = (1) Constantine X
1067–71   1059–67

(2) Nicephorus III = Maria = (1) Michael VII
1078–81   1067–78

Constantine

Andronicus

Constantine

John Caesar

Maria = Andronicus   Constantine

Irene Ducas = Alexius I
1081–1118

The two families were united when Alexius married the grand-daughter of John Ducas, the Caesar, in late 1077 or early 1078.

APPENDIX III

George Maniaces avenged the defeat of Romanus III near Antioch by routing the Saracens. Shortly afterwards he captured Edessa (1032) and found there the famous letter said to have been addressed by Our Lord to Abgarus, the king of that city. This precious relic Maniaces presented to the emperor. In 1035 he was sent by Michael IV Paphlagon to carry on the war with the Saracens in South Italy. The conquest of Sicily followed and a great victory over the enemy (1040). Stephen, the emperor's brother-in-law, commanded the Roman fleet and apparently allowed the Saracen admiral to escape. There was a quarrel, Maniaces justly accusing him of negligence, and Stephen appealed to the emperor: he claimed that Maniaces was aiming at the imperial throne. The latter was promptly recalled in disgrace and imprisoned. It is noteworthy that in his Sicilian campaigns Maniaces had under his command the Russian Varangian Druzhina and the Scandinavian hero, Harald Haardraade. It was not long before he (Maniaces) was once more a free man; Michael V Calaphates released him and in 1042 he was leading the Byzantines in Italy. He quickly restored the province to some semblance of order, although outnumbered and despite the terrible reverses suffered by his predecessors Doceianus and Boioannus. However, he was once more the victim of jealousy. According to Cedrenus (756-7, pp. 547-8) he was attacked by Romanus Sclerus, whose sister was concubine to the new Emperor Monomachus. It seems that Maniaces had possessions in the East and Romanus was a neighbour. Possibly owing to some insult he had endured in the past, more probably because he saw in Maniaces a serious rival for honours that he coveted himself, he plundered the general's estates in Anatolia and seduced his wife. Not content with that he slandered him and Maniaces was deprived of his title (*magister*). It was only then that rebellion was seriously considered: Pardus, sent to relieve Maniaces of his command, was murdered and Maniaces himself was proclaimed emperor by his soldiers after the victory near Ostrovo (1043). His sudden death on the field of battle undoubtedly changed the course of Byzantine history: the military party had lost a great champion, the civil element could now carry on the unpopular centralization of government in the capital. Within a few years Maniaces' victories were forgotten and Byzantium was threatened by new and more formidable enemies.

APPENDIX IV

Greek Fire was the secret weapon of the Byzantine emperors. It is said to have been invented by a Syrian engineer, one Callinicus, in the seventh century. The 'liquid fire' was hurled on to the ships of their enemies from siphons and burst into flames on contact. As it was reputed to be inextinguishable and burned even on water, it caused panic and dread. The secret formula was handed down from emperor to emperor, jealously preserved for seven centuries. For a thorough investigation of the weapon the reader should consult Professor J. R. Partington's excellent volume, *A History of Greek Fire and Gunpowder*, published by Heffer in 1960; much has been written on the subject, in many languages, but Partington quotes the ancient authorities *in extenso*, with a first-class commentary, and also examines medieval and modern theories on the composition of this 'artificial fire'; his is the most detailed and up-to-date treatise.

GLOSSARY

Curopalates. One of the three highest honours, with *Caesar* and *Nobilissimus*, and normally conferred only on members of the imperial family. E. A. Sophocles (*Greek Lexicon of the Roman and Byzantine Periods*) defines the position as 'major-domo of the imperial palace'.

Drungarius. Commander of a *drungus*, a body of infantry.

Druzhina. A corps of soldiers. Usually applied to the famous Varangians who formed the emperor's personal bodyguard.

Eparch. The Greek equivalent of the Roman *praefectus* ('one in charge', a governor or commander). The Eparch was 'father of the city', the most important civil official in Constantinople after the emperor himself.

Logothete. In charge of financial accounts, a chancellor. The Great Logothete occupied a position of growing importance in the bureaucratic organization of the eleventh century.

Magister. A high court official. The Roman word means 'master' and the title was conferred on many persons, each with his own sphere of action.

Nobilissimus. See under *Curopalates.*

Nomophylax. 'Guardian of the Law.' The Head of the Legal Faculty in the University of Constantinople.

Orphanotrophus. The supervisor of the large orphanage in the capital.

Parakoimomenus. Literally 'one who sleeps near [the emperor]'. The Lord Chamberlain was a eunuch.

Protospatharius. The commander of the *spatharii* ('sword-bearers'), who formed part of the imperial bodyguard.

Protovestiarius. In charge of the emperor's wardrobe and the monies concerned with it.

Rhomphaia. A one-edged heavy sword of iron.

Strategus. The Greek word for 'general', 'commander'. The military title was also given to governors of the *themes* ('provinces').

INDEX

Index

Index

Stypes, 165
Sultan (of Egypt), 253; (of Parthia), 314; (of Seljuq Turks), 354–5, 358
Synod, 316
Syria, 67, 348, 352

Tarsus, 258
Tauro-Scyths, 138, 283, 289
Taurus, 35
Telamon, 374
Themis, 245
Themistocles, 226
Theodora Augusta, 121, 142–271 *passim*, 283, 309
Theodora (daughter of Constantine X), 334, 340
Theodorus (*eunuchus*), 282–3
Theodorus Alopus, 285
Theodorus Alyates, 361
Theodorus Chryselius, 298
Theodorus Doceianus (nephew of Isaac Comnenus), 324
Theodosius (father of Constantine IX), 161
Theometor, 70, 74
Theophano, 27
Thetis, 326

Thrace, 332
Thucydides, 191, 270
Tornicius. See under *Leo Tornicius*
Trajan, 63, 376
Trebizond, 254, 343
Triballi, 341
Troy, 221, 374
Turks, 278, 317, 332, 348, 352
Tyre, 174
Tyropoeum, 33, 361
Tzimisces. See under *John Tzimisces*

Uzes, 332, 352

Varangians, 35, 359
Vladimir of Russia, 35, 201

Xenocrates of Chalcedon, 304
Xiphilinus, John, 254, 343, 347

Zeus, 326
Zeuxis, 72
Zoe Augusta, 58, 63, 65, 75–81, 87–240 *passim*, 250
Zoe (daughter of Constantine X), 334, 340

Index

Index

Maria (wife of Michael VII and Nicephorus Botaneiates), 372
Mary, St Peribleptos, 88
Medes, 352
Megarian School, 73
Michael IV Paphlagon, 75–81, 87–118, 143, 160, 163, 200, 309
Michael V Calaphates, 100, 103–4, 121–51, 164, 193
Michael VI Stratioticus, 271, 275–302, 309, 312, 335
Michael VII Parapinaces, 334, 340, 345, 367–80
Michael Anastasius, 298
Michael Attaliates, 131
Michael Burtzes, 276
Michael (brother of John the Orphanotrophus), 75
Mitylene, 130, 161, 164
Monobatae, 130
Monomachus. See under *Constantine IX*
Moses, 313, 341
Muslims, 367
Mysians, 317, 341

Naziraeans, 270
Neoplatonism, 257
Neoptolemos, 374
Nestor of Pylos, 374
Nicaea, 279, 283
Nicephoritza, 370–1
Nicephorus Phocas, 28, 29, 30, 31, 49
Nicephorus (son of Bardas Phocas), 30
Nicephorus (gòvernor of Bulgaria), 259–60
Nicephorus (nephew of Michael Cerularius), 298
Nicephorus Botaneiates, 332, 348, 372, 377
Nicephorus Palaeologus, 353

Nicetas (brother of John the Orphanotrophus), 75
Nicolaus, 156
Nicomedia, 177, 282, 286
Nile, 306
Nireus, 221
Nomophylax, 254
Normans, 367
Novel of January 996, 44

Odyssey, 244, 265
Olympiads, 191
Olympus, Mt, 256
Opsaras, 277
Ostrovo, 196
Outis, 73

Pancalia, 31
Pantherius, 333
Paphlagonia, 75, 254
Pardus, 194
Parthia, 306, 314
Patriarch, Oecumenical, 269
Patzinaks, 314, 317, 332, 348
Peleus, 326, 333
Peribleptos. See under *Mary, St*
Pericles, 226
Persia, 98, 352
Persians, 167, 351, 355, 364
Petrion, 143
Pheidias, 72
Philip (father of Alexander the Great), 68, 310
Philip Opuntius, 175
Phocas (Nicephorus Botaneiates), 377, 379
Phocas family, 30
Phoenicia, 177
Phrygia, 311, 352
Plato, 174–5, 304, 313, 370
Pliny Major, 304
Plotinus, 174

395

Index

Index